Praise for *The CRM Handbook*

"Want to avoid being one of the estimated 70 percent of companies who have tried implementing standalone CRM systems and failed? Confused by what your IT suppliers are telling you about 'CRM'? Then you need to read this book! Jill provides a comprehensive , practical, and easy to understand view of CRM and shows you how to successfully implement an enterprise customer-focused solution."

> **—Kevin Bubeck**
> **Director, North America Information Strategy, Coca-Cola**

"CRM could be viewed as the ERP of the 2000's. As such, there will be multiple winners and losers as the marketplace places some large and strategic bets on this technology. In any case, Jill Dyché has captured the importance of the concepts and value derived through CRM solutions. Those needs will evolve, of course, but companies will always need the basics that have been discussed."

> **—Brian Berliner**
> **Co-founder & EVP, Product Development, Acies Networks**

*"**The CRM Handbook** provides information for the business person who is trying to understand CRM and how it can effect his/her business. It goes beyond the hype of the acronym and dives into the real issues that a company needs to consider before implementing a CRM solution."*

> **—Joy Blake Scott**
> **Director, Marketing and Communications, Fastwater, LLP**

"I haven't read anything that has such a practical approach. I view the book as having multiple benefits. It gives a good definition of CRM functionality but also gives detailed guidance of how to approach CRM in your organization."

> **—Francine Frazer**
> **Principal Consultant, Net Perceptions**

"Even better than defining CRM, Jill took on all of the hyperlanguage around CRM and clearly differentiated the various incarnations of CRM. It's also useful to know what can go wrong and the potential affects of such missteps. Too few authors level with readers about pitfalls!"

> **—Linda McHugh**
> **Director, Professional Services, Cygent Inc.**

The CRM Handbook

Addison-Wesley Information Technology Series
Capers Jones and David S. Linthicum, Consulting Editors

The information technology (IT) industry is in the public eye now more than ever before because of a number of major issues in which software technology and national policies are closely related. As the use of software expands, there is a continuing need for business and software professionals to stay current with the state of the art in software methodologies and technologies. The goal of the Addison-Wesley Information Technology Series is to cover any and all topics that affect the IT community: These books illustrate and explore how information technology can be aligned with business practices to achieve business goals and support business imperatives. Addison-Wesley has created this innovative series to empower you with the benefits of the industry experts' experience.

For more information point your browser to http://www.awl.com/cseng/series/it/

Sid Adelman, Larissa Terpeluk Moss, *Data Warehouse Project Management.* ISBN: 0-201-61635-1

Wayne Applehans, Alden Globe, and Greg Laugero, *Managing Knowledge: A Practical Web-Based Approach.* ISBN: 0-201-43315-X

Michael H. Brackett, *Data Resource Quality: Turning Bad Habits into Good Practices.* ISBN: 0-201-71306-3

Frank Coyle, *Wireless Web: A Manager's Guide.* ISBN: 0-201-72217-8

James Craig and Dawn Jutla, *e-Business Readiness: A Customer-Focused Framework.* ISBN: 0-201-71006-4

Gregory C. Dennis and James R. Rubin, *Mission-Critical Java™ Project Management: Business Strategies, Applications, and Development.* ISBN: 0-201-32573-X

Kevin Dick, *XML: A Manager's Guide.* ISBN: 0-201-43335-4

Jill Dyché, *e-Data: Turning Data into Information with Data Warehousing.* ISBN: 0-201-65780-5

Jill Dyché, *The CRM Handbook: A Business Guide to Customer Relationship Management.* ISBN: 0-201-73062-6

Dr. Nick V. Flor, *Web Business Engineering: Using Offline Activites to Drive Internet Strategies.* ISBN: 0-201-60468-X

David Garmus and David Herron, *Function Point Analysis: Measurement Practices for Successful Software Projects.* ISBN: 0-201-69944-3

Capers Jones, *Software Assessments, Benchmarks, and Best Practices.* ISBN: 0-201-48542-7

Capers Jones, *The Year 2000 Software Problem: Quantifying the Costs and Assessing the Consequences.* ISBN: 0-201-30964-5

Ravi Kalakota and Marcia Robinson, *e-Business 2.0: Roadmap for Success.* ISBN: 0-201-72165-1

David S. Linthicum, *B2B Application Integration: e-Business-Enable Your Enterprise.* ISBN: 0-201-70936-8

Sergio Lozinsky, *Enterprise-Wide Software Solutions: Integration Strategies and Practices.* ISBN: 0-201-30971-8

Joanne Neidorf and Robin Neidorf, *e-Merchant: Retail Strategies for e-Commerce.* ISBN: 0-201-72169-4

Patrick O'Beirne, *Managing the Euro in Information Systems: Strategies for Successful Changeover.* ISBN: 0-201-60482-5

Mai-lan Tomsen, *Killer Content: Strategies for Web Content and E-Commerce.* ISBN: 0-201-65786-4

Bill Wiley, *Essential System Requirements: A Practical Guide to Event-Driven Methods.* ISBN: 0-201-61606-8

Ralph R. Young, *Effective Requirements Practices.* ISBN: 0-201-70912-0

Bill Zoellick, *CyberRegs: A Business Guide to Web Property, Privacy, and Patents.* ISBN: 0-201-72230-5

Bill Zoellick, *Web Engagement: Connecting to Customers in e-Business.* ISBN: 0-201-65766-X

The CRM Handbook

A Business Guide to Customer Relationship Management

Jill Dyché

PEARSON
Education

Copyright © 2002 by Pearson Education, Inc.
This edition is published by arrangement with Pearson Education, Inc. and Dorling Kindersley Publishing Inc.

ISBN 81-7758-762-5

First Impression, 2006
Second Impression, 2006
Third Impression, 2007

This edition is manufactured in India and is authorized for sale only in India, Bangladesh, Bhutan, Pakistan, Nepal, Sri Lanka and the Maldives. Circulation of this edition outside of these territories is UNAUTHORIZED.

Published by Dorling Kindersley (India) Pvt. Ltd., licensees of Pearson Education in South Asia.

Head Office: 482, F.I.E., Pataparganj, Delhi 110 092, India.
Registered Office: 14 Local Shopping Centre, Panchsheel Park, New Delhi 110 017, India.

Printed in India by Anands Sons.

To my mother June Dyche,
who set the book-writing precedent early, and well.

Contents

CHAPTER 3   CRM AND CUSTOMER SERVICE   75

CHAPTER 4   SALES FORCE AUTOMATION   10'

CHAPTER 5   **CRM IN E-BUSINESS 127**

CHAPTER 6   **ANALYTICAL CRM 143**

Part II: Delivering CRM 175

CHAPTER 9   MANAGING YOUR CRM PROJECT   257

Acknowledgements

A business writer, trying to consolidate and make sense of the varied disciplines that comprise the intricate apparatus of even the simplest new technology trend, incurs many debts. I am grateful to those who have contributed to this book and proud to acknowledge their help.

Thanks first and foremost to the subjects of my case studies, and to those who guided me to them: Beth Leonard of Verizon Communications; Monica Tyson of Harrah's Entertainment; Harry Egler of Eddie Bauer; Kari Opdal of Union Bank of Norway; Regina Wallace of juniper Bank; and Mike Overly and Ed Magin from Hewlett Packard. These people had the generosity and authority to say yes. Thanks too go to Bill Prentice and Nelle Schantz of SAS; Kim Stanick and Carrie Ballinger from Teradata; Susan Poser and Susan Umphrey from Oracle; and Mary Chan, fellow management consultant and world traveler.

My reviewers represent the best and the brightest in the CRM industry, and share credit for this book's real-world perspective. Hats off to Brian Berliner, Joy Blake, James Craig, Capers Jones, Kelly Mooney, Robin Neidorf, Marcia Robinson, David Linthicum, and Anne Thomas Manes. Thanks, too, to Kim Moutsos, editor of DB2 Magazine, for letting me reclaim text from an article I wrote on clickstream analysis. And to the vendors who provided examples of real, working products-Brian Hoover of Touchscape, Fadra Nally and Mary Gros of Teradata, Yancy Oshita from Oracle, and John Gill from Channel Wave-you've enriched the Handbook immensely.

I feel as if I have a personal troop of CRM gurus in Fran Frazer, Linda McHugh, and John Earle, who together corner the market on personalization, voice recognition and wireless technology, and CRM planning expertise, and who plowed through my drafts with the patience and understanding of good friends. Evan Levy lived through the writing of this book, revealing his own CRM battle scars at aberrant hours and without complaint. I'm grateful to him for many things, foremost of which is that he's still talking to me now that the book's finished.

Addison-Wesley's Mary O'Brien, whose imagination and creativity were the seeds of the Handbook, was indispensable in its development, as was editorial assistant Alicia Carey, copy editor extraordinaire Malinda McCain, and the inimitable Addison-Wesley production staff.

And a final shout out to my colleagues at Baseline Consulting Group, who picked up the slack when the going got tough, in particular Gordon Levy and David Rankell. You are CRM best-practices personified!

About the Author

Jill Dych6 is a partner with Baseline Consulting Group, a firm specializing in the implementation and analysis of customer databases. As vice president of Baseline's management consulting practice, Jill leads teams through front- and back-end reviews of strategic technology initiatives, including data warehousing, database marketing, and CRM planning and implementation.

Jill speaks regularly at marketing and technology conferences, and her writings on technology and workplace issues have been featured in Information Week, EAIjournal, Oracle Magazine, DM Review, The Chicago Tribune, and The Washington Times. She is the author of the acclaimed book e-Data: Turning Data into Information with Data Warehousing (Addison-Wesley, 2000), which has been translated into Spanish, Korean, and Japanese. Jill was recently named a WITI Woman by Women in Technology International.

Introduction

On one of those preternaturally warm spring afternoons, when many of their colleagues had forsaken them for the beach, around 500 conference attendees packed themselves into a hall at the Los Angeles Convention Center to hear about Customer Relationship Management. A group of high-profile experts was assembling to deliver a heralded panel discussion on the current and future state of the CRM market. Attendance swelled to standing room only.

On the panel were executives from both established and emerging CRM vendors. One panelist headed a company that sold an Internet storefront product. Another ran a sales-force automation company. A third represented a major database vendor. There was a call center system vice president and, to his left, a chief privacy officer. At the end of the line sat a renegade technology analyst.

As they began talking, it became clear that each of the panelists had a different perspective on CRM. The president of the database company talked at length about connecting databases to applications, after the privacy officer had finished weighing in on the risks of opt-in marketing. The call center executive discussed new advances in live chat. The analyst inveighed against CRM vendors who didn't offer sufficient analytics, making a few of his co-panelists shift in their chairs.

In fact, the discussion topics were so far removed from one another that the panelists might as well have been speaking different languages. As the moderator quickly learned, integrating the discussion in any meaningful way was a more significant undertaking than a mere hour would allow. As with the CRM marketplace, there was no holistic message-just different conversations. Shuffling out of the auditorium, none of the attendees left with a clear CRM vision they could take back to work and begin promoting.

Nevertheless, we all have our eyes on the CRM ball. Aberdeen Group's "Customer Relationship Management: Year 2000 Edition" report predicts the CRM market will grow from $8 billion in 1999 to more than $24 billion by 2003. Such pronouncements—and there are many—represent sufficient ammunition for many companies to target CRM before thoroughly scoping it.

The problem is the noise. Companies worldwide are declaring themselves "customer-focused" and forking over millions of dollars on CRM-related technologies. Over-hyped vendor products clash with varied interpretations of CRM objectives, leading many companies to simply automate ineffective marketing and customer support processes. And because many of these processes rely on sporadically gathered data and shoddy business practices ("I can't help you; you'll have to talk to our billing department—and they're closed"), these firms were no closer to building solid customer relationships than prior to adopting CRM.

Likewise, customers have more choices than ever before, and a vendor's arch competitor is often—as the current sound bite goes—just a mouse-click away. Without customers, products don't sell and revenues don't materialize. And without establishing customer loyalty, a profitable customer can be as fleeting as a dot-com Web site. Suddenly, customers matter.

Thus, banks have succeeded in automating their marketing processes and calculating customer value. Communications companies are busy trying to reduce churn. Retailers and e-tailers alike are launching customer loyalty programs with alarming speed. And everyone has an Internet strategy for stimulating purchases. The only thing many of these forward-thinking companies have in common is their struggle to separate the truth from the hype.

This book seeks to mitigate the spin rampant in the CRM marketplace, first by defining CRM and its various components and then by providing a guide to successful delivery of a CRM program. It will serve both as a resource, defining and illustrating key CRM concepts, and as a field guide, directing you in the best approaches for adopting and implementing your own CRM solution. In the latter role, the Handbook points out mistakes as well as successes, allowing you to learn from those who fell too early for the hype ("We're your one-stop CRM shop!"). In the former role, it will help clear the clutter and provide straightforward explanations of the various types of CRM, as well as how they can work together.

And, like a good CRM initiative, the book revolves around the customer's experience. After all, no matter how informative the material or how knowledgeable the source, the message should always be geared toward the right audience. CRM conference panel organizers, take note!

How to Read This Book

This book is written for a wide range of readers, from executives to practitioners. Part 1 is geared toward executives, project managers, and businesspeople interested in understanding the components of CRM and their definitions, as well as how those components are being used. Part 2 is for project managers, consultants, business analysts, and technical practitioners who need practical tips on CRM planning and implementation.

Readers with specific areas of interest can skip to individual chapters. Table I-1 briefly explains each chapter and its audience focus.

Table I-1: The Handbook's Chapters and Their Intended Audiences

Part 1: Defining CRM	Part 1 explains types of CRM—offering real-life examples of how businesses are using them—and explains how they fit together.	
Chapter	**Description**	**Intended Audience**
Chapter 1: Hello, Goodbye. The New Spin on Customer Loyalty	Introduces CRM's value proposition from a business perspective and explains why companies are rushing to jump on the CRM bandwagon.	Any reader needing an introduction to CRM and its role in business strategy should read this chapter.
Chapter 2: CRM in Marketing	Explores marketing's recent history and transition from product focus to customer focus to the latest craze: improving the customer's experience.	For executives in charge of planning and funding customer loyalty, acquisition, and retention programs and for marketing staff, including product, segment, and campaign managers. Sales management might consider starting here prior to reading Chapter 4.

(continued)

Table I-1: The Handbook's Chapters and Their Intended Audiences (*continued*)

Chapter	Description	Intended Audience
Chapter 3: CRM and Customer Service	Covers why customer service is the locus of most CRM programs and how new customer service strategies and technologies promise to enhance customer loyalty—not to mention a company's revenues.	Customer support staff members at all levels will enjoy comparing their company contact center environments with the best practices outlined in this chapter. Also of interest to marketing staff considering other customer touchpoints.
Chapter 4: Sales Force Automation	The birthplace of CRM, SFA includes a variety of tactical and strategic functions. This chapter goes from managing customer leads and accounts to sharing customer knowledge via wireless media.	Sales managers and sales reps alike can use this chapter as a benchmark for how they're managing their customer contacts and leads. Also valuable for field service personnel.
Chapter 5: CRM in e-Business	Given the challenges e-business presents, this chapter discusses where the customer fits in the supply chain for both B2B and B2C relationships.	For managers and developers responsible for delivering e-business, particularly eCRM, as well as users and developers of ERP and supply chain management systems.
Chapter 6: Analytical CRM	Analytical CRM leverages the data gathered from cross-functional customer touchpoints to help companies make strategic decisions. This chapter covers the risks and rewards of analyzing and acting on new customer knowledge.	For business people for whom decision support is a critical job function, as well as data analysts using sophisticated predictive techniques. Also helpful for marketing managers who rely on data analysis for launching new programs.

Part 2: Delivering CRM	Part 2 describes the key components of a CRM program and offers examples and checklists for ensuring they are performed thoroughly and in the right sequence to mitigate risk and ensure successful CRM delivery.	
Chapter	*Description*	*Intended Audience*
Chapter 7: Planning Your CRM Program	Explains how to evaluate your company against CRM critical success factors. This chapter also describes how to gauge the complexity of your CRM initiative and how that complexity determines a range of planning and development activities, including requirements gathering and ROI calculation.	For business analysts and consultants who will be gathering and documenting CRM requirements, as well as project managers who will be charged with translating them into a working CRM system. Also helpful for CRM sponsors and end users who must understand the tasks and resources necessary in CRM planning.
Chapter 8: Choosing Your CRM Tool	Discusses CRM technology software features and explains requirements-driven technology selection. This chapter contains checklists and interview questions for both CRM software vendors and application services providers (ASPs).	For IT executives and project managers charged with leading CRM technology selection efforts, as well as stakeholders who need to understand CRM technology-selection best practices. The vendor evaluation questions might help vendors better prepare for prospect and client presentations.
Chapter 9: Managing Your CRM Project	Describes how to delineate, prioritize, and staff CRM projects and highlights some common roadblocks to successful development. Discusses	Technical staff, CRM development team members, and project managers will be interested in the roles integral to CRM projects, as will CRM

(continued)

Table I-1: The Handbook's Chapters and Their Intended Audiences (*continued*)

Chapter	Description	Intended Audience
	establishing success metrics and measuring against them, and includes a CRM Implementation Roadmap.	stakeholders who want to learn more about where to begin.
Chapter 10: Your CRM Future	This chapter introduces some of the main roadblocks known to sabotage CRM programs. It also covers some controversial CRM trends.	Business sponsors and project managers interested in ensuring the success of their CRM programs, as well as business users who want a preview of CRM features on the horizon.
Further Reading	A compendium of books, magazines, journals, and Web sites to aid readers in their CRM research.	
Glossary	Definitions for the CRM-related terms used throughout the book, as well as coverage of some current business and technology buzzwords.	

Toward the end of the content chapters, you'll find a "Checklist for Success," describing the best practices involved in achieving the objectives discussed in that chapter. (If you're underway with CRM, use this checklist as a tool to perform gap analysis against your current project.) In addition, because CRM is inherently a business management initiative, each chapter concludes with a section titled "The Manager's Bottom Line," summarizing the discussion for managers and executives who might be sponsoring CRM in their companies.

PART I

Defining CRM

CHAPTER ONE

Hello, Goodbye: The New Spin on Customer Loyalty

The so-called typical customer no longer exists, and companies have been learning this lesson the hard way. Until very recently, business was more concerned about the "what's" than about the "who's." In other words, companies were focused on selling as many products and services as possible, without regard to who was buying them. Most corporations cling to this product-centric view even today, basing their organizational structures and compensation plans on the products they sell, not the customers who buy.

The Burger King slogan of the 1970s inviting the fast-food consumer to "Have it your way" was positively unorthodox for its era, as companies across industries offered standard products to the consumer population at large. Moreover, 1960s and 1970s corporate America bet their profits on classic marketing tactics-primarily television ads, mass mailings, and billboards-and then sat back and waited for the customers to pour in.

But the baby boomers came of age and competition burgeoned. Consumers had more choices than ever before about where to do their banking, their grocery shopping, and their vacationing. Deregulation increased competition even further as it drove prices down. Companies were forced to invent new methods of interacting with customers to reduce costs and gain market share. Use of automated teller machines (ATMS) and interactive voice response (IVR) systems increased. But customers weren't necessarily more satisfied than before.

Executives soon realized cost-reduction tactics weren't enough to satisfy either customers or shareholders, who continued to call them on the carpet for eroding margins. Maximizing profitability was the real name of the game. The paradox was that companies couldn't very well increase profits while simultaneously enticing new customers with price breaks. AT&T and MCI learned this the hard way in the 1980s as they and other long-distance companies mailed millions of $100 checks out to consumers, who switched their long-distance service and switched it back again.

The Cost of Acquiring Customers

Nowadays, the competition is just a mouse-click away. Embattled companies are slouching toward the realization that without customers, products don't sell and revenues don't materialize. They have been forced to become smarter about selling, and this means becoming smarter about who's buying. Companies are reading the competitive writing on the wall and looking to technology for a leg up.

This, combined with the oft-quoted factoid that it costs a company six times[1] more to sell a product to a new customer than it does to sell to an existing one—the old "bird in the hand" thus coming to roost—has motivated businesses to try to maximize existing customer relationships. And the main way to squeeze every drop of value from existing customers is to know who the best customers are and motivate them to stay that way. Indeed, a good starter definition of **customer relationship management (CRM)** is

> The infrastructure that enables the delineation of and increase in customer value, and the correct means by which to motivate valuable customers to remain loyal—indeed, to buy again.

As we'll see throughout this book, CRM is about more than simply managing customers and monitoring their behaviors. CRM has the potential to change a customer's relationship with a company and increase revenues in the bargain.

The most forward-thinking companies have recognized from past failures that CRM smacks of strategy, and thus technology alone can't address high-profile issues such as new-customer acquisition and Web-based marketing. To these companies, CRM is much more than a standalone project accounted for

---

1. Although six times is acknowledged as the prevalent figure, reports on new-customer acquisition costs vary, from as low as three times to as high as thirteen times.

by a single organization, it's a *business philosophy* that affects the company-at-large. (We'll see examples later of companies who practice CRM without even using the term.) These firms have articulated their ultimate visions for CRM to communicate them to every facet of operations. The following list represents a set of legitimate CRM business objectives from several of my clients currently in the throes of their CRM programs:

- "We want to thoroughly understand our customers' needs—even before they know them themselves."—A mid-market financial institution
- "Decreasing customer churn by increasing customer satisfaction."—A competitive local exchange carrier
- "Motivating customers to initiate revenue-generating contacts with us."—An online insurance company
- "Increasing the likelihood of the 'right response' by a given customer or customer segment."—A catalog retailer
- "To use technology to improve customer service and enable a greater degree of customer differentiation in order to deliver unique customer interactions."—A data services firm
- "We want to attract customers—both old and new—through more personalized communications."—An online retailer

The point here is that there is not one but many visions for CRM success. CRM promises to help companies get to know their customers well enough to understand which ones to keep and which ones they should be willing to lose—and why—and how not to overspend in the meantime. CRM also means automating many of the business processes and accompanying analysis and saving precious time in the bargain.

And saving money. Charles Schwab's multimillion-dollar investment in Siebel's CRM product, which the brokerage firm uses to track each interaction with a customer or prospect, was recouped in less than two years.[2] Stories of wildly successful CRM programs have invaded both print and cyberspace, spurring otherwise cynical executives to turn their heads in the CRM direction. After all, who could argue?

Who indeed? The estimated 70 percent of companies who have tried implementing standalone CRM systems and failed, as well as the legions of

---

2. Roberts-Witt, Sarah L., "It's the Customer, Stupid!" *PC Magazine,* June 27, 2000, 26.

other companies who have taken missteps on their e-business journeys might have a few comments. As with enterprise resource planning (ERP), supply chain management (SCM), and other wide-reaching corporate programs that mandate a combination of innovative technologies, new business processes, and organizational buy-in, CRM's failures are vast and visible.

From Customer Acquisition to Customer Loyalty

In his book *Why We Buy,* self-described retail anthropologist Paco Underhill notes that if consumers purchased only what they really needed, the economy would collapse. Indeed, one could argue that the heady mixture of good times and popular fads from protein bars to same-sex fragrances to sport utility vehicles has created a veritable buying frenzy.

But consumers are fickle, and more cynical than ever before. We no longer believe what we read and see, and for large purchases we're more inclined to do our own research. Your company has just announced another strategic alliance? You've got a cool new animated logo? You're on your fourth round of venture funding? So what, so what, and so what?

Consumers are also busier than ever and have consequently placed a premium on their leisure time. After all, why tramp through aisle upon aisle of merchandise when I can order groceries off the Web and spend more time with the kids? And pizza? And dog food? And even that sport utility vehicle?

In a recent *Information Week* survey[3], of the companies actively implementing CRM, 93 percent claimed increased loyalty and customer satisfaction would justify their CRM investment. The second-highest percentage, 83 percent, stated the need to demonstrate increased revenue. The implied mandate for most of these early adopters seems to be "customer loyalty at any cost—even if we don't see a return on investment."

It certainly doesn't take much for a consumer to turn her head to a competing product or vendor. A jazz buff has a mental list of the CDs she wants to buy. When CD Now e-mails her a discount code for the new Dave Brubek recording, she goes to the site and buys it despite her hefty "wish list" on Amazon.com.

---

3. Sweat, Jeff, "Lots of Companies Are Thinking About Customer Relationship Management, But Progress Can Be Very Slow—CRM Under Scrutiny," *Information Week* via COMTEX online, September 15, 2000.

But just as loyalty is becoming the mantra on every executive's lips, customer satisfaction rates are plummeting. It's practically routine these days for consumers to vow never to do business with a particular merchant. Regardless of their frenetic embrace of the customer, companies seem to be angering customers at a faster pace than they are serving them. In June 2000, *Fortune* columnist Stewart Alsop wrote a scathing piece on Sprint PCS and its poor service. The column, titled "Dear Sprint: You Ticked Off the Wrong Guy," provoked hallelujahs from Sprint PCS customers, one of whom responded:

I hate Sprint and spend way too much time fantasizing about its demise. I have friends who have Sprint too, and we talk to one another like members of a support group. Whenever I'm in line at Sprint stores, I feel it is my duty to reach out to and dissuade as many prospective customers as I can.

Another reader weighed in with this:

To list all my horrifying experiences would render this letter too long for publication.

And another (with graphic metaphor):

I'm sure you're getting a million thank-you letters from the rest of us who have been lied to, hung up on, over-billed, underserviced, and treated like cattle on the way to the slaughterhouse.

Treating customers like cattle is the antithesis of CRM, the goal of which is to *recognize and treat each customer as an individual.* That said, if one individual is dissatisfied, odds are he'll tell a collection of other individuals—one widely accepted marketing rule-of-thumb claims the average unhappy customer tells eight other potential customers about his negative experience. Such spreading of consumer disapproval turns the world of viral marketing, which depends on word-of-mouth from true believers, upside down. (*Viral marketing*—a phenomenon in which consumer buzz trumps advertising as the means of a product's adoption—accounts for the popularity of such products as Razor scooters, *The Blair Witch Project,* and MAC Spice lip liner, to name a few.) Web sites such as www.planetfeedback.com and www.downside.com are expanding the reach of these "viral complainers" and even speculating on the demise of companies that proffer poor service. The influence of such groups could in fact impact whether a product, indeed an entire company, succeeds or fails.

. . . to Optimizing the Customer Experience

Companies are spending millions of dollars trying to prevent acerbic customer testimonials like the ones we've been talking about and to figure out tactics that will not only help them keep customers, but keep their customers coming back. Throughout the book, scenarios such as the following will illustrate such tactics from customer-focused companies around the world:

Scenario

You've spent two grueling weeks of nonstop business in London and are ready to head home. Virgin Atlantic Airways sends a driver to fetch you at your hotel and bring you to the airport. Upon arrival at Heathrow, the driver stops at an outdoor kiosk. Your window magically rolls down to reveal a uniformed Virgin associate, who politely requests your ticket. As the associate checks you in, the driver retrieves your luggage from the trunk—the "boot," in the local vernacular—tags it, and deposits it on the baggage conveyor belt. The Virgin associate smiles and hands you your boarding pass.

The driver then proceeds to the terminal, pointing the way to the entrance of the Upper Class lounge, which features sleek décor, laptop hookups, and a beauty salon. As you enter and stow your carry-on bag, a waiter asks for your drink order. Midway through your haircut, Peter Frampton walks by on his way to the bar and gives you a little wave. Once in flight, you are offered a pair of fleece pajamas and a free massage.

Everyone's been super friendly. In fact, you've made no special requests since you left the hotel, have barely lifted a finger, and still have the cash you left the hotel with. (Declaring this a far cry from your typical airport experience would be an understatement.) As you take the last sip of your complimentary cosmopolitan and prepare for preferred boarding, you make a mental note: You'll be flying Virgin Atlantic again.

Notice that this particular customer experience involved no Internet access. Indeed, as much as CRM technologies tend to usurp its other components, customer relationship management can be as simple as saying, "Thanks for your business." Although some customers require a level of personalized service and customized products that make them feel special, others simply appreciate good manners. And this is the crux of CRM: how to differentiate customer treatment according to individual preferences.

The Virgin Atlantic scenario exemplifies the ultimate goal of CRM. When you recall your trip home from London, your knee-jerk recollection isn't your aisle seat or the cost of your ticket. You remember the entire experience, from what the airline did (the limo, the massage) to that serendipitous extra—in this case, Peter Frampton acknowledging your existence. Indeed, a recent Virgin advertisement wondered aloud to a fed-up traveling public: "Never hear of anyone cursing out the on-board masseuse, now do you?"

In fact, many companies have recently appended their CRM or customer care initiatives with the goal of "owning the customer experience." The implication is less about controlling what happens during a customer interaction than it is about the ability to influence how a customer perceives her contact with the company, be it through an advertisement, ordering a product, or calling customer support with a problem. CRM can allow the company to surmise a customer's *unspoken needs.*

Inciting a chance encounter with a '70s rock star is probably not in most companies' marketing plans. But there are subtler ways to give customers an experience they will remember and look for again.

The most visionary businesses understand that singular customer experiences will drive loyalty to levels unknown. Those who have already adopted a customer-focused culture understand that CRM done well influences customer emotion. It makes customers feel good, personally connected. It *humanizes* their purchase or service request or complaint. These companies define the truly loyal customer as someone who feels such good will toward the company that he "sells" its products to others, in effect acting as a voluntary (albeit unpaid) company agent. Moreover, he takes pleasure in proselytizing the company and its products, thus repeating his own positive customer experience each time he relates his story. Harley-Davidson has mastered the use of its customers as company agents. Harley owners, who consider their "hogs" less a means of transportation than a way of life, are more than happy to proselytize the company's brand—and their loyalty to it—on everything from embossed leather jackets to tattoos bearing the company logo.

In their book *The Experience Economy: Work is Theatre & Every Business a Stage,* B. Joseph Pine and James Gilmore argue that providing customers with a memorable experience, along with a useful product at a reasonable price, will become a key differentiator for companies striving to avoid the commoditization of their services. Pine and Gilmore cite NikeTown and Hard Rock Cafe as two successful establishments that lure customers for reasons beyond their mere product offerings. The authors assert that the evolution from a service-based to an experience-based economy is not only natural but also inevitable. No wonder companies have embraced CRM as a strategic imperative: it helps serve customers' *unspoken needs.*

How the Internet Changed the Rules

Talk to a marketing executive for a large bank or credit card company and she might claim to have been doing CRM long before the term was invented. Indeed, large financial institutions were at the forefront of relationship marketing, which—as we'll discuss in Chapter 2—is a subset of CRM.

The emergence of the Internet heralded a new opportunity for customer relationship building. For one thing, search engines made it easier for customers to find online merchants and interact with them. And, once found, those merchants offered customers more streamlined ways of ordering and receiving products and services.

Moreover, the Internet simplified bidirectional communication, for the first time offering a better way for consumers to relay personal information to the merchant. Instead of waiting to be mailed a form to open an account or order a phone line, a prospective customer needed only to send an application through cyberspace, resulting in shorter delivery time, improved accuracy, and quite often a higher positive perception.[4] In fact, the Internet is an environment of zero latency, offering real-time information and often on-demand product delivery.

Internet users appreciate not having to go out of their way to buy what they want, and the simpler the process, the higher the potential for customer satisfaction. Indeed, the Web offered customers options they hadn't had with other delivery channels, namely:

- 24-hour access
- Up-to-the-minute information (on, for example, stock levels, product features, and prices)
- The ability to research a product or merchant *during* a shopping trip

---

4. In 1999, 77 percent of customer questions were handled online and customer satisfaction levels increased by 20 percent over 1995, according to *Customer Service on the Internet* by Jim Sterne (Wiley, 2000).

- Online customer support
- Online self-service
- Personalized content

Consider the old way. A customer needs a new set of window blinds. He goes to the kitchen, finds the yellow pages, and calls his local blind company. The representative explains they can have someone come out and measure for the blinds a week from Thursday. The rep arrives from the blind company, measures, and shows the customer photos of various blind styles and colors. Then the rep takes another two days to write up an estimate. Almost two weeks later the customer has the pricing information he needs. Now he must decide whether to get another estimate or take his chances with the only vendor he's contacted.

Compare that to the Web version. The customer enters "mini blinds" in his favorite search engine, which returns the Web sites for several catalog window treatment firms. He chooses a company, which displays a series of blind designs and prices-per-inch. The customer chooses a design he likes, enters his window measurements, and receives a price online, including tax and shipping. Before purchasing, he browses a couple of other window-ware Web sites for additional blind designs and prices, eventually placing his order in less than an hour.

Although basic, the above examples illustrate why the Web has made doing business easier than ever. For the customer, the time savings—even if he has to measure the window himself—is improved by orders of magnitude. Plus, while he awaits delivery he can revisit the Web site to validate measurements or refresh his memory on his chosen style.

For the blind retailer, the order arrives electronically, decreasing sales time while reducing the chance of error. (The measurements, after all, are now the customer's responsibility.) Furthermore, the company has captured other information—the customer's preferred blind style, his neighborhood, his interior color scheme—for potential use in follow-up communications.

At the 2000 Comdex conference in Las Vegas, Cisco CEO John Chambers put a new spin on leveraging customer loyalty with the Internet. Chambers demonstrated a Web-connected gas pump that allowed a customer to swipe a "loyalty card." Swiping the card not only starts the gas flowing, it also illuminates a digital screen displaying personalized messages such as traffic reports while the customer pumps her gas. A customer's initial reluctance to subscribe to such services can be more than offset by the value they provide.

What's In a Name?

Being the *de rigueur* buzz-term of the moment, CRM was bound to spawn similar acronyms. Following are some CRM-related terms you will come across in this book and elsewhere in your CRM readings:

- *eCRM (alternatively, e-CRM).* eCRM refers to "electronic" customer relationship management or, more simply, CRM that is Web-based. For instance, when you log on to golf retailer chipshot.com to see if they've shipped your new titanium driver, that's eCRM.
- *ECRM.* Somewhat confusingly, many experts and publications are using ECRM, alternatively coined "ERM," to refer to "enterprise" CRM, meaning a CRM program that spans an enterprise-wide view of a customer. (We'll spell out enterprise CRM to avoid any confusion with electronic CRM.)
- *PRM.* "Partner relationship management" allows a company to manage its alliance partner and reseller relationships to provide customers with the optimal sales channel while streamlining the sales process. Determining incentives for various Web referral sites based on the profitability of the customers they send your way is one PRM tactic.
- *cCRM.* "Collaborative CRM" denotes situations in which customers can interact directly with the organization, usually through the Web. Dell, for instance, allows customers to choose their own workstation components, essentially designing their own PCs.
- *SRM.* "Supplier relationship management" resembles PRM in that it focuses on keeping external vendors happy, but SRM limits its focus to actual suppliers. Often operationally focused, SRM helps companies evaluate and categorize suppliers for given projects to optimize supplier qualification and selection, thereby streamlining the supply chain.
- mCRM: "Mobile CRM" suggests the provision of data to customers, suppliers, and business partners via wireless technologies.
- xCRM: You're bound to see other letters preceding the CRM acronym, and the "x" is simply used as a placeholder for other CRM hybrids to come.

Irrespective of the type of CRM a company is looking into, the common denominator is motivating the right customers to continue doing business with you. We'll see the various types of CRM at work in the next several chapters.

Another important CRM distinction is "operational" versus "analytical" CRM. The distinction is an important one, because it speaks to the tactics a company is taking in implementing its CRM strategy. As we'll see in Part 2 of the Handbook, there is no one right answer to CRM implementation as long as business requirements drive the initiative.

Operational CRM, also known as "front-office" CRM, involves the areas where direct customer contact occurs. We'll refer to these interactions as customer "touchpoints." A *touchpoint* can be an inbound contact—e.g., a call to a company's customer support hotline—or an outbound contact—e.g., an in-person sales call or an e-mail promotion. The majority of self-described CRM products on the market today fall into the operational category. Figure 1-1 illustrates the various levels of operational CRM.

Operational CRM enables and streamlines communications to and from customers, but this doesn't necessarily mean optimizing service. Just because a banking customer checks her balance on your Web site won't conclusively establish that she doesn't prefer to perform her transactions in the branch. But how do you know for sure?

Analytical CRM, also known as "back-office" or "strategic" CRM, involves understanding the customer activities that occurred in the front office. Analytical CRM requires technology (to compile and process the

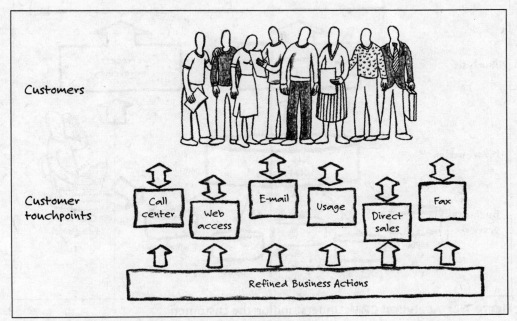

Figure 1-1: Operational CRM: Touching the customer

mountains of customer data to facilitate analysis) and new business processes (to refine customer-facing practices to increase loyalty and profitability). Under pressure from analysts and industry experts, most of today's CRM vendors are either creating analytical CRM capabilities or partnering with business intelligence (BI) vendors to incorporate analysis into their offerings. Figure 1-2 shows how the data and processes combine to refine business actions.

As we'll see throughout the Handbook, the refined-business-actions piece of the puzzle is the most difficult of all to put in place. The greater the number of missing pieces, the harder it is to construct a meaningful CRM picture. Put another way, if enhanced customer loyalty is the door, integration is the key.

CRM and Business Intelligence

Analytical CRM, when done right, involves large amounts of cross-functional data. This data is often stored on a *data warehouse,* a repository of corporate data from various sources intended to facilitate business analysis. (We'll talk more about data warehouses in Chapter 6.)

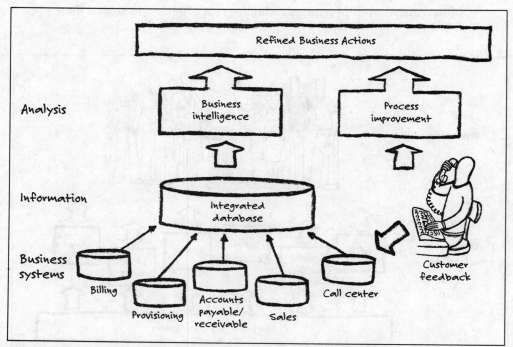

Figure 1-2: Analytical CRM: Understanding the customer

Data warehouses continue to deliver critical knowledge in a range of industries, generating returns on investment in the hundreds of millions of dollars. (My first book was about how data warehouses are providing businesses with information about their customers and products that was previously impossible to locate, let alone provide to business users, and the resulting tremendous payback.) The practice of using data warehouses to analyze business performance is known as *business intelligence*.

Data warehousing is not CRM, and neither is business intelligence.

Although this might seem obvious, even heretical to some, read a magazine article or attend a conference presentation on CRM and you'll likely hear at least one of the following claims:

- We're using data mining to execute our corporate-wide CRM initiative. It allows us to predict what customers might buy next!
- Our new CRM system allows us to analyze customer behaviors and to give our salespeople global customer information, rather than select bits and pieces like they had before.
- Once we started doing CRM, we could access all of our customers from one system.
- Customer relationship management allows the company to analyze claims data to better understand which types of claims are most prevalent for a given customer segment.
- Hallelujah! We finally know which customers are buying which products!

Valuable as they are, none of these capabilities requires a CRM product. In fact, companies from brokerage houses to pharmaceutical firms were performing these duties long before the CRM acronym came along. The combination of data warehouses and analytical toolsets has given companies the ability to drill down into integrated data to reveal interesting—even competitively differentiating—findings. Rather than extrapolating what types of promotions to launch and guessing who would respond, companies have begun relying on business intelligence analysis to provide them with hard facts that help them make better, more informed decisions and reap unforeseen rewards.

But even the experts are confused about the differences between business intelligence and CRM, and the media often exacerbates the misunderstanding. Publications and conference presentations routinely confuse the two terms. Data warehouse vendors whose markets are waning—most large companies already have at least one data warehouse—are hanging out the CRM shingle without refashioning the message. Likewise, CRM vendors who realized too late that data analysis capabilities were vital are now pitching CRM data marts along with their core products.

One popular CRM book concentrates the majority of its text and all its case studies on decision support analysis. In August 2000, a high-profile management journal dedicated an entire issue to CRM, featuring a dozen "best practices," most of which involved analyzing customer data rather than focusing on deployed CRM applications. And there was the well-attended CRM conference presentation offering the "nine types of CRM," four of which—database, decision support, analysis and data mining, and "rules repository"[5]—smacked more of business intelligence than of the overarching business strategy of CRM.

Although often misrepresented, the differences between business intelligence and CRM are distinct. Yes, they both involve critical business decisions and both rely on information technology to deliver value. The examples in Table 1-1 illustrate the distinction.

Your first impression might be that CRM is more complex than business intelligence. In fact, at most companies the number of true CRM users is a mere subset of the business population using business intelligence. However, business intelligence, when not exploited to its full potential, can result in analysis for analysis' sake.

The major difference between BI and CRM is that *CRM integrates information with business action.* In each of our examples, the CRM action will be tested and further refined. CRM combines data analysis with the deployment of specific business actions. The ability to access data is, by itself, immensely powerful, but many business intelligence environments simply use data to confirm already held hypotheses. The mandate of CRM is the ability to *act* on that data and to change fundamental business processes to become more customer-centric.

---

5. "Rules repository" refers to the storage of business rules that describe data and how it's used. For instance, a business rule that ensures a discount for a high-value customer could be executed at the time the customer places an order or could simply define that the term "revenue" refers to booked revenue rather than billed revenue.

Table 1-1: Business Intelligence versus CRM

Business Intelligence	CRM	CRM Rationale
Display the name and address of business customer TechCo.	Display TechCo's most recent inbound contact on my personal digital assistant (PDA), along with their current corporate address.	Salespeople become aware of existing or in progress issues before meeting with the customer.
Display customers who visit one of the video stores in our chain on a weekly basis.	Once a month for the next six months, send a direct-mail solicitation to customers most likely to rent next month's new features who are not weekly visitors to the store.	Convert casual visitors to frequent visitors.
Display a list of customers who have lodged a complaint within the past 30 days.	Contact all high-value customers who have lodged a complaint. Generate retention recommendations for each customer (using CRM product feature).	Focus on retaining high-value customers.
Analyze the top five most popular office supplies and compare approved vendors' prices to prices of other potential suppliers.	Identify the top five purchased office supplies and trial-run an automated Web request-for-quote (RFQ) system for limited quantities to test price improvements.	Increase the likelihood of price improvements on commodity purchases.
List the e-mail addresses for registered customers who abandoned their shopping carts during their last Web visit.	Send profitable registered customers a $5 online discount if they fill in a form explaining why they abandoned their shopping carts. Send 10 percent off to unknown visitors if they complete the form.	Reward repeat customers who are profitable and gather valuable prospect behavior data.

The Manager's Bottom Line

Operational aspects aside, CRM is first and foremost a business strategy, one that helps a company tighten its business practices across organizations while forging an ironclad connection with its customers. It is not only a response to competitive pressures facing every industry—from deregulation to supply-chain efficiencies to the massive demand for Web-based customer interaction—it is also considered a strategic imperative, garnering executive-level attention and equally lofty budgets.

In the business-to-consumer (B2C) space, CRM means keeping pace with a savvy and increasingly impatient consumer base that is closer than ever to finding your main competitor and more willing than ever to share their bad experiences with your prospects. As for the business-to-business (B2B) segment, as we'll see in Chapter 5, optimizing supplier and partner communications is more critical than ever. Making it all work together and seamlessly involves nothing short of organizational choreography.

That CRM is a business strategy is now a well-worn maxim. That it involves much more than information technology is sometimes disheartening news to many a manager gunning for that elusive quick win. The CRM best-practice company is the one that understands how to improve business practices and customer relationships by using CRM technology and customer data as part of an overarching program that also involves process and organizational changes, with the ultimate aim of differentiating itself through superior customer relationships.

As we'll see throughout the Handbook, defending customers and profits while inspiring loyalty takes more than just CRM vendor tools. It takes understanding which type of CRM can best foster high-impact relationship improvements. The following four chapters present the various types of CRM and their components so you can decide on the best definition of CRM for your organization.

CRM in Marketing

I n the 1960s, the practice of motivational research sought to understand what made people tick. The hope was that company researchers could discover how to better market their products. Motivational research involved everything from scientists showing volunteers a series of advertisements and measuring the subtle physical responses to administering Rorschach tests and extrapolating visceral reactions to conducting traditional focus groups, a practice that endures today in the consumer packaged goods and entertainment industries.

The scope of these efforts remained unwavering in its product focus, however, with the customer acting as an ancillary component of the purchase cycle. Brand was king, as the saying went, and it would take many iterations of the marketing lifecycle for companies to understand the importance of a customer-focused business strategy.

From Product to Customer: A Marketing Retrospective

In fact, product marketing became a study unto itself, its students testing the waters with a variety of gimmicks and promotional ideas. Part research, part guessing game, and part leap of faith, the practice of product marketing evolved into a formalized organization in most companies, and the process, as shown in Figure 2-1, was predictable.

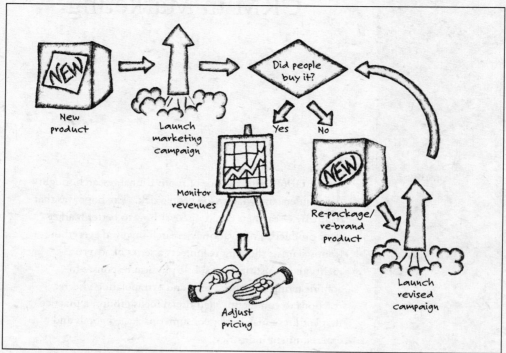

Figure 2-1: The process of product marketing

Product marketing campaigns were designed to reach as many people as possible. Mass marketing campaigns not only treated all customers as if they had the same needs and wants, but also focused on the product being pitched, not on its potential buyer. Mass marketing a product means stocking the same shelves across all stores with the same product and alerting potential customers in the same way. The underlying assumption was that the availability and choice of products a company offered consumers was the principal determinant of its success.

A product focus nevertheless does not imply a lack of market understanding. On the contrary, as companies launched and re-launched their products, they began analyzing the responses to determine the success of marketing campaigns. Business journals waxed poetic on product distribution strategies, and statisticians were suddenly in demand as companies began institutionalizing such data analysis practices as product revenue analysis and price-elasticity modeling.

The 1960s introduced the phenomenon of "direct marketing." Direct marketing involved communicating with large numbers of consumers—usually through promotional mailings or magazine advertisements—and inviting them to respond to the promotion ("Send check or money order . . .") by ordering the product through the mail. Based on the principles of mass marketing, direct marketing usually focused on selling a mass-produced product, be it 8-track tapes, porcelain plates, or glass-encased stamp collections, to as many consumers as possible.

But direct marketers were pioneers in one respect: they monitored responses to their ads, often creating several versions of the same campaign and launching it in different areas of the country. They then analyzed relative response rates, whittling away the marketing messages that didn't work and refining other campaigns based on those learnings. Direct marketing stood the world of conventional advertising on its head, for the first time suggesting that messages could be tailored and consumers had preferences.

Despite its sophistication relative to the more general mass marketing campaigns, a direct marketing promotion was considered a smash if it generated a 2 percent response rate. In fact, according to the Direct Marketing Association, if a company's direct mail campaign touches 100,000 customers and costs $98,000, the company nets a significant loss.[1]

Target Marketing

As consumers began purchasing and using products, more data became available about them. Data analysts began associating products to the customers who were buying them. And it was through these analysis activities—as well as rising temperatures in the competitive climate and a few timely magazine articles—that companies began to understand that their (usually inert) customer data could be as valuable as the product data they were busy probing. Thus evolved the term "target marketing," the practice of promoting a product or service to a subset of customers and prospects.

Technically, the size of a target market can range from the sum of all customers to a single individual, but during the early days of target marketing when companies began using information technologies in creative new ways, market segmentation was the most widely adopted approach. Although many data

---

1. As reported in *CIO* Magazine, August 15, 2000.

points across the organization from products to sales channels might be segmented, segmentation is most often associated with dividing customers into categories based on their demographics: age, gender, and other personal information.[2] Even 20 years after customer segmentation had been embraced by marketing departments, many still divided their customers on the basis of whether they were business or residential.

Modern companies assign a variety of segments to their customers, often dynamically defining segments and temporarily regrouping customers for specific campaigns. Marketing departments routinely group customers into the following categories:

- Geography or regionality
- Psychographics[3]
- Firmographics[4]
- Infographics[5]
- Preferred sales channel
- Profitability
- Number of products
- Sales territory
- Tenure
- Lifetime value
- Household demographics
- Risk score
- Life stage
- Privacy preferences

By segmenting customers, companies could begin more specialized communications about their products. Much of this relies on the company's

---

2. In March of 1964, author Daniel Yankelovich wrote about "New Criteria for Market Segmentation" in the *Harvard Business Review,* arguing that demographic segmentation, while valuable, was not the only way a company could categorize its customers.

3. "Psychographic" segments define groups of customers with similar interests, opinions, and preferences.

4. "Firmographics" characterize a business and are used especially often in business-to-business (B2B) communications.

5. "Infographic" segments delineate customers according to how they want to be communicated with (via e-mail? direct sales? a proprietary Web site?), as well as how they prefer to interact with the company.

understanding its business strategies to the extent that it knows its most desirable segments. For instance, if a bank has set its sights on deriving most of its profits from fee-income products offered in its investment services line, customers of this organization will likely have different preferences and characteristics from those opening savings accounts. Segmenting customers based on their preferred line of business or desired product features can reveal interesting facts about their different preferences and behaviors.

For instance, Boots, a U.K. retailer, segments customers who respond to promotions based on whether they are "deal seekers," "stockpilers" (who buy in bulk when an item goes on sale and then don't visit the store until they need to stock up again), loyal existing buyers (whose purchase patterns increase for sale items), or new market customers (who buy a sale item and continue to buy it after it reverts to its regular price).[6]

Many companies with the ability to analyze detailed customer data tend to segment customers on the basis of how likely they are to purchase a new product or service. One of my clients, a leader in cable television, segments its customers based on their "propensity to buy," as illustrated in Table 2-1.

Based on this segmentation, the cable company trying to up-sell customers to digital TV service offers customers in its Skeptics segment digital cable for the price of standard cable service for a three-month period. The net cost is only

Table 2-1: Propensity-to-Buy Segments

Segment:	Early Adopters	Pragmatists	Skeptics	Laggards
Description:	Most likely to buy newly offered products and services. Especially attracted to technology innovation.	Will purchase new products after value is well understood. Might need to see the product in action.	Only purchase if value is proven. Chances increase with rebates or money-back guarantees.	Await mass-acceptance of product prior to purchase. Not likely to respond to new promotions.
Percentage of customer base:	11	46	28	15

6. According to "Taking Advantage," *1:1 Direct* magazine, September 2000.

sixty dollars—twenty dollars more per month—and there is a high likelihood of retention. The Early Adopters receive an e-mail offer—"For a limited time only!"—for digital cable plus 500 minutes of free long distance per month for six months. The value of this service is $50 per month to the consumer—the cost to the cable company is negligible. The Early Adopters end up keeping the digital cable and will most likely remain long distance customers as well.

The advantage of target marketing is that, if the company has 50 million customers, only 14 million or so—28 percent—will receive the promotional mailing for digital service. At a bulk rate of eight cents per mailing, target marketing saves the company almost $3 million in postage alone. (The company might incur labor and mail service costs, which would also be sharply reduced.) This allows the cable company to steer clear of disinterested prospects and avoid the all too common practice of over-communicating to customers. It fosters the customer's perception that marketing is a tailored service, not an annoyance.

Through the significant cost savings and increased response rates, target marketing justified increased expenditures for information technology. In fact, the better companies became at analyzing data about their customers, the more effective their campaigns became, creating the closed-loop effect illustrated in Figure 2-2.

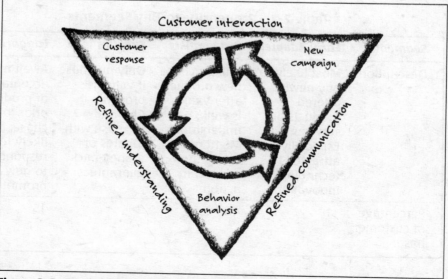

Figure 2-2: Refining marketing campaigns

Figure 2-2 illustrates that the more a company knows about its customers, the more detailed its marketing messages can be. Refined marketing campaigns, targeted to customer segments rather than to the mass populace, became the marketing Holy Grail.

Relationship Marketing and One-to-One

That is until relationship marketing came along. Popularized by Regis McKenna in his 1993 book, *Relationship Marketing: Successful Strategies for the Age of the Customer,* relationship marketing was embraced as a way for marketing departments to get to know their customers more intimately by understanding their preferences and thus increasing the odds of retaining them. Target marketing, cross-selling, and customer loyalty programs evolved from one-off pilot projects and became formalized as part of core marketing and sales processes.

Also in 1993, Don Peppers and Martha Rogers predicted the demise of the mass marketing tactic of relying on economies of scale to churn out huge quantities of standardized products. They declared the need to focus less on products and more on customer relationships. In their watershed book *The One to One Future,* Peppers and Rogers argued that in coming years

> . . . you will not be trying to sell a single product to as many customers as possible. Instead, you'll be trying to sell a single customer as many products as possible—over a long period of time, and across different product lines. To do this, you will need to concentrate on building unique relationships with individual customers, on a 1:1 basis.[7]

Peppers and Rogers rounded out marketing's evolution from mass-marketing standard products to segmenting customers to true relationship marketing, or one-to-one. Figure 2-3 shows the stages and their differences.

One-to-one means not only communicating with customers as individuals, but also developing custom products and tailored messages based on customers' unspoken needs. It relies on a two-way dialog between a company and its customers to foster a true relationship and allow customers to truly express the desires the company can help fulfill. It relies as heavily on the customer's experience of the company as it does on the specific marketing messages he receives.

---

7. Peppers, Don and Martha Rogers, Ph.D., *The One to One Future: Building Relationships One Customer At a Time.* New York: Doubleday, 1993.

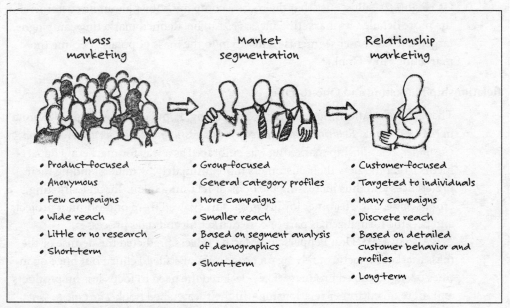

Figure 2-3: Marketing evolving

The concept of "permission marketing" goes hand-in-hand with one-to-one: customers not only need to be communicated with as individuals, they themselves should be able to stipulate how and when. After all, as Seth Godin says, "You can't build a one-to-one relationship with a customer unless the customer explicitly agrees to the process."[8] Permission marketing implies that the customer will decide when and for what reason she will accept to be interrupted with a marketing message. Most of the time, it's when the customer perceives there is value to her in such an interruption. A current example is Amazon.com's notification of Oprah's new Book Club selection to subscribers who have opted in.

The vision of one-to-one and permission marketing relies even more heavily on information technology to track individual customers, understand their differences, and acknowledge their interaction preferences. The purveyors of these visions often stop short of discussing how exactly a company can not only differentiate each discrete customer, but also put the business processes and

---

8. Godin, Seth, *Permission Marketing: Turning Strangers into Friends, and Friends into Customers.* New York: Simon and Schuster, 1999, 65.

organizational structures and technologies in place to treat them differently (see the definition of CRM in Chapter 1). Fortunately, companies had begun analyzing customer data even before the advent of relationship marketing, and thus the possibility of managing individual customer interactions based on the requirements of those individuals is becoming ever more realistic. The trouble has been that they've underestimated the extent of the work necessary to realize the promise.

Campaign Management

If traditional marketing is, as the saying goes, part art and part science, the marketing of the future is pure science with a bit of flourish. The success of corporate marketing programs has become directly proportional to a company's ability to capture and analyze the right data.

In days of mass marketing with its "batch and blast" mentality, most companies would decide on a marketing campaign based on someone's interesting idea. A team of product managers would plan the campaign, coming up with hit-or-miss media guesses and sound bites. Then they'd pull the ripcord and pray. It could take months to figure out whether a campaign was working, and months more to repair and re-launch it.

Why the throw-it-at-the-wall-and-see-if-it-sticks approach? For one thing, finding, entering, storing, and tracking individual customer data records was beyond most companies' capabilities, not to mention their budgets. Paradoxically, the larger the company, the greater the number of customers and thus the more cumbersome and expensive managing customer data became. Large companies began undergoing the Herculean task of collecting and storing customer data in primitive databases. In the 1980s, the advent of relational databases and data warehouses (databases expressly designed to hold large amounts of corporate data) promised to ease the pain of amassing detailed customer records and availing them to business users. Chapter 6 discusses how data warehouses have gone from a large-company luxury to a CRM necessity.

Another challenge was the sheer labor involved in launching new marketing campaigns, rendered all the more difficult with the increasing frequency of smaller, more targeted promotions. Marketing departments needed to conceive of and plan the campaign, define the targeted consumers, determine the channel—how the campaign would be communicated—and then launch the promotion, as shown in Figure 2-4.

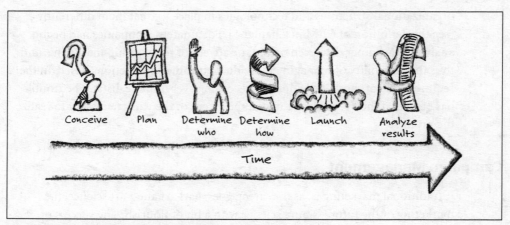

Conceive   Plan   Determine   Determine   Launch   Analyze
                    who   how   results

Time

Figure 2-4: A linear campaign management process

But only those with the necessary data can really monitor the results of that campaign, and use those results to refine future campaigns, a process known as "closed loop" campaign management. This means the ability not only to analyze and understand whether a campaign is a success and why. It means using that new knowledge as the basis for future campaigns, in effect closing the loop with evolving customer information, as in Figure 2-5.

It could be months or even years before companies understood whether a marketing campaign was successful. No wonder the practice of campaign management mandated large marketing organizations and even larger marketing budgets! Many companies relegated the cumbersome work to marketing service bureaus or direct marketing agencies, whose turnaround time was less than stellar. Many stayed in their marketing comfort zones, executing ad-hoc, point-in-time campaigns that generated short-term revenues but did nothing to reveal customer preferences or improve customer relationships.

The time and cost being spent on these campaigns and the opportunity cost associated with ad hoc or experimental promotions were noted by technology vendors, many of them database product companies, who began devising ways of automating key pieces of the campaign management process.

The initial developments in campaign management software were list generators. Leveraging current customer information in existing databases, list-generation software dynamically segmented customers for certain campaigns, using standard database queries. The result was a list of customer names and addresses that fit the specified boundaries.

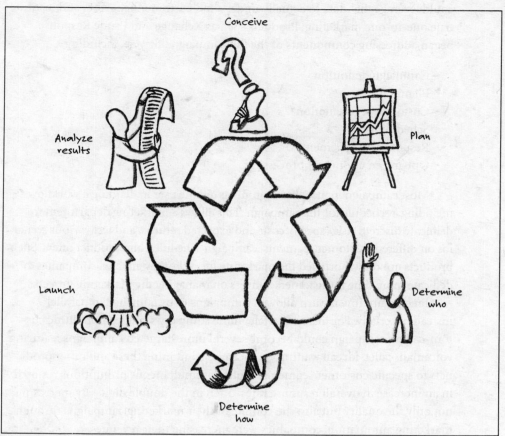

Figure 2-5: Closed-loop campaign management

For example, a marketing department at a bank wants to offer frequent depositors with large balances access to low-interest lines of credit. The specification "Display the names and addresses of all customers with checking account balances of over $25,000 who have an average deposit amount of $5000 or higher" could easily be translated into a query and submitted to the bank's customer database. The resulting list would become the basis for a mailing offer to those customers. The bank saves money not only by applying the principles of target marketing and segmentation—communicating to a proscribed and thus smaller group of customers—but also by avoiding the cost and time involved in searching out those customers manually.

As campaign management software became more popular, its features became more robust. The richer a company's customer database, the more it could leverage that data to actually understand customer behaviors and institute true one-to-one marketing. Products such as Xchange and Prime Response began addressing components of the full campaign lifecycle, including

- Campaign definition
- Planning
- Customer segmentation
- Scheduling
- Response management
- Opt-in versus opt-out processing

Most campaign management products aid the user in defining a workflow, including a schedule for the campaign. This allows a marketing department to delineate discrete tasks, specify costs and expected returns, and test various scenarios on different customer segments, campaign schedules, and product offers. Such products not only shortened the marketing lifecycle, they enabled companies to dedicate more time to customers and less on managing the marketing process.

Freeing up time in turn allowed campaigns to be launched in parallel instead of serially. For instance, a telephone company's single, monolithic custom-calling campaign could become several more-targeted campaigns featuring voicemail, caller-id, call waiting, or packages combining these and other products to specific customer segments. Multiple simultaneous promotions resulted in an increase in overall response rates, often in the double digits. By increasing not only the quality but also the volume of their marketing campaigns through marketing automation, companies were increasing their revenues.

CRM products offering campaign management present savings of time, labor, and cost and often demonstrate quantifiable returns on investment, as they have to the following companies:

- An outdoor products catalog company that customized catalogs for specific customer segments (segments include "Day-trippers," "Clotheshorses," and "Roughnecks") has boosted its average purchase by segment to 23 percent, thereby increasing its overall catalog revenues by a staggering 500 percent.
- An online brokerage firm's cross-selling of its new checking account offering to holders of Keogh retirement accounts generated a 32 percent response rate from its targeted base of customers, versus 4 percent from a control group.
- An e-tailer specializing in lifestyle products saw sales of its languishing line of house-brand women's clothing nearly double when the company

promoted select casual outfits with a well-known brand of baby products favored by new mothers.

When mastered, automated campaign management is like a good wine: it gets better with age. With marketing campaigns targeting increasingly smaller customer segments, companies can increase the number of campaigns simply to ensure that they continue interacting with as many customers as possible. And by tracking the success of campaigns over time, companies can refine them, resulting in even higher response rates and thus greater corresponding revenues. The practice of closed-loop campaign management—using the results of campaigns to refine future campaigns—has become an acknowledged CRM best practice.

CRM Marketing Initiatives

Companies simply don't purchase CRM products to automate campaign management without a clear view of what they want to do. After all, companies devoid of a marketing vision rarely have sufficient budget for CRM software. Those who do, have a variety of tactics in mind for increasing customer value and loyalty.

Cross-Selling and Up-Selling

Cross-selling is the act of selling a product or service to a customer as a result of another purchase. The example of new mothers purchasing products for their babies at the same time they buy clothes for themselves is an example of cross-selling. Cross-selling is all the rage nowadays, because selling more services to an existing customer increases revenue from that customer and costs less than acquiring a new one.

Likewise, companies are frantically looking for opportunities to up-sell, or motivate their existing customers to trade up to more profitable products. The youthful voice at the drive-thru window predictably asking, "You wanna super-size that?" is the best quotidian example of up-selling.

The art of cross-selling and up-selling is understanding which products will increase, rather than decrease, a customer's overall profitability. Simply cross-selling a customer an unprofitable product might actually render that customer less profitable than he was prior to the sale.

Cross-selling done correctly means selling the right product to the right customer. It also means understanding that not every customer is a good candidate for cross-selling. For instance, credit card customers have proven to be poor cross-selling candidates because favorable interest rates and low fees—not the card itself or even the issuer—are the dominant determinant of consumer response to credit card offers. Understanding the ways by which customers evaluate how and whether to respond to such promotions is critical. Not surprisingly, the desire to improve cross-selling business practices accounts for much of the popularity of CRM marketing automation technologies.

Customer Retention

In 1996, author Frederick Reichheld wrote that U.S. corporations lose half their customers every five years.[9] Indeed, banks and telephone companies were already in the throes of analyzing customer attrition to understand why customers were leaving for competitors.

Understanding that customers have left, and knowing specifically who, is non-trivial. Understanding why they have left is even more difficult. Harder yet is stemming the tide of customer attrition by applying this knowledge to business tactics that encourage customers to stay.

Analyzing customer attrition operates on the aphorism established in Chapter 1 that keeping an existing customer is far more cost effective than acquiring a new one. After all, the more customers leave, the greater the loss of revenue, loss of the initial acquisition investment, and loss of a stable market base for selling new products.

Although this business tenet hasn't arrested the frenzy to acquire new customers, it has resulted in millions of dollars being spent to analyze not only why customers leave, but also which customers are the most desirable and thus worth keeping. In the 1980s, companies began focusing on who had left. In the 1990s, they began applying characteristics of customers who had left to existing customers, thereby pinpointing those customers who might be leaving next. Reducing customer defections by even a fraction has been proven to increase profits exponentially.

Currently, companies are using sophisticated predictive technologies that compare like attributes of similar customers to delineate customers who are "likely to churn," and they're simultaneously personalizing tailored marketing interactions designed to motivate those customers to stay.

---

9. Reichheld, Frederick F., "Learning from Customer Defections," *Harvard Business Review,* March-April 1996.

The trouble with customer retention strategies is that, once you've identified customers who might leave, how do you keep them? Despite sophisticated churn prediction products, most companies still don't really know whether product give-aways and add-on perks—whose initial cost outlay often exceed the resulting revenue contribution—really result in profitability. Will the cost of the free mobile phone be recouped in the customer's service spending? How often are customers continuing their digital cable subscriptions after the first 3 (free) months? Will that first-class upgrade ensure that a given customer will fly with you again?

While they figure out the best way to keep customers who are on the brink of leaving, companies are working on designing marketing campaigns to bump low-value customers to a higher value band rather than allowing them to churn by default. Churn prediction is one of several uses of technology and data that aid marketing in predicting customer behavior.

Behavior Prediction

Although not so much a marketing practice as a marketing enabler, behavior prediction helps marketing departments determine what customers are likely to do in the future. Using sophisticated modeling and data mining techniques—we'll discuss some of these in more detail in Chapter 6—behavior prediction uses historical customer behavior to foresee future behaviors. This analysis includes several variations:

- *Propensity-to-buy analysis.* Understanding which products a particular customer is likely to purchase.
- *Next sequential purchase.* Predicting what product or service a customer is likely to buy next.
- *Product affinity analysis.* Understanding which products will be purchased with other products. Also known as "market basket analysis," it can be viewed as examining products in a shopper's basket to understand possible product associations.
- *Price elasticity modeling and dynamic pricing.* Determining the optimal price for a given product, often for a given customer or customer segment.

By understanding how a customer is likely to behave, a company can make a host of marketing decisions based on this knowledge, including these:

- Preemptively offering discounts or fee waivers to existing customers who are at risk of churning

- Refining target marketing campaigns to smaller customer segments or specific products
- Packaging certain products together and fixed-pricing them to sell more products and increase their profitability
- Cross-selling products likely to be purchased with other products

The key to all this analysis, and especially to the actions that result, is knowing who your best customers are.

Customer Profitability and Value Modeling

Calculating overall customer profitability was nirvana for financial institutions in the late 20th century. But it wasn't easy. These businesses first had to understand the costs of their various products, then roll those products up to the account level, and then associate a single customer with multiple accounts and perhaps with a household. The extensive processing and detailed data required to calculate customer profitability combined with the high cost of specialized profitability-modeling products kept it out of reach for even mid-market banks until recently. For the first time companies could quantify that price-sensitive customers—those who bring in paper-thin margins—might never recoup their value, irrespective of their purchase volume, yet certain low-volume customers were nevertheless highly profitable.

But profitability is only a piece of the revenue puzzle. A customer can be unprofitable but could have referred three high-value customers to your firm, thereby rendering himself very valuable. Despite not being currently profitable, a recent college graduate shows several signs of emerging profitability and thus might be considered valuable over her lifetime.

Different companies in different industries will have different value metrics. Customer value is a pregnant phrase, variously referring to a customer's lifetime value (LTV), potential value, or competitive value (also known as wallet share). Many firms have formalized the practice of value modeling, allowing them to score a customer based on her relative worth to the company over time. The score is then used in a variety of ways to tune communications with that customer.

For instance, a brick-and-mortar retailer recognizes a shopper with a frequent-buyer card who nevertheless visits the store only during advertised sales. The customer has been assigned a low value score. The retailer sends the customer a preapproved credit card to increase his value and thus his corresponding revenue contribution. The credit card might result in raising the number of monthly shopping trips, as well as boosting the customer's average purchase amount.

Irrespective of the level of customer value being modeled, customer value measurement is data-intensive. The challenge of value modeling is that it is only as accurate as the customer data is rich—and the analysis statistically robust. Historical customer behaviors, product costs, support costs, customer profitability, and channel usage should all figure into the overall value of a customer. Basing customer value on only a single metric puts companies at risk of making erroneous decisions about how to communicate with customers and what to say, which could ultimately decrease customer satisfaction and increase attrition. As we'll see in Chapter 3, companies can use the result of customer value analysis to differentiate customer service.

Channel Optimization

The goal of marketing automation is to offer the right message to the right customer at the right time. With the advent of the Internet, many firms are appending "through the right channel," to this maxim (denoted by "Determine How" in Figure 2–4) as customers' interaction preferences evolve.

For instance, a new customer whose use of online banking services has steadily increased might prefer to be e-mailed a new offer along with her regular statement, whereas a retiree who enjoys visiting the neighborhood branch might be delighted when the branch manager offers her a cup of coffee and a brochure on a new annuity product. Indeed, banking customers have a range of choices when it comes to their preferred channels, as Figure 2-6 illustrates.

Understanding the channels through which specific customers prefer to interact with your company is only a slice of the pie. Your company must also decide how best to communicate with your customers. Just because a valuable customer prefers making his deposits in the branch doesn't mean he won't demand comprehensive online statements. Channel management means optimizing a company's "inbound" channels with its "outbound" means of customer interaction and knowing how to choose the best approach for each.

Personalization

Practically all of us have purchased something over the Internet, be it books, large appliances, or a pizza. But have you ever noticed that sometimes one of those Web sites seems to be talking right to you? Personalization is the

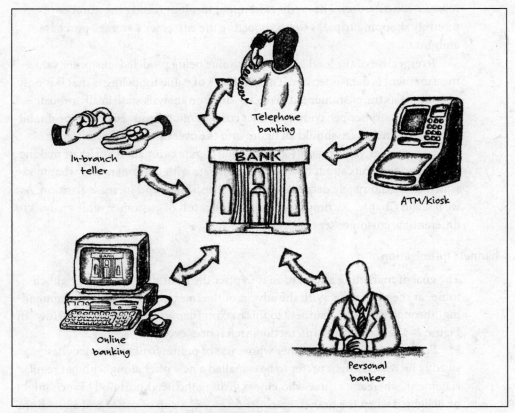

Figure 2-6: Various banking service channels

capability to customize customer communication based on knowledge preferences and behaviors at the time of interaction. It can take any of the following forms:

- You log on to your favorite music Web site. The site greets you with "Hi, Jill, welcome back! We have some new picks for you!" You scroll down and see a variety of new CDs you've had your eye on but have been too busy to browse through at the record store. You double-click on the cover of the new Beastie Boys anthology and listen to one of the cuts.
- While channel-surfing, you come across a hedge trimmer being featured on a home shopping station. You know your wife would love it. You call to

order it and the operator greets you by name and asks for the item number. After confirming that the hedge trimmer can be sent overnight, she asks you whether you'd like to use your Visa card. She already has the number. You say yes. (Obviously, your wife has shopped here before.)

Although both of these examples are leveraging personalization, the first example is personalization as most people know it: online messages tailored to a particular customer or customer segment.

Such tailored messages can involve anything from inserting the Web shopper's name into the message—known as "variable insertion"—to using detailed customer data to personalize Web site content. For instance, a cosmetics e-tailer might want to promote de-frizzing shampoo to shoppers in the humid southeast and a conditioner with SPF protection to shoppers in Palm Springs.

More specifically, personalization technologies can tailor messages to individual customers, accessing current personal data each time the customer visits the site and using it to create custom content. These technologies enable analysis of each customer over time and across all channels, using customer profile data, past purchases, clickstream data, and Web survey responses to determine, for instance, what product the customer is most likely to purchase next or whether the customer is at-risk and thus deserving of a discount offer to lure him back. A personalized message reflecting the results of that analysis is then delivered in real time when the customer visits the Web site.

The following two screens illustrate personalization functionality from the Teradata CRM product. The screen in Figure 2-7 depicts the text from a pending e-mail marketing campaign, along with a range of possible account balances. Instead of sending the same offer to all the bank's prospects for this campaign, the campaign administrator can scale the offer according to the customer's current account balance.

Figure 2-8 shows the first screen as it would be seen by the prospect, having been "filled in," with the actual offer. The prospect is proffered additional high-margin products, allowing the bank to maximize the opportunity for cross-selling.

Personalization technologies can apply their learnings—if the customer responded to a discount on skis, it's likely she'll be interested in cold-weather apparel—to future personalized messages, having proven improved response rates over time as the customer's behavior data becomes ever more enriched. This removes the guesswork, resulting in a creeping understanding of customers

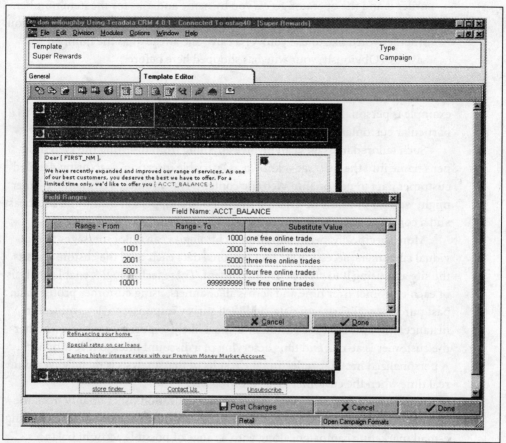

Figure 2-7: Applying Personalization (Courtesy of Teradata CRM)

and their preferences over that customer's relationship with your company. Known as "adaptive personalization," it's a critical factor in making it as difficult as possible for your customer to switch to a competitor. For example, Wine.com uses personalization to tailor unique e-mail newsletters to certain customers based on past purchases.

Personalization in the B2C space is largely based on the analysis of a customer's clickstreams, his navigation path through a company's Web site. By monitoring a customer's clickstream, a company can see not only what a customer purchased but how the customer reached the site in the first place (a partner Web site? A banner ad?), how he traveled through the site after he got there, how much time he spent on each page, and which products might have

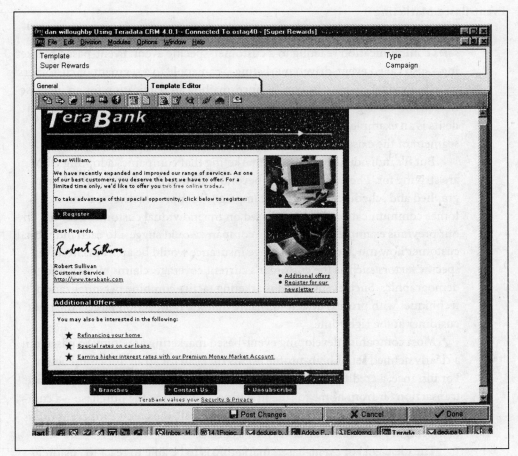

Figure 2-8: A personalized marketing message (Courtesy of Teradata CRM)

stimulated purchases of other products. In short, clickstreams can shed light on a customer's Web experience.

For now, it's important to note that analyzing clickstreams can trigger dozens of new tactics, including

- Changes to Web impressions (images on the Web site) according to a customer's navigation patterns and past purchases
- Custom promotions or discounts based on past purchases or research
- Customized Web pages according to the visitor's use of the site

Chapter 6 features a real-world scenario of clickstream analysis at a specialty e-tailer and how it presented a choice of business actions.

Event-Based Marketing

The best definition of event-based marketing is a time-sensitive marketing or sales communication reacting to a customer-specific event. Event-based marketing—also called event-driven marketing—can apply to a segment of customers or to individual customers. For instance, mailing an application for an increase in collision damage insurance to all customers who've recently had traffic accidents is an example of event-based marketing to a largely undifferentiated segment of the existing customer base.

But it's individual event-based marketing that companies adopting CRM are striving for. They want to move beyond traditional, painstakingly choreographed and scheduled marketing campaigns to more reactive, real-time customer communications highly focused on the individual customer's profile. In our previous example, the insurance company would suggest to each individual customer how much collision damage insurance would be appropriate, given specific factors such as the customer's current coverage, claims history, and demographics. Such event-based marketing tactics combine personalization techniques with process design to ensure that the right action targets the right customer at the right time.

Most companies developing event-based marketing are doing so based on a clearly defined set of high-profile events that call for straightforward action. For instance, a credit card company calls a customer who has made a purchase transaction far from home for the first time, confirming the purchase—a common fraud-avoidance tactic. During the phone call, the credit card agent offers to overnight the customer free traveler's checks.

The ideal goal of event-based marketing is to be able to react to customer events in near real-time, soon after the actual event occurs. A simple example of this is the grocery store receipt featuring coupons on the back for merchandise you're likely to be interested in, but might not readily buy if unprompted. Such real-time, event-based marketing means detecting and responding to events quickly, often using complex data-mining capabilities (see Chapter 6), and requires an intimate understanding of possible events and their desired outcomes. Dynamic event-based marketing means reacting to a customer event in the optimal time frame—which could differ from one event to another.

Event-based marketing requires solid process automation and a well-calibrated workflow to be effective. For instance, a communications company wants to formalize a "preemptive strike" strategy for all high-value customers—18 percent of the total customer population—when they experience dropped calls or mobile phone outages. The company has set the following success metric: the customer who experiences the outage must be contacted within one hour of the event, giving the company a shot at service recovery while it's still fresh in the customer's mind.

As a manual process, this would be virtually impossible. Automation is required to detect the dropped call, route the information (including the cause) to a qualified customer service representative, and suggest the appropriate compensation for that customer. To effectively automate this process, the wireless provider must first understand the process as well as its desired outcomes. After all, for one customer the objective of the call could be customer retention, but for another it might be the chance to up-sell newer equipment.

The term "event-based marketing" is often used erroneously to replace "life stage" or "life event" marketing, in which a company determines where a customer is in the continuum of her life span in order to deliver the appropriate marketing message. For instance, a newly married couple won't respond to a promotion for a home-equity line of credit if they aren't yet homeowners; however, the couple might be interested in a joint interest-bearing checking account. Tracking such life events can enrich your customers' profiles over time, providing better and better clues about how to effectively market to them.

No matter what type of customer communication a company sends for marketing purposes, the ultimate goal is to get the customer to visit the store, catalog, or Web site; to buy products they're happy with; and to return often. Preeminent companies that have excelled at this strategy have actually succeeded in convincing customers to *pay them* for the privilege of being loyal customers. Disney's new Disney Club program charges its members a membership fee plus an annual payment for access to new Disney products and promotions. The company's chief strategic officer told *The Wall Street Journal* he expects to have at least a million members by 2002.[10]

Customer Privacy—One-to-One's Saboteur?

Although we'll talk more about the privacy issue's potential to foil customer relationship management initiatives in Chapter 10, the subject of privacy deserves mention in the context of customer marketing. After all, the success

---

10. "Customer Affinity Club Targets Firm's Loyalists," *The Wall Street Journal*, November 15, 2000.

of the marketing programs this chapter discusses hinges on the availability of customer data, and privacy is becoming an increasing concern for both consumers and the companies who market to them.

If the indiscriminate use of individual consumer information is at the heart of the privacy debate, the speed of change is its lifeblood. CRM technologies such as data-mining engines and personalization tools enable their users to not only understand a consumer's behavior history and preferences, but to predict what she might do next and to share this information without the consumer's having a say. The increasing sophistication of such technologies and incendiary reports on identity theft, villainous Web crawlers and Web bugs, and so-called Trojan horses (software programs that purport to be innocuous but in reality are scanning your hard drive or turning on your PC camera) fan the flame of consumer paranoia. Witness the title of the book, *Cybercrime . . . Cyberterrorism . . . Cyberwarfare . . . Averting an Electronic Waterloo.* The scare tactics are working.

Aside from the growing practice of posting privacy policies on their Web sites, companies are doing little to assuage consumer fears. Latanya Sweeney, assistant professor of computer science and public policy at Carnegie Mellon University, recently told *Newsweek* that "87 percent of the population of the U.S. can be uniquely identified [only] by their date of birth, gender, and five-digit ZIP code."[11] Although this was a backhanded compliment to the developing prowess of database marketing, it was nevertheless a battle call to consumer privacy advocates.

And companies who blow the privacy issue are getting unwanted attention for often-innocent errors. It's not only the ubiquitous consumer protection agencies vying for more privacy restrictions, but government regulators as well. The Gramm-Leach-Bliley Act in the United States established mandatory measures for U.S. financial institutions and their use of data, and many consumer advocates believe it's the harbinger of privacy legislation for other industries. Almost all European countries now have federal agencies dedicated to protecting privacy, with the European Economic Union guaranteeing individual compensation in instances of privacy abuse.

"Consumers shouldn't have to reveal their life story every time they surf the Web," said California congresswoman Anna Eshoo in a press release announcing

---

11. Sherman, Erik, "Tinker, Tailor, Software, Spy," *Newsweek,* October 16, 2000.

her proposed legislation[12] requiring companies to adopt "opt in" policies. The Shelby Act recently barred state motor vehicle agencies from sharing driver registration information without explicit consent, reversing the previous opt-out policy. Corporations fear such legislation because it will require them to receive explicit customer permission to solicit and use their personal data. Not only will such opt-in policies thwart many extensive and intricately planned marketing strategies, they will result in millions of dollars being spent on process and technology modifications to support it.

Add to all this the fact that consumers are feeling harassed. It's no longer enough to post a privacy policy on a Web site—companies are being blacklisted by consumer organizations for contacting customers more frequently than they're comfortable with, or for simply sending duplicate mailings.

The point to incorporating privacy measures into a CRM initiative is this: the customer doesn't care about your company's *intent*—it's the *behavior* that counts. A duplicate mailing or unwanted phone call can be the innocent result of an incomplete customer profile or simple data error. But from the customer's perspective, it could mean all your outbound communications are suspect. Using a customer's data without her permission need occur only once before that customer is lost.

Companies are increasingly limiting the number of messages they send to their customers in an effort to maintain good will. But if your company believes every customer is indeed an individual, contact preferences will be different too. Understanding the type of marketing message and its optimal channel aren't enough—you must understand each customer's preferred interaction *frequency* as well.

Simply put: Each customer's privacy preference should be solicited and incorporated into his customer profile and should then be unequivocally honored. As we mentioned earlier in this chapter, customers have unspoken needs, some of which you'll have to infer from their past interactions with you. Aside from the numerous marketing possibilities offered by CRM and its accompanying customer understanding, the ongoing privacy controversy alone makes integrating detailed customer behavior and preference data worth the time and effort.

---

12. The bill, co-sponsored by Reps. Chris Cannon of Utah and Anna Eshoo of California, was introduced in January 2000.

A Marketing Automation Checklist for Success

The goal of campaign management products, whose vendors inevitably lay claim to the more pervasive rubric of CRM, is to automate marketing processes, not to replace them. This raises three important points about how an organization conducts its marketing:

1. The marketing processes themselves should be sound. As with other technologies, speeding up a broken or inefficient process simply means faster mistakes, otherwise known as "paving the cowpath."
2. Marketing practices are very industry specific. A bank usually has enough information about its customers to send a specific message to an individual customer based on her existing product set. A general merchandise retailer, however, doesn't necessarily know who's shopping and thus relies more on mass marketing techniques and encouraging customers to sign up for loyalty cards so it can gather more personal information. Each of these companies will have different service channels, different strategies, and very different ways of communicating.
3. The greater the variety of campaigns and the more robust the analysis, the greater the choices for future campaigns. As companies run more campaigns and increase their expertise at analyzing the results, recurring findings will result in even more creative campaigns to other sets of customers, not to mention providing the company the capability to increase its number of campaigns while at the same time decreasing the audience size of each one in an effort to move toward true one-to-one marketing.

Given these three factors, selecting a CRM tool to automate campaign management is easier said than done. A good campaign management tool is flexible enough to support existing marketing processes and not enforce its own. It should also be able to sustain current campaigns, yet support the evolution of the business and its customer knowledge while at the same time leveraging other campaign details such as the campaign's chosen media, its manager, or its seasonality. Some of the more advanced products even include so-called decisioning capabilities that support the translation of customer profitability, value, or future behavior scores into automated actions (for example, suggesting the waiver of a service fee for a particular customer).

Companies in the midst of planning or using CRM technologies to automate marketing are nevertheless still struggling with basic questions about how to optimize their marketing expenditures. Even those in the heat of implementing CRM are still asking themselves these questions:

- How do we focus our marketing campaigns on customers with whom we'd like repeat business?
- How do we migrate customers to lower-cost channels?
- How do other organizations in the company see customers differently than we do and how does that influence our campaign messages?
- How can we anticipate which products and services a customer might want?
- What is the best means of communicating with customers on an ongoing basis?
- What tactics do we use to entice prospects to become customers?
- How do we tie what we've learned about customers to improving overall customer satisfaction?
- What keeps our most loyal customers coming back?

CRM technologies alone can't help companies answer these questions. As we'll see in later chapters, companies implementing CRM must make staffing and technology decisions that transcend CRM.

Case Study: Eddie Bauer

Summary: Customer relationships are important to any retailer. But for a member of the exclusive group of retailers who have successfully integrated their brick-and-mortar, Web, and catalog channels, customer relationships are about more than just understanding behaviors: They're about making them happen.

Back in 1920 when the first Eddie Bauer store opened its doors, personalized customer service was one of the company's trademarks. One can imagine Seattle shoppers being greeted by name and offered suggestions by helpful sales staff who understood their tastes and remembered their past purchases. The company has certainly changed since then—Eddie Bauer has grown to over 500 stores in 49 states, with a catalog circulation of 105 million across the United States and Canada—but its service mentality is surprisingly consistent: understanding the merchandise customers want and providing it to them in the optimal way.

Indeed, the company—now a division of the Spiegel Group—is one of a tiny handful of retailers who can lay claim to a bona fide channel triumvirate that includes brick-and-mortar stores, a catalog business, and an acclaimed Internet site for Web shoppers. Although most brick-and-mortar retailers are still struggling to find their Internet sweet spots, Eddie Bauer's three channels are thriving and, as the company's data suggests, complementing one another.

WHAT THEY DID:

Harry Egler, Vice President of CRM for Eddie Bauer, explains the company's CRM strategy as being centered on a two-way dialog with its customers. "Our customers are coming to us with certain needs and wants," Egler explains, "so we have to provide relevance, as well as be able to have an intelligent dialog with them. Retailers aren't usually set up to accommodate this type of interaction."

In the mid-1990s, the company began to realize its knowledge of its customers was rudimentary, as was its ability to respond to customer requests. "It was like pulling teeth for a brick-and-mortar customer to get one of our catalogs," Egler recalls. Initial research suggested opportunities were falling through the cracks due to a lack of an integrated view of the customer. Indeed, customer data was dispersed across the company and not easy to find, let alone gather and analyze. Eddie Bauer began exploring what it would take to attain the 360-degree customer view.

As the company began developing new metrics for understanding customer behavior, it also invested in the technologies that would enable the inevitable customer analysis considered by executives to be a critical next step. The company began building a strategic infrastructure to deliver sophisticated analytics, including a powerful Sun platform and an IBM DB2 data warehouse, along with analytical technologies that included SAS and its accompanying decision-support and data-mining capabilities. The new business intelligence environment enabled Eddie Bauer not only to examine customer behavior but also to apply the findings to predict future behaviors through what the company calls its rapid modeling environment.

The company now has a complete view of its customers and their shopping behavior and has reached the proverbial retailing brass ring: channel integration. Eddie Bauer recognizes a customer regardless of whether she orders from a catalog, in a store, or over the Internet. Moreover, Eddie Bauer can segment that customer's spending to determine her most profitable channel, in turn helping optimize customer profitability across all channels. Not putting too fine a point on it, Egler adds that this gives Eddie Bauer the flexibility to manage each channel autonomously and still gain an overarching view of total cross-channel profitability.

Such newfound knowledge has crossed the transom from research to tactics. Marketing can choose which of the company's 44 catalogs best fit a customer's profile and likely needs. The company can also analyze data to determine how frequently it can and should communicate with its customers.

Although Eddie Bauer bases most of these decisions on the goal of communicating to the customer through the right channel at the right time, there's also the very real issue of cost. "We can afford to send our most valuable customers a broader assortment of products," explains Egler, referring to the company's diverse offerings of not only men's and women's apparel but an assortment of home soft-good and furnishing products. The company's ability to score customers based on their propensity to respond to campaigns gives it the intelligence it needs to get customer interaction decisions down to a science.

THE CHALLENGES:

Despite being ahead of the curve, Eddie Bauer is a testament to CRM's complexity. With its lofty multichannel and one-to-one goals—goals, the company would point out, that are being achieved—Egler admits they might have been a little too ambitious. "We wanted to get to Mecca right away," he says. He cites three different CRM tactics: evolutionary, where each step is logical; revolutionary, which involves significant business change; and interdisciplinary, leveraging CRM to a diverse set of decision-makers.

"Everyone wants to get to 'interdisciplinary' immediately," Egler explains, "but there are incremental steps across CRM development. We probably tried biting off more than we could chew early on." Eddie Bauer has also had its share of business process issues as a result of its CRM strategy, but the resulting changes ultimately contributed to a greater degree of customer-centricity. If he had it to do over again, Egler says he would have made sure organizational and business processes were considered earlier in the CRM lifecycle.

GOOD ADVICE:

Eddie Bauer is intimately aware that the rules of retailing are changing. In these days of hypercompetition, market fragmentation, and Internet speed, Harry Egler considers a learning relationship with customers to be a cornerstone of the company's competitive advantage. Such a relationship begins with the objective of building overall customer value (see Figure 2-9).

Like the CRM program itself, such a learning relationship is a never-ending journey: The fact that Eddie Bauer has replaced disparate customer data and outdated legacy systems with over a terabyte of online customer information—from names and addresses to itemized past purchases to channel preferences—makes that journey a lot easier.

THE GOLDEN NUGGET:

Since it began practicing the learning relationship model, Eddie Bauer has discovered that customers who shop across all three of its channels can spend up to five times more than customers who shop through only one channel. The company can then understand which of its three channels contributes the highest profit for each customer, driving tailored content to its catalogs and more personalized offers to its shoppers.

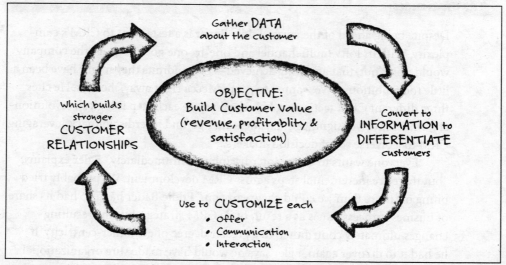

Figure 2-9: The learning relationship (Courtesy of Eddie Bauer, Inc.)

Like other CRM best practices, Eddie Bauer has institutionalized its conviction that CRM is about more than mere technology—it's about business strategy. "CRM has fundamentally changed the way we market," says Harry Egler, who insists the strongest marketing strategies fuse CRM with the company's brand. As the self-described custodian for customer focus, Egler credits the mix of technology, business process and organizational change, and data with helping Eddie Bauer get CRM right. "We now realize what we don't know," says Egler, citing what could be Eddie Bauer's most powerful CRM finding so far.

The Manager's Bottom Line

Despite the foreseeable payback of CRM in marketing, a recent survey of 175 companies with immediate CRM plans in place indicates marketing automation lags behind other CRM initiatives such as customer support.[13] Why the slow start?

Money, for one thing. According to the same survey, 72 percent of the large companies responding planned on spending $1 million or more on their CRM initiatives. Relationship marketing tactics such as customer segmentation and automated campaign management pay off only if a company is ready to use the results to improve customer interactions.

And if a company isn't clear about its business processes, CRM can backfire. Differentiating customer treatment based on partial customer data can result in the wrong message to a customer, ultimately doing more harm than no interaction at all.

Successful marketing tactics use the results from customer interactions to improve future interactions, paving the way for high-impact decisions such as these:

- Shifting marketing dollars toward campaigns more likely to generate high responses
- Understanding the characteristics of high-value customers, finding such characteristics in customers who have a high value *potential,* and changing interactions accordingly

---

13. "Lots of Companies are Thinking About Customer Relationship Management, But Progress Can Be Very Slow—CRM Under Scrutiny," *Information Week,* September 15, 2000.

- Improving the effectiveness of high-cost channels (such as face-to-face sales) to maximize their revenue streams
- Institutionalizing personalized communications for specific customer segments
- Understanding research and purchase patterns and further delineating segmentation criteria to improve future interactions or stimulate one-to-one marketing

The goal of CRM in marketing is to move C-level customers up to B-level customers and B-level customers up to A-level customers and to motivate A-level customers to stay that way—indeed, to buy more. It is to ensure the optimal type and frequency of communication, regardless of how "sticky" the Web site, the number of free giveaways, or the cost of the advertising campaign. It is to ensure that the company is the customer's first choice.

To succeed on this distinguished mission, a company's marketing process must be well defined. It must institutionalize the practice of customer differentiation. It must act on the information it analyzes. Moreover, it must not exist in a vacuum, but must support the other business processes that surround it, including the customer support and sales processes described in the next two chapters.

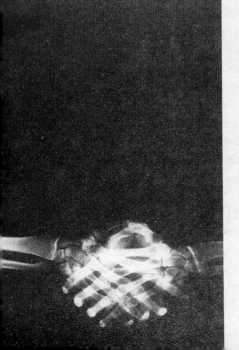

CHAPTER THREE

CRM and Customer Service

Scenario

Last May you subscribed to an online consumer product evaluation service so you could evaluate different brands of dishwashers. The monthly subscription cost was automatically billed to your credit card.

Trouble is, it's now November and you haven't used the service since, though the $3.95 fee shows up on your monthly credit card bills. Because you have no plans to evaluate other products, you decide to cancel the subscription. You log on to the site and navigate to the Customer Support screen, which requests your username and password.

You haven't used the service lately, so you don't remember your password and you're not sure whether the username is even right. You try a couple of variations but realize it's not going well when your dog's name doesn't do the trick. Why haven't they put some sort of 'cookie' on your workstation like everyone else? You jump to several screens that promise to explain how to change or cancel service, only to be greeted by a request for your username and password. Not even the FAQs (Frequently Asked Questions) page is accessible without a password.

(continued)

> You decide to phone the company and request cancellation, but no phone number is displayed on the site. To contact the company via e-mail, the site requires your user ID and password. There would be no easy way to cancel the service. The toll-free operator has no listing for the online service. You are condemned to online hell. And—irony of ironies—it's with a consumer advocacy company!

The above scenario is a good example of a well-meaning company failing to put itself in its customers' shoes. And it's not the only one. Companies who trip up on customer service do so at their peril, because they risk alienating the very constituencies they want to attract.

Despite the CRM frenzy, good customer service is harder to come by than ever before. Everybody seems to have a service horror story and, as we discussed in Chapter 1, everybody's more than happy to share it. No wonder most companies planning CRM projects begin with the goal of improving customer support. If anything can affect a customer's experience, it's the service—or lack thereof.

The Call Center and Customer Care

Leading CRM vendor Siebel Systems parodies the nightmare of poor customer service in their recent TV spot, in which a concerned operator listens attentively as a frantic customer shrieks about the company's failure to respond to her problem. When the operator politely asks the customer to describe her problem, the customer becomes so hysterical she hangs up, leaving the dismayed operator wondering what has just happened.

Not so humorous are the anecdotes scattered across the Web and print media bemoaning the decline in customer service. Last July, the *New York Times* asked the question "Is the Customer Ever Right?" in an article profiling the service nightmares of disconsolate consumers who had dedicated a disproportionate amount of their lives to resolving disputes. The article pointed its editorial finger at corner-cutting companies guilty of hiring unqualified Help Desk staff, portraying the telephone and Web support infrastructures of several companies as "infuriating mazes."[1] In October, a *Forbes* cover article lamenting outrageous wait times in lines and on hold asked readers, "Shouldn't profits and customer service go hand in hand? How did we get to the point where a company thinks it can improve its prospects by wasting customers' time?"[2] Withholding its diplomacy that same month, *Business Week* proclaimed on its cover, "Why Service Stinks."

Twenty years ago, most consumers complained by writing letters, mailing them, and awaiting a response whose arrival was hit-or-miss. The 800 number sparked a revolution in customer service, offering consumers real-time dispute resolution and the accountability of a company representative. Now e-business has upped the ante.

To its dismay, Dell Computer recently uncovered the fact that customers who ordered their PCs from the company's Web site made an average of two and a half calls to the company's support center.[3] (So much for the Web's efficiency.) And scathing news reports began citing shoddy customer service as ground zero for why online retailers had lost a combined $6.1 billion in 1999. E-tailers were accused of intentionally omitting contact phone numbers from their Web sites and print ads to avoid costly telephone calls, in effect, forcing customers to interact with a company via its lower-cost Web channel. The fact is that with the Internet, the call center often represents the customer's only opportunity to interact with a real human being.

Call centers, increasingly known as contact centers, customer interaction centers, or—somewhat optimistically—customer care centers or even knowledge centers, were around long before customer databases, and friendly service was the hallmark of such companies as the Walt Disney Company and State Farm Insurance even before the Web made its mark. Companies have long known that customer support is critical to both keeping existing customers and acquiring new ones.

What they haven't always known is how to perform it effectively. Until recently, executives considered their companies' contact centers a necessary cost of doing business and treated them as if they served the sole purpose of

1. Hafner, Katie, "Is the Customer Ever Right? Service's Decline and Fall," *The New York Times,* July 20, 2000.

2. Barron, Kelly, "Hurry Up and Wait," *Forbes,* October 16, 2000, p. 158.

3. According to *Sales and Marketing Management,* June 2000.

weighing down corporate profitability. Call center hiring involved merely testing how fast a job candidate could type.

Call center operators had been responding to each call as if it were unique, in effect, proving their executives partially right. The reality is that up to 50 percent of call center contacts are duplicates. Call center effectiveness was measured by how quickly the operator could get the customer off the phone. When the customer's call required research, tracking down a product specialist who could work on the problem could take days or even weeks. Because calls were rarely monitored, some operators took liberties in inventing their own ersatz solutions to turn over as many calls as possible.

Call center technologies entered the marketplace to effectively alleviate some of the repeat work and increase efficiencies, allowing companies to handle escalating call volumes. Call center products offered the creation of trouble tickets for customer complaints and provided tracking of trouble tickets from the seminal call through its resolution. CSRs (customer service representatives) could look up similar calls and resolutions while a customer was on the phone without having to repeat research. Products such as Remedy and Clarify enable companies to run statistics on their calls, categorizing them by call type, time-to-resolution, escalation percentages, and average call duration. Such products also provide forecasting of call volumes to ensure adequate call center staffing.

Such vendors legitimately aid their clients in increasing agent productivity and turnover rates, expediting training, gauging the effectiveness of solutions offered, and—ideally—shortening problem-resolution times and reducing costs. (One popular maxim advises that any customer interested in bankrupting a company need merely phone the call center on a regular basis.) Most companies use statistics from their call center products to track CSR performance, compensating them according to the volume of calls they can support.

Notwithstanding consistent improvements in call center software, business processes have still played a larger role than customers do.

In Figure 3-1, the customer is not happy. The airline had promised to mail him a ticket, which never came. The CSR is authorized to reissue the ticket and log the customer's complaint. Lucky for the customer, the fare hasn't changed. And lucky for the airline, the customer accepts his new ticket. However, the focus here is not on the customer's happiness but on the process of ensuring that the complaint is recorded, with the goal of post facto analysis and comparison. Soothing the customer is up to the call center agent—standard

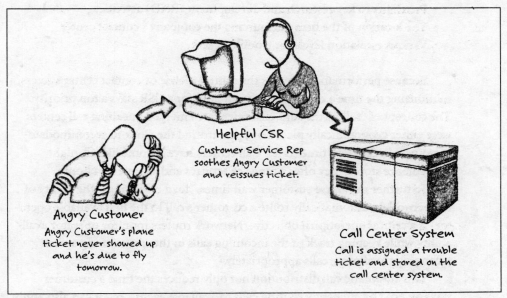

Figure 3-1: The typical call center process

operating procedure in most of today's call centers. Indeed, the customer hasn't figured into the call center infrastructure at all until very recently.

The Contact Center Gets Automated

Contact centers have evolved quickly from a group of local workers answering phones during business hours to a dedicated organization providing on-demand global support and sales through several different channels. Companies are realizing increasingly that their customer relationships are only as good as the quality of their support and are adopting computer telephony integration (CTI) features that automate various communication processes.

Call Routing

A company's customer support "help desk" might actually be made up of several—or many—geographically dispersed contact centers. These contact centers might be segregated based on

- The location of the company's regional offices
- Staff expertise or product specialization

- Proximity to key research and development (R&D) activities
- The location of the firm outsourcing the company's contact center
- Various escalation levels for trouble tickets

Because performance remains the central metric of contact center success, minimizing the time a customer waits on hold for a CSR stays a top priority. The concept of "follow the sun" customer care emerged, meaning call centers were either geographically placed or open around the clock to accommodate customers in different time zones. Call centers have become like all-night convenience stores: they offer a range of services and are open 24 hours.

To further minimize customer wait times, "load balancing" (the ability of the network to automatically route a customer's call to the first available operator) is a critical operational objective. Network routers monitor operator availability while keeping track of the incoming calls in the queue, using switch technology to allocate calls appropriately.

This automatic call distribution not only reduces the time a customer stays on hold by efficiently routing calls to available agents, but it can also apply intelligence about the customer to its decision about where to route a call. For instance, by using caller identification, a call center system can route a call from a multicultural city such as Los Angeles to a bilingual CSR.

Of course, companies were routing incoming calls long before CTI technologies automated the process. However, in these cases, it was frequently the customer who had to navigate the often complex alleyways of a company's organization. Many companies—most notably the airlines—still routinely provide their best customers with a separate 800 number that guarantees they'll reach specially trained service agents.

More sophisticated automatic call distribution, also known as precision call distribution, facilitates calls to be routed to agents who have access to specific information or with particular areas of expertise. It can delineate a company's valuable customers by mapping the incoming phone number to the customer profile, thus prioritizing customer calls to favor repeat customers or routing customers to specialty agents who are instructed in ways to differentiate treatment based on the customer's assigned segment. Saks Fifth Avenue's parent company Saks Incorporated bases its call routing on CSR skill sets, ensuring that customer support staffers receive calls on the subjects they know well. Saks ensures that its high-value customers—those who spend over $2000 annually—reach an operator in one second or less.

Interactive voice response (IVR) systems provide round-the-clock routing based on a customer's response to questions typed on her telephone keypad. The now-pervasive instructions ("Press 1 if you would like your account balance; Press 2 if you are responding to our ad; Press 3 . . .") delay contact with a human being, allowing CSRs to dispense with qualifying a caller before helping her.

Automated speech recognition features can offer customers even more options by allowing callers to communicate their troubles without having to navigate an often-cumbersome, multilayered phone menu. Speech recognition technologies deconstruct the words in a sentence string to provide a call center with more choices offered through the digits and "yes/no" options available from a numeric keypad. For instance, United Airlines has adopted speech recognition technology to support higher call volumes from customers inquiring about flight availability, improving throughput for these frequent calls while easing the burden for reservations agents.

CTI features such as IVR and call routing, although considered technical, can nevertheless play a key role in an overall CRM strategy. Providing multi-modal access to customers is great, but understanding which mode a customer prefers is even better. "A fundamental flaw is that companies apply speech recognition everywhere, instead of where it will provide the most value," says John Earle, president of Chant, a leading provider of speech technology development tools and services.

Earle stresses the importance of knowing a customer's preferred mode of interaction, be it via a telephone operator, e-mail, fax, or handheld device. "In theory, a customer should be able to customize his own interface: Maybe he prefers voice response when using his cell phone on the freeway because of bad reception or because his hands are on the wheel. At such times he prefers saying 'one' to pressing '1'—and that preference should be part of his customer profile." Earle adds that such automated services haven't reached their full potential because they're being implemented to emulate humans rather than to drive further efficiencies.

Contact Center Sales Support

Your customer has just purchased a diamond solitaire necklace and would like to know if there are matching earrings. Such an interaction could be just another customer inquiry or an opportunity to generate additional revenue. With the right information—often displayed via a little window called a "screen pop" on the customer service rep's workstation—a rep can gauge an incoming call to determine whether the customer on the other end of the phone line is a good candidate for another product or service. The call center as a point-of-sale is a relatively new practice that requires a combination of robust customer data and CSR finesse, because the CSR needs to transcend his traditional role of answering questions, landing smack in the middle of revenue generation.

This type of sales support not only saves the company money by preempting an in-person sales visit, but it can also provide more information to the customer than a direct sales call—after all, the CSR has product information at his fingertips—and can even push through an in-progress sales activity.

You have probably been at the receiving end of such an effort yourself. How often have you heard one of the following?

"That's a great pair of shoes. Would you like a belt to match?"

"Sorry you're having problems sending e-mail, Ms. Smith. For only $49.95 per month, we can get you DSL and it's always on. Plus, this month we're offering free installation. Interested?"

"While I'm confirming your trade, Mr. Rankell, can I tell you about our new precious metals sector fund?"

Or seen during your Web visit:

"Click here to learn more about today's savings-of-the-day!"

"If you'd like someone to contact you about converting from the individual to the family plan, enter the information in the boxes provided, as well as your preferred contact method, and someone will be in touch shortly."

The CSR or Web site acting as adjunct salesperson frees up the bona fide sales staff to concentrate on opportunities more likely to be won based on face-to-face interaction. (Remember "infographics" in Chapter 2?) The idea is to use CSRs to focus on the existing customer base—where they already have experience—and free up more sales time for prospects.

Even if a customer chooses not to respond to a contact-center cross-sell or Web promotion offer, the simple act of mentioning a complementary product or service is a way to provide product information to customers who might not have otherwise known about it, thereby establishing "mind share." Sometime in the future, the customer might decide she needs a new pair of bindings to go with those brand new skis, and she's likely to call the company that initially suggested a complementary brand.

To optimize the customer's experience with call center sales support, companies must have the right information about a customer. Simply suggesting the latest commodity product over the telephone or aggressively pitching a new service while the customer is complaining can actually backfire more often than not. It is for this reason that CSRs must be well trained on when to engage a customer in a cross-selling dialog and when to refrain entirely.

Web-based Self-Service

Customers are both refreshed and annoyed by company Web sites re-intermediating the support process. After all, the shortest distance between two points is a straight line—shouldn't you be able to talk to a human being when you want?

The previously mentioned redundancy of calls to customer support centers has initiated the automation of customer support processes, not only increasing support efficiencies but also allowing customers a greater degree of access to important information via the Web, any time of day, for a variety of questions.

For instance, sites such as FedEx.com allow customers to track their shipments. Testing this theory, I recently called the FedEx support center to track a package. The time from initial call to answer was 93 seconds. By comparison, the FedEx Web site took 17 seconds from the time of access. Multiply the improvement by the number of people every day who want to know where their packages are, and it's easy to see why FedEx automated their package tracking.

But customer self-service has as much to do with obtaining general information as it does with tracking specific orders. Most Web sites have made FAQs—Frequently Asked Questions—a site staple. FAQs answer questions such as these:

- Where is the company headquartered?
- How do I return an item?
- I've moved—how do I update my profile?
- How do I review my account?
- How do I change my password?
- I have a question about my bill; what do I do?

The more choices customers have in how they can deal with the company, the more likely they will be satisfied with that company's service. This can mean something as simple as a company e-mail address provided on the Web site so customers can provide the company with details on a question or problem.

It can also mean the inclusion of a "Call me" button that allows the customer to request an in-person conversation with a company representative, on the company's nickel. Indeed, many companies have taken person-to-person electronic support[4] one better by offering customers the ability to chat online with a customer care representative. Lands' End is famous for this. Its Lands' End Live™ service offers customers the capability to ask questions of a company rep either by telephone—a Lands' End agent will call the customer after she enters her phone number—or by live text chat—the customer can engage in an e-mail dialog with a representative. (Lands' End reps have even been known to ask whether your child has grown a size since you ordered those overalls last March.)

CRM application services provider TouchScape customizes self-service screens for its customers. The FAQ screen in Figure 3-2 not only displays the most frequently asked questions; it also categorizes the top five most frequent questions so visitors can more easily scan questions similar to their own.

"Live person chat" features bring customer support to real time; customers with a single phone line need not log off the Web site to call an 800 number. Likewise, CSRs staffing live chats can service more than one customer simultaneously. Live chat helps ensure that the customer stays on the site and takes his online shopping cart through checkout rather than abandoning it. This increases the likelihood not only of sales, and thus revenues, but of customer satisfaction as well.

Of course, breakthrough technological capabilities alone won't ensure stellar customer service. Studies show many companies still can't handle the volumes of phone calls they receive. A Southwest Airlines spokesperson told *The Dallas Morning News* the company would not move toward e-mail support until it could guarantee the same level of service it could provide to its telephone customers. (Customers calling the airline's Customer Service Department rarely wait more than 60 seconds before speaking to a human being, and the company's Web site is exemplary for its ease of use.) Other companies, such as

---

4. In Chapter 1 we introduced the term "eCRM," usually meaning the capability to contact a customer service rep through the Web—by e-mail, live chat, or high-speed Web telephone line.

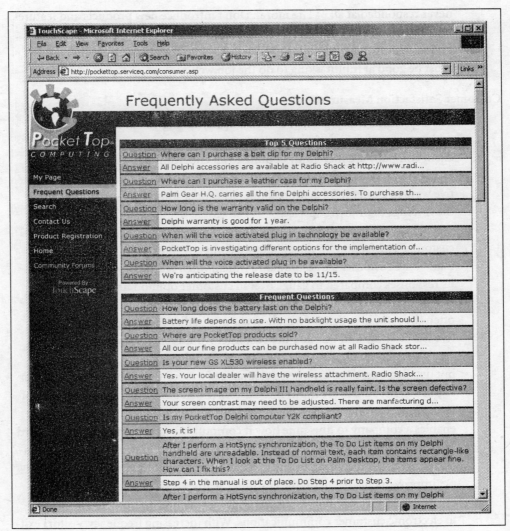

Figure 3-2: Frequently Asked Questions

Baltimore's All First Bank, only allow customers in top segments to use live chat features on their Web sites. Indeed, with limited human resources a fact of life for most call centers, companies are constantly evaluating new ways to mitigate customers' need for human contact.

A recent survey showed that 56 percent of all financial services companies either failed to respond to customer e-mails in a timely fashion or never responded at all.[5] (The moral: Don't introduce new products and features until you're serious about supporting them.) Like their telephone counterparts, online customer service reps must have excellent communication skills and must be good at multitasking to do the job well.

Customer Satisfaction Measurement

The days of the independent survey company calling you at dinnertime and asking you to "answer a few questions about your recent purchase" with its client company are mercifully coming to an end. Although the demise of customer surveys has been greatly exaggerated, companies are using more innovative ways to gather information about customers' impressions and leveraging the findings to improve service.

Survey mailings endure as the principal way for companies to monitor customer satisfaction. In the old days, a company or external survey firm mailed the customer a questionnaire which, when remitted, was analyzed and its responses compared to gauge overall customer opinion. In the past, such surveys have been innocuous and geared toward a general audience. Most often they would solicit information about whether the company representative was friendly and whether the customer would remain loyal.

These days such survey forms not only monitor customer satisfaction, but detailed questions are often personalized to specific customers or customer segments. Responses are input into customer databases and included as part of individual customer profiles. Such tracking of customer satisfaction over time enables a company to fine-tune how it communicates with its customers according to their preferences. Companies who have detailed customer databases can also map survey responses to customer value, thus prioritizing requested product improvements based on the customer segments they will affect.

But with the advent of e-business, paper-based surveys are ceding ground to electronic customer communications. With increasing frequency, visitors exiting a Web site are being greeted with pop-up screens inquiring about their experience on the site. Some companies design online surveys to solicit customer feedback that can directly affect how a company improves its customer communications. Such surveys are designed, distributed, and analyzed to discover

- What will make customers return to a company's Web site
- How customers found the site

5. Study done by Celent Communications, reported by *Bridge News,* August 24, 2000.

- Why customers did or didn't make a purchase during the visit
- Why customers did or didn't register on the site
- Which features the customers found particularly useful onsite
- How the customers' impressions about the company or the brand was affected by this visit
- How customers would rate the site in comparison to the Web sites of the company's competitors

Such electronic surveys are becoming increasingly sophisticated, serving as the technical equivalent of the focus group, albeit with more science and sans the overhead. Companies can randomize their surveys and achieve detailed response reports. Many companies who might have developed their own Web sites and the accompanying infrastructures have nevertheless chosen to outsource their customer surveys to firms that specialize in designing custom questionnaires, tallying responses, and mapping survey results to the client company's overall strategic goals.

Call-Scripting

As customer contact centers become more automated, the infrastructure improves. Customer databases become richer, and customer behavior and preferences can actually be predicted by comparing them to the behaviors of similar customers over time.

Because of this increased customer intelligence, the capability to provide CSRs with situational scripts is emerging as a must-have for many contact centers. Such scripts eliminate agent guesswork by providing the CSR with a logical series of talking points and guiding her through a dialog with the customer based on such factors as

- The reason for the contact
- The customer's value
- Cross-selling opportunities and propensity-to-buy data
- Current product promotions or discounts
- Past-due bills or accounts payable issues

Some products actually provide natural language support, meaning the agent can enter a sentence or phrase ("Customer needs laundry instructions for flannel sheets") and be supplied with the appropriate response ("Cold water, tumble dry on low"). Others feature logging of transcripts, allowing a company to retain a running text log of each customer's chat. Saving such information allows call center reps to e-mail transcripts of customer conversations to subject matter experts or even call up past chats in real time while the customer is online.

Even vendors of CRM products designed to support scripting admit there's no such thing as a "canned" response, and their software can't possibly make up for a CSR with deep product knowledge and a good disposition. However, scripting helps a company's contact center present a uniform image of the company by ensuring that the company responds in a consistent way to common problems so two different customers don't get two different answers.

The flip side to this, of course, is that your high-value customers might deserve different answers than the customer population at large. Consider the illustration from Figure 3-1 as revised in Figure 3-3 to accommodate a high-value customer.

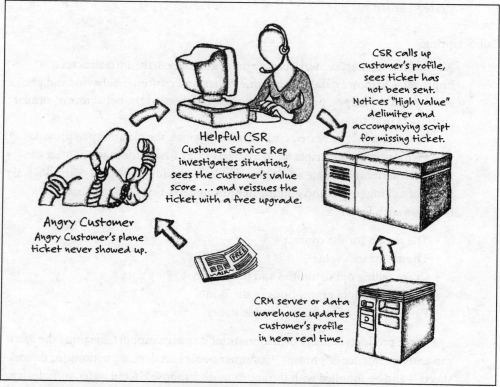

Helpful CSR
Customer Service Rep investigates situations, sees the customer's value score . . . and reissues the ticket with a free upgrade.

Angry Customer
Angry Customer's plane ticket never showed up.

CSR calls up customer's profile, sees ticket has not been sent. Notices "High Value" delimiter and accompanying script for missing ticket.

CRM server or data warehouse updates customer's profile in near real time.

Figure 3-3: Adding customer intelligence to customer support

In this example, the angry customer's profile is maintained on a CRM server or, more likely, on an enterprise data warehouse that contains a superset of information about that customer, not simply his calls to the contact center. Such a database might include information about the marketing promotions the customer has received, his travel history, how he books his tickets, his seating and meal preferences, and his use of partner products and services. In this case, the customer's profile indicates most of his ticket purchases are "Y" fares, he has flown over 60 segments in the past seven months, and he belongs in the top 3 percent of the airline's frequent fliers.

This information in turn dictates a script that guides the CSR in offering the customer a free upgrade along with his overdue tickets. The customer is more likely to remain loyal and consider the airline's error an anomaly rather than a reason to churn.

The ability to differentiate treatment of different customers based on their value is not only the Holy Grail for contact centers; it is the crux of CRM.

Cyberagents

Some CRM vendors are taking the concept of self-service one better by introducing cyberagents, lifelike "representatives" normally depicted on a company's Web site as a real person—CompUSA's "Jill" being one of the archetypes.

Cyberagents attempt to pull together the best of both personalization and advanced technology. On the one hand, the cyberagent is given a personality—complete with voice and facial expressions—often communicating with the Web visitor by her first name. On the other hand, the cyberagent can draw from a wealth of detailed information to answer basic FAQs as well as guide a customer to the appropriate screen for making a purchase or checking an order.

Although still relegated to rudimentary customer support functions, the vision for the cyberagent is to go from providing information to actually making decisions based on a combination of the customer's request, heterogeneous and detailed information about the customer, and complex rules-based logic to guide the cyberagent in making recommendations. The anthropomorphic qualities of a particularly effective cyberagent could one day further retention and loyalty initiatives by providing the customer with a personal company representative all his own. Until then, cyberagents are emerging as a viable means of providing basic customer support.

Workforce Management

Staffing the contact center has traditionally been a matter of determining who can work when. The contact center with three people dedicated to the Top 100 customers, six more covering the next tier of 500, and so on, is bound to fall short of customers' expectations, not to mention employees'. It's great that the best customers are getting better service, but is it good enough?

Workforce management tools specialize in staff planning and optimization, and several products are specific to contact center staffing. Optimizing staff around high call volumes, different communication channels, and customer types is the surest means of guaranteeing that the right customers receive the appropriate levels of support. Such products can combine operational contact center tasks, such as call routing, with planning functions including

- Ability to forecast contact volumes to predict busy periods
- Recommendations for the optimal number of CSRs for certain peak periods

"Things were done very differently on the farm when I was your age, Kenny."

- Performance tracking by customer value, customer satisfaction, priority level, or other metrics
- Employee scheduling based on skills, tenure, or preferred work hours
- Global monitoring of multiple contact centers, with the ability to combine findings into single reports for staff or performance fine-tuning

With staffing issues claiming up to 70 percent of a contact center's operating budget, the ability to track performance against customer satisfaction levels and fine-tune staffing choices accordingly is the goal of customer support executives worldwide, many of whom are now being compensated based on such measurements. Indeed, increasing customer satisfaction should be the overarching goal of every contact center employee.

A Customer Service Checklist for Success

World-class customer service is more than a practice; it's a series of corporate policies that should be defined, refined, and repeated across the organization. As the following scenario illustrates, listening to the customer is more important than ever.

Scenario

It's Friday morning and you're at home waiting for the DSL rep to install a third line, so you're teleconferencing into your biweekly staff meeting. Each of the eleven team members gives a brief status about his or her department. Just as you're about to report on profitability for Q4, your second phone line rings.

Thinking it's the DSL rep—finally you can nail down a time!—you beg forgiveness, put your waiting teammates on hold, press line 2, and hear a friendly voice.

"Hi there!!! It's Colleen!" says the voice. Colleen is warm and enthusiastic, and it takes you a minute to realize you don't know a Colleen. By this time, Colleen is gushing about the fantastic prices on gemstone jewelry that will be featured this weekend on home shopping television.

You hang up and return to your meeting. "Who was that?" an indiscreet staff member asks.

(continued)

"Colleen," you say in spite of yourself, unknowingly raising more questions than you've answered.

When the conference call wraps up, you call the home shopping channel and request to have your phone number removed from their automatic telemarketing list. The operator is pleasant and helpful and promises he'll remove your name from the mailing list. He requests your e-mail address, and you decline. You're cleaning up your life, getting rid of unsolicited marketing messages from companies you don't care about. Your call to the home shopping company eliminated one more unwanted phone call. You hang up, feeling you've accomplished something.

A few hours later, the DSL rep calls. He'll be showing up at . . .

The second line rings. You interrupt the DSL rep and take the call. It's Colleen again. She's perky as ever, this time flogging an upcoming kitchen appliance show, and you now hate her guts.

It's no surprise that, in spite of revolutionary advances in call center software functionality, established industry best practices have nevertheless failed to promote the infrastructure necessary to support evolving customer needs. Indeed, according to one recent survey, not even technology companies are immune:

> Many dot-coms also actively avoid the considerable investment necessary to build an adequate customer service center to answer phones and e-mails from disgruntled customers.[6]

So what can your company do to ensure your call centers are able to respond to customers in the optimal way, recognizing who they are and providing a consistent level of service? Following is a checklist for customer support success:

- *Choose your technologies carefully.* Understand your business needs before you invest in an expensive and complex call center system and all its extensions. For instance, if your company's Web site isn't tied to inventory yet, it

---

6. Olsen, Stefanie, "Customer Disservice: E-tailers Dodge Calls to Cut Costs," CNET News.com, September 14, 2000. (www.cnetnews.com)

makes no sense to offer customers Web-based self-service and risk unmet expectations. Likewise, if your company's most valuable customers land in voice-mail hell at every contact attempt, something's wrong. Have the call center evolve with the business, which might mean a building-block approach to implementing your call center infrastructure. Just be sure your call center technology is a step or two ahead of your business' evolution so there are no awkward surprises.

- *Provide CSRs with everything they need to know about customers.* Although this metric implies the integrated customer data from a variety of contact points (see Chapter 6 for more on this), it also mandates that a company be aware of what various call centers might require so they can provide the best service. For instance, if past-due customers are routed to a collections operator, that operator should have easy access to the customer's payment history, including the date and amount of the most recent payment. Likewise, if a company expects its call center CSRs to cross-sell products while customers are on the phone, agents should see a prominent product recommendation displayed on their screens.

- *Establish processes for call center staff.* Given the fast-paced increase in service expectations, companies can't afford to let CSRs experiment with customers. Providing two different customers with two different answers to the same question should be a studied practice based on data analysis of those customers and their differences, not on a CSR's best guess. Have escalation procedures in place for cases when a CSR needs additional information to answer a customer's question. And have a process in place with which the CSR can get back to the waiting customer with that answer.

- *Agree on success metrics.* Many companies use CRM to provide call center agents with easier data access, the goal being increased call efficiency. However, I know a large automaker with two different sets of success criteria. For its traditional car brand, CSRs are compensated for keeping phone calls brief and directing customers to information on the Web or to their local dealer. For luxury car models, CSRs are actually *encouraged to stay on the phone* with the customer for however long the call takes. It's not surprising that in the former case the average call duration is 4 minutes but in the latter case the typical call lasts 25 minutes. Nor is it a shocker to learn that customer satisfaction among drivers of the high-end brand is significantly higher. Companies should be clear about their metrics for customer support interactions, and policies should be established to address acceptable time on hold, optimal call lengths, desired call outcomes, customer follow-up procedures, and information provision.

- *Understand the issue of service recovery.* Once in a while, a customer on the brink of churning gives a company one last try, usually through the contact center. Service recovery means the company must do what it can to make things right with that customer, whether he's having a service problem or just having a bad day. Contact center staff must be able to identify these service recovery opportunities and understand the procedures necessary to win over those customers. Ideally, this involves the ability to examine customer value information so the CSR knows just how far to go to retain a customer who's at risk. The fact is, sometimes fixing a problem does more to cement a customer relationship than never having goofed up in the first place.

- *Ensure that your contact center reps are properly trained.* What was once a routine telephone call for your CSR is now a series of often-complex computer screens and data drill-down. Technology is allowing customer support staff to communicate with multiple customers simultaneously and availing more information about those customers. Make sure your CSRs are comfortable with the tools the company is asking them to use, as well as knowledgeable about the products it offers. (The Container Store provides 235 hours of training to its CSRs, and was—not coincidentally—voted one of Fortune's "100 Best Companies to Work For."[7]) Also ensure that employees are given incentives, financial or otherwise, to provide customers with consistently excellent service.

- *Staff the contact center at appropriate levels.* Web shoppers requesting live customer support routinely receive messages that say something like this: "There are currently no agents available to assist you. Click on the question mark below to send us an e-mail." If your company is going through the expense of providing multichannel customer support, it should be willing to optimize support resources for individual channels. Use existing call center software to monitor and track call volumes according to time of day and channel and then plan staff accordingly. For more complex environments, find a workforce management tool that can help you take the guesswork out of staffing your call centers.

- *Share key learnings.* After all, customers don't call the marketing department when they need help. Sharing contact center activity reports with other areas

---

7. According to *1 to 1 Direct,* January/February, 2001.

of the company can aid the company not only in better understanding its customer base, but in improving its products as well. Forward-thinking companies with centralized customer data actually enter important facts learned from customer interactions into those customers' profiles, rendering the information available to the company at large. When the right processes are in place, redundant trouble tickets and frequently logged complaints can make their way into R&D, resulting in product improvements and differentiation—"closing the loop" on high-profile problems.

- *Improve CSR compensation.* After all, how much can someone earning a low hourly wage realistically care about an unhappy customer, particularly if she's just been trained to cross-sell products and survey customers in addition to solving their problems? Customer service is stressful, rarely rewarding, and extremely visible. Balance CSR compensation with realistic business development opportunities. If the company wants its contact center reps to go the extra mile, so should the company.

- *Last but not least, if your company hasn't already determined its corporate personality, it's time.* If you're a securities company, you'll probably want to encourage your contact center agents to be professional and courteous. But if you're selling video games, you might consider being a bit more casual. There are countless moves afoot by corporations seeking to "humanize" their call centers, and the payoff matters. I once placed an order with a delightfully irreverent CSR at The Pottery Barn's baby catalog. Not only was he funny, he complimented my choice of crib sheets ("Good going!") and ended with the great line, "Now, I'll just read you back your order, Jill, and then we'll part friends." But he—and, by extension, The Pottery Barn—had me at "hello."

Case Study: Juniper Bank

Summary: It's one thing to take an existing enterprise from a product focus to a customer focus. It's another thing to start a brand new company around an entire customer-focused culture. Juniper Bank's employees don't concentrate on how to deliver customer relationship management—they just go about their everyday customer-centric business.

Walk into the main offices of Juniper Bank and the first thing you notice is the posters. The artwork decorating the walls of the company's headquarters in Wilmington, Delaware, doesn't depict the requisite sunsets or the abstract brushstrokes of local artists. Like the company it adorns, the artwork focuses on customers, posters in hallways and break rooms instilling such messages as "Keeping the Customer First!" and "Improving the Customer Experience." It's a testimonial not only to the company's culture of customer commitment but to the very tenets on which the company was founded.

WHAT THEY DID:

Richard Vague has always been known as an industry thought leader. Vague was the former Chairman and Chief Executive Officer of First USA, the market leader in affinity credit cards that was purchased by Bank One in 1999. In co-founding Juniper Bank, Vague envisioned combining an online bank with a mission to simplify consumer banking and provide stellar service. Indeed, the company's flagship product is its futuristic transparent credit card, a product its founder declares is the best vehicle for obtaining rich customer information. Vague has described his vision for Juniper as being "genuinely fair to consumers, easy to access, and simple to use." All this even before the company had opened its virtual doors.

Now that it has—Juniper Bank was launched in October 2000—it faces the same customer service challenges faced by most online businesses. But building a company from scratch presents some unique opportunities, as Regina Wallace, Juniper's Director of Customer Service and Operations, can testify. Wallace, who before joining Juniper was instrumental in constructing the Internet bank at Wells Fargo, is responsible for Juniper's entire service culture, from establishing the company's call center to directing the selection of its support technology infrastructure.

After joining Juniper in June 2000, Wallace made crafting customer-focused business processes one of her first priorities. "Not many companies can establish the ideal business processes before they're deployed," says Wallace, who acknowledges that such work is much more difficult to accomplish after a bank is already in business. Wallace and her team designed business rules and processes from the customer's viewpoint. The organization then automated them for customer service reps—known as relationship managers, or "RMs"—through a high-touch, integrated customer desktop.

The word "integration" was key for Wallace. After all, unlike typical financial service call center reps, Juniper's RMs are trained on all Juniper products, from the core credit card to electronic billing and payment to the company's new wireless banking service. Moreover, an RM is required to know how to communicate with a customer regardless of whether the preferred channel was the telephone, Internet chat, or e-mail. In fact, 85 percent of calls to Juniper customer support can be handled by a single RM, resulting in faster turnaround and more satisfied customers.

In addition, Juniper's preliminary customer behavior analysis indicates that the typical customer contacts the company three to four times a year. "We don't have branches," Wallace explains, "so we have very few opportunities to actually leave an impression on our customers." Wallace made the decision not to outsource Juniper's call center for the same reason. "We definitely feel that our competitive advantage is to have our service in-house. There's a lot of customer intelligence that originates in Customer Service."

Taking the service culture one step further, Wallace empowers her RMs to resolve issues in what they believe is the optimal way for each individual customer, embracing the practice of one-to-one dialog. For instance, an RM can decide to waive a service fee in an extenuating circumstance for a valuable customer. In addition to maintaining an online database that provides RMs with customer profiles, the company tracks service outcome statistics to determine whether RMs are making the best decisions possible.

THE CHALLENGES:

The luxury of being able to build a company's support infrastructure from scratch is also its difficulty. True, Juniper has no neighborhood branches with lines of impatient customers spilling out the door. Nor is there an easy way for Juniper to provide its customers with an intimate human experience. There are no unwieldy legacy systems to grapple with, but that means little established data to direct the best decisions. "We were always tempted to revert to our past experience," Wallace reflects, "and sometimes we had to guess. But our products are different, and so are our customers."

All things being equal, Wallace estimates Juniper is between 12 and 18 months ahead of the industry curve simply because she didn't have to undo existing business processes to establish effective ones. She plans on tackling the organizational issues next: "We're moving toward organizing more around the customer so that we can continue to evolve our customer focus."

GOOD ADVICE:

Wallace also credits her success to the tight relationship between customer support and marketing. The classically tense relationship often sees service reps accusing marketing of being unrealistic about its promotions, and marketing accusing customer service of being unresponsive and foiling its campaigns.

Not so at Juniper, where product managers in marketing can regularly monitor how their campaigns affect inbound customer contacts, and RMs can openly provide feedback to marketing about campaign improvements. The two organizations meet regularly and maintain a weekly performance scorecard.

The organizational missions of both Juniper's Customer Support department and its Marketing department are centered on the customer experience. As Juniper understands more about its customers' behaviors and preferences, RMs can influence them. For instance, if a customer purchases a Juniper credit card through a direct-mail promotion, an RM would highlight the benefits of Internet banking in his welcome call to that customer, potentially steering her toward a more profitable channel and evolving her toward online bill payment. Indeed, when Juniper communicates with a customer on his palmtop, reminding him that his telephone bill is due and offering to pay it for him, the line between marketing and service becomes refreshingly blurred.

THE GOLDEN NUGGET:

Since its launch, Juniper Bank has begun receiving unsolicited customer feedback. "I can't tell you how many times in the past four months that our customer contacts have resulted in a 'wow' response," says Wallace. The resulting word-of-mouth has been rewarding for both Wallace and Juniper. The company recently received the Number 1 spot in Gomez Advisors' Internet Credit Card Scorecard for providing "accurate and timely responses via phone and e-mail." American Banker reported a Speer & Associates Internet survey that rated Juniper "the best financial Web site, beating out American Express Corp. and Citigroup Inc."

Not bad for a company so customer focused it doesn't need a formal CRM program. "CRM is more of an assumption," explains Regina Wallace. "We don't really talk about it; it's a behavior we're trying to instill into our culture. You know, 'Are we pleasing the customer from the customer's viewpoint?'" Judging from the industry praise and hearty consumer response, the answer is an absolute Yes.

The Manager's Bottom Line

Customer service is a set of business processes aided by new technologies but fundamentally practiced by human beings. Notwithstanding all the new CRM tools on the market that support call centers, companies can retain their customers by simply giving them an unforgettable service experience.

My friend Drew, a professor of psychology who personifies the term "even-keeled," flushes noticeably when telling the story of returning a faulty automatic tie rack to a high-end gadget store, only to be told he was merely eligible for store credit. His voice hardens as he relates the failure of the second tie rack. He gets positively irate when he gets to the part about the cashier not accepting the second return, this time for a refund. When he finishes the story—he and his wife finally located a district manager who grudgingly agreed to the return "despite company policy"—Drew looks utterly defeated. In more ways than one, Drew has churned.

In their book *Emotional Value: Creating Strong Bonds with Your Customers*, authors Janelle Barlow and Dianna Maul contend that people are driven by their emotions, thus companies can do a better job at retaining and satisfying customers by using this knowledge when providing customer service. The authors explain companies should develop an emotional bond with their customers, one that transcends products or pricing. (The company I work for, for instance, advertises the charities it funds annually in its proposals and on its Web site.) Customer service strategies, they argue, should be receptive to emotion and involve not only efficiency but also friendliness and empathy, two terms that play a larger role in CRM than they're given credit for and that even the most cutting-edge CRM technologies will never provide.

CHAPTER FOUR

Sales Force Automation

C RM's metamorphosis from a focused application into an enterprise-wide business initiative has everything to do with its beginnings in sales force automation (SFA), so why not discuss SFA up front? Because in many ways, the various customer-focused projects in marketing and customer support act as input into an SFA project. After all, a company that can collect and understand customer touchpoints from its marketing and contact center organizations can feed this new knowledge to its sales group, fostering relationship and revenue improvements.

SFA products were originally meant to improve sales force productivity and encourage salespeople to document and communicate their field activities. However, sales force automation products are becoming increasingly focused on cultivating customer relationships and improving customer satisfaction, as the following two scenarios illustrate.

Scenario Number One

You're on your way to a meeting with one of your best customers. Shoot, Jim's not only one of your best customers-he's one of the company's best. This guy and his firm account for 2 percent of this year's revenues. Hopefully, after this meeting it'll be 3 percent.

You arrive at the customer's building early-you're always a few minutes early-show your

(continued)

badge, and take the elevator to Jim's office. Jim is talking with a member of his staff, but when he sees you he dismisses his employee and motions to you to sit down. Good old Jim. Always has time to hear a pitch and place an order.

But Jim isn't placing an order today. In fact, he might never place another one. As he explains it to you, his entire firm has been at a standstill for the past 48 hours because of **your** product. **Your** product is still on the fritz, and Jim and his people have been on the phone to **your** customer support center for the past day and a half.

Your face betrays your surprise. "No one told me about it, Jim," you stammer as you strive to recall any voice-mail messages you might have prematurely erased. Jim stands up from behind his desk, a wordless acknowledgement that he's far too busy to hear about **your** communication breakdown. After all, he's got a big one all his own to worry about.

As you stride across the hot parking lot, you begin thinking about how to make up for the 2 percent in revenue you and your company are about to lose.

Scenario Number Two

You're on your way to a meeting with one of your best customers. Truth be told, Jim's your very **best** customer. This guy and his firm account for 2 percent of your company's revenues this year. Hopefully, after this meeting it'll be 4 percent.

En route to the customer's site, you turn on your PDA computer, which begins beeping. The screen display reads: *Priority 1 alert! Customer impacted!* You pull to the side of the road and press the Down Arrow key to read more. According to the message, the customer you're about to see has just experienced a major outage. A field service rep has been contacted and is now working on the problem.

Ten minutes later you park your car at the customer's building. You're early, so instead of going upstairs to see Jim, you walk to the back of the building and find your service rep busily repairing equipment.

"Been here since yesterday," he answers your unspoken question. "Broken part just showed up," he smiles, patting the wireless PDA device hanging from a belt loop. He was able to order the part remotely and have it dispatched by courier. The device is currently displaying instructions that guide him through installation of the part. "'Spect I'll have it working in 30 minutes or so."

Relieved, you take the stairs to Jim's office. He asks you to wait for five minutes, during which time you power up your laptop and refresh your memory about Jim's current product model and installation date. Jim appears in the doorway and motions you in. Preemptively, you begin:

"I know all about it, Jim. We should have everything working again within the hour."

Jim looks at you and smiles. "I knew you would," he says. "We might just be overloading the system. We'll probably need an upgrade. How soon can **we** put that together?"

Forty-five minutes later, you leave Jim's office and head downstairs to confirm with your field rep that service has been restored. As you exit the building and walk across the parking lot, you realize you're leaving behind a relieved customer—and, in the bargain, increasing his revenue contribution to 4 percent.

Not to put too fine a point on this example, but guess which company is using CRM for sales force automation?

Sales Force Automation: The Cradle of CRM

The timeline goes something like this: In the early 1990s, a handful of software vendors realized that companies—specifically those with field sales forces—needed help. The more business they closed, the more information they had to keep track of about their customers. Meanwhile, salespeople had various means of recording this customer information and communicating critical account news back to the home office. And those who left simply took their little black books along with them, forcing the company to locate and re-collect customer data, starting at ground zero.

Likewise, salespeople needed better tools to help them manage their accounts, track opportunities, establish and monitor the sales pipeline, and organize their contact lists. After all, the alternative involved a lot of manual effort for both the sales reps and their home office counterparts.

Multiply the scenario in Figure 4-1 by the number of sales reps working for the company and you have an infrastructure nightmare on your hands.

Moreover, the scenario assumes that headquarters possesses the necessary information and can communicate it quickly—many didn't and still can't. The promise of sales force automation was in putting account information directly in the hands of field sales staff, making them responsible for it, and ultimately rendering them (and the rest of the company) more productive.

SFA likewise helped managers in both the front and back offices who, lacking timely sales forecasts, struggled to keep up with demand. Organizations needed a way to be sure that up-to-date sales data, including sales forecasts, could be communicated across the organization from the manufacturing floor through to company executives. Management considered the potential for sales force automation to increase productivity and provide consistent information as nothing short of a competitive weapon.

Salespeople took a little more time to warm up to the idea. To be fair, some are still warming up. Sure, they could now keep track of product inventories, customers' names and addresses, org charts, and marketing plans. And they now had slick new laptops, which they could use to dial in to headquarters

Figure 4-1: Before sales force automation

to synchronize their information with the corporate client/server database. But salespeople need to be convinced of the value of SFA, which means having an acceptable answer to the question, "What's in it for me?"

Here's how a salesman I know describes his experience using an early SFA:

No argument that it was more information than I ever had before. And I loved that first laptop. But I was spending a lot of time downloading. I mean, how could I be sure of current pricing plans or product updates? I had to have the latest and greatest information about my customer contacts or product release dates *before* I walked through my customer's door. Plus, the application wasn't really intuitive. Sometimes—okay, often—I'd just pick up the phone and call someone I knew at the office who could answer my question. A lot of guys I was working with didn't even bother, which made me nervous because maybe their customers were getting better deals than mine were, and mine would find out.

Arguably, an even bigger problem existed: because of the client/server model, communications between the sales force (the front office) and the headquarters customer database maintained by the Information Technology (IT) department (the back office) was one-way. This meant that although salespeople were getting updated information from corporate databases, they weren't necessarily providing their own information back to those databases to maintain current data and close the information loop.

This phenomenon resulted in outdated corporate information that didn't reflect the most recent customer contact activity. After all, the salesperson in regular contact with the customer is more likely to know about a job change or office move than the IT administrators managing the customer database. Critical and useful account information was often being left on the table.

Although improving the sporadic and often seat-of-the-pants sales process for many companies, SFA still had flaws, including the fact that companies hadn't enforced its use as a basic job requirement. Of course, this is easier said than done, especially for salespeople who are above quota. Would you rather have your salespeople spend their time keying in data or closing the next big deal?

Today's SFA

SFA product vendors set out to automate the answers to some basic sales rep questions that, when answered, could help them be more productive. Sales force automation products run the gamut from rudimentary calendar support and scheduling to real-time alerts about customer events. Irrespective of the vendor or product, most sales force automation tools claiming the CRM moniker fall into one or more of the following categories.

Sales Process/Activity Management

Many SFA products depict a sales methodology that can usually be customized to the company's specific sales policies and procedures. Known as *sales process management,* such tools include a sequence of sales activities that can guide sales reps through each discrete step in the sales process.

This not only makes certain sales reps consider each step in the sales cycle, providing a unified sales process throughout the company, but also ensures that follow-up activities are performed—indeed are assigned and scheduled automatically (see Figure 4-2).

Sales process management tools by themselves aren't that sophisticated. When they're deployed across the country or around the world, however, they can serve as an effective training aid, minimize human error, and ultimately result in greater productivity for both individuals and entire teams.

Activity management tools offer calendars (optionally visible to fellow team members) to assist in the planning of key customer events such as proposal presentations or product demonstrations. Alarm reminders can signal important tasks as they become due, generate documents as they are needed, or make decisions based on the user's input. For instance, an SFA tool can generate a mailing suggestion for a customer who's been inactive or hasn't

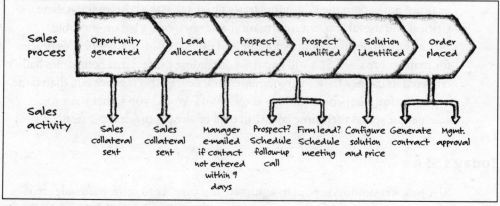

Figure 4-2: Sample sales process

made a purchase for over six months. These products also offer the ability to "check off" activities after they're complete.

The ability to oversee activities within the sales process enables management staff to schedule and assign discrete tasks, in effect, automating both an individual and organizational to-do list. This streamlines team-selling and ensures company-wide consistency of the sales cycle. Team collaboration tools let remote team members chat in real time, using a Web browser, further ensuring synchronization of effort and rendering sales meetings and training updates more timely and practical. Managers can save chat sessions to a central server for absent team members or later reference.

Activity management tools can also provide valuable post facto analysis of a sales cycle, allowing the sales team to examine the duration and procedures involved in critical tasks. The sales organization thus comes to understand the success factors that contribute to closing a sale, leading to refining of processes over time.

Most salespeople will tell you just how differently their company does things. Like most SFA functionality, sales process and activity management tools are only as good as their ability to be tailored to the user company's individual sales methods. Forcing the adoption of broad-brush processes and generic activities will fail to provide value to the salesperson or team chartered with using them. And at worst, CRM products can impede the very sales processes they were meant to enhance.

Sales and Territory Management

Which salespeople are assigned to which accounts? Who's already reached quota? What's the pipeline look like in the Southwest? Sales managers overseeing tens or hundreds of sales teams can't possibly keep abreast of every active sales initiative, let alone the individuals in their organizations. Sales management tools enable them to do just that, offering data and reporting options to give sales managers and executives on-demand access to sales activities—before, during, and after the order.

From a team management perspective, many sales force automation products enable managers to set up sales teams and link individuals to accounts, regions, and industries. Such teams can include both field account teams and telesales organizations, and can even integrate Web sales data into the results for a robust view of the corporate sales environment. Teams can also be linked to headquarters specialists such as industry experts or product managers. Some

SFA tools support personal data about each individual to generate staff and team profiles.

Likewise, sales managers can track territory assignments and monitor pipelines and leads for individual territories. Most SFA tools offering such territory management capabilities provide security features that limit an account manager's activities to her own territory. When necessary, however, sales management tools can provide a host of information on one account, or many, freeing geographically dispersed staff from having to request or run cumbersome reports to understand account status or prior order history.

Overall, sales and territory management capabilities allow managers not only to understand sales activities as they occur, but also to optimize individual teams according to critical mass and skill sets appropriate for the client or prospect, increasing the odds of closing the deal.

Contact Management

Contact management is the subset of sales force automation that deals with organizing and managing data across and within a company's client and prospect organizations. Contact management software can contain various modules for maintaining local client databases, displaying updated organization charts, and allowing salespeople to maintain notes on specific clients or prospects. Many also allow users to query remote databases for supplementary information or to synchronize laptop-local data with a corporate customer database.

With contact management tools, salespeople can answer the following types of questions:

- Who is our contact individual for Client X? Who is the contact for each department?
- What is Client X's mailing address? Billing address?
- In which office is the client's Accounts Payable department?
- Who is the client's purchasing agent? What is her phone number?
- Which customers were included in the most recent promotion for Product X?
- Who already has a brochure?
- When is my next sales call? When was the last time I called on that customer?

Much of the CRM software available today that falls under the contact-management rubric interfaces with Microsoft Outlook or similar products. This linkage allows sales reps to supplement their phone lists and calendars with fulfillment features to track customer mailings or automated workflow programs that can assign and route appointments.

As part of a larger CRM product suite, many contact management tools enable salespeople to communicate their schedules to the organization at large. The real value of contact management CRM is in its capability to track not only where customers are but also *who* they are in terms of their influence and decision-making clout. Many contact management tools can interface with sales management functions to help optimize the number and skills of team members involved in high-profile sales efforts. CRM suite products can then leverage these features to map sales activities back to resulting revenues.

Lead Management

CRM vendors claim that the capabilities described in the previous section push sales prospects through the pipeline more quickly. But who's in the pipeline, anyway, and how long will they be there?

Lead management (also known as "opportunity management" and "pipeline management") aims to provide foolproof sales strategies so no sales task, document, or communication falls through the cracks. Thus salespeople can follow a defined approach to turning opportunities into deals. Many lead management products not only track customer account history but also monitor leads, generate next steps, and refine selling efforts online.

Some sales force automation products enable a company's marketing or sales management organization to automatically distribute client leads to a field or telemarketing rep based on the rep's product knowledge or territory. Because the organization has presumably already qualified these leads through marketing campaigns or client referrals or via an internal customer support rep, this type of lead distribution can result in faster deals and higher close rates.

In addition, SFA tools can track other prospect attributes such as known product interests, discretionary budget amounts, and likely competitors, providing a real-world view of each lead and its likelihood of becoming a full-fledged sale. This information can feed sales forecasting software and result in more accurate predictions than relying on traditional spreadsheets of past performance.

Other SFA products bring the sales process full circle, tracking leads against orders to provide a view of close rates and salesperson productivity. This information can then be reported back to the marketing manager who originally designated the lead. This enables marketing to compare a campaign's result to actual sales of that product and refine future campaigns over time.[1]

Such capabilities can result in answers to questions that previously depended on guesswork or analysis of incomplete data, for example:

- At which step in the sales cycle do we lose most of our prospects?
- How many sales appointments did Adrianna have with TechCo? How many were cancelled?
- What percentage of leads resulted in sales in the northwest region last month?
- How long is the average sales cycle overall? How does that compare to the sales cycle for the health care industry?
- How did order amounts for the San Francisco branch office compare to those in Seattle last year?

Of course, lead management analysis is only as good as the data that feeds it, and different products provide different levels of sophistication. Advanced lead management tools even calculate the probability of the sale based on the success factor information stored in the prospect's profile, and others can alert the salesperson when a problem arises that thwarted a similar opportunity with another prospect.

Configuration Support

Because many of these tools allow a salesperson to input client and prospect information into an easy-to-use tool, CRM products have evolved to leverage this information by providing product-specific configuration support to companies who must "build" products for their customers. Such companies— computer technology vendors, appliance manufacturers, and telephone companies among them—no longer undergo the painstaking process of factoring in complex customer attributes and requirements to build a solution from scratch.

---

1. The ability to record campaign results and leverage them for future campaigns is one example of "closed loop" campaign management.

CRM vendors providing this type of functionality often use the graphical sales process like the one pictured in Figure 4-2 as a way to consider each step of the cycle. After the "order" stage has been reached, the tool can calculate a product configuration and price quote automatically. When this is finished, a configuration tool can provide forms that facilitate electronic communication of the information to other areas of the company. For instance, an account manager can generate a configuration and price, e-mail his district manager the price quote for approval, and check inventory for stock, *all while sitting with the customer.*

Siebel Configurator from CRM heavyweight Siebel Systems also supports headquarters marketing staff and product managers who might create new product bundles for the field. Instead of field salespeople combining products and selling them as ersatz units, marketing staff can use the Configurator tool to build unique product packages, brand them, and distribute them to field sales staff with a few mouse clicks.

After the product has been configured and a quote calculated, the information can automatically populate a standard contract resident on the salesperson's laptop. Such automation dispenses with paper-based contract generation and validation steps so fraught with error they can bog down or even kill an order.

Knowledge Management

As field salespeople know all too well, a lot more than customer data is necessary for selling, and the more information available, the better. Organizations have a plethora of information an account rep can use sometime during the sales lifecycle. Accessible internal documents can provide the sales force with the information it needs to understand a variety of components in the sales lifecycle. Such information might include

- Corporate policy handbooks
- Sales presentation slides
- Company phone list
- Proposal templates
- Contract boilerplate
- Expense report forms
- Regulatory standards and recent compliance reports
- Historical sales and revenue reports

- Partner and supplier profiles
- Transcripts of sales meetings and executive briefings
- Digitized video of sales presentations or executive briefings
- Industry and competitor data
- News articles and press releases
- Trade show and promotional event schedules
- Thank you notes and other client correspondence

How effectively salespeople use this disparate information depends on how easily they can access it. More and more companies are developing corporate intranets for headquarters and field staff alike, facilitating the dissemination of critical corporate knowledge.

Systems that can locate and store such information and provide users with a means of communicating about and adding to its contents from a single application are known as knowledge management (KM) systems. Many CRM tools geared to SFA include functions specific to accessing and conversing on a range of corporate documentation to supplement sales efforts and provide fast data during the heat of the sale. Most knowledge management systems do all of this:

- Include a means of granting individuals control or editing rights over a document to avoid users working on the same material simultaneously
- Provide a history of who has modified material, and when
- Offer a search engine, allowing users easy file lookup by keyword
- Allow users to view various files and documents via a portal that unifies materials that in fact exist in many different places

Although not exclusive to sales organizations—knowledge management systems are increasingly popular with large companies such as consulting firms that have geographically dispersed employees—the existence of a consolidated view through which the field force can access a variety of information delivers increased efficiencies.[2] No more mailing binders to the entire North American sales team! Let's give them access through the KM system! Knowledge management can mean the difference between losing and retaining key sales staff who are hungry for information but strapped for time.

---

2. The documentation and information resident in knowledge management systems are usually displayed via an enterprise portal, a type of "window" into the system that makes the information appear centralized.

SFA and Mobile CRM

The subtext of the various sales force automation features discussed so far is that the information needs to be disseminated to the field sales rep in order for him to use his SFA tools. But the days of not knowing whether the most current data is on the corporate server or your own laptop are thankfully behind us.

From Client/Server to the Web

For one thing, the Web has simplified information availability. Instead of being resident on each salesperson's laptop, SFA functionality now rests on a headquarters Web server running CRM software, and the salesperson can access that server remotely. Information local to a single server is consistent across geographical regions and multiperson teams. Cumbersome synchronizations between the client laptop's data and the headquarters database are a thing of the past.

The intranet infrastructure also eliminates the traditional support costs of managing communications, instead delineating the work to the company's chosen Internet service provider (ISP). Resource expenses are dramatically less than those needed to support the old client/server model, which involved expensive modem banks, numerous dedicated phone lines, and the capacity planning that accompanied them. The Web simplifies access by allowing a company to outsource remote access to the ISP and focus instead on running the application and maintaining the data, arguably its core competencies. Laptop configuration and support costs are also reduced. Salespeople no longer need act as systems programmers, setting up their communications options, modem settings, and the like.

Most important, browser-based technology shields the company's data asset—one of its key competitive weapons. Instead of the account rep having to ensure security, experienced IT staff now manage and protect critical customer data in a central location at headquarters. The data is no longer propagated, but remains in one place. The risks of deleted files, smashed laptops, or lost sales reps are thus dramatically reduced.

SFA Goes Mobile

Having reduced the responsibility of the laptop in sales force automation, CRM vendors intend to unburden it altogether. The time is coming when IT staff won't have to provision and configure laptops, and nary a rotator cuff will be torn by a heavy briefcase hanging from an account rep's shoulder.

Just about every CRM vendor is vowing to support access from a variety of handheld devices to the precious customer data in its database. Many already do. Scenario 2 at the beginning of this chapter illustrates the SFA mission:

> To provide data to headquarters and field-based personnel (not only about customers but also about products, inventory, pricing, and other key company information) on-the-fly from a variety of equipment, thereby allowing them to qualify and close opportunities faster and better than our competitors do.[3]

Handheld device technology is evolving at a fast clip. According to the Aberdeen Group, 74 million people will have access to the Web via wireless technology by the year 2004. Personal digital assistants (PDAs), cell phones and Web phones, two-way pagers, tablet PCs, and any other device with a display screen and the appropriate communications features can support anytime/anywhere access via wireless networking. The benefits are boundless.

- Deals can be won or lost based on who can respond the fastest. With wireless technology, configuring a product, pricing it, and creating the contract can all be done remotely and in much less time than by traditional fax and e-mail based processes.
- Not only can field staff access important information, they can also enter updates to that information that are relayed back to a corporate server accessible by other organizations. Companies get smarter about their customers as they witness the creeping customer intelligence that accompanies such a closed-loop information exchange.
- As in Scenario 2 at the beginning of this chapter, an account rep can be alerted about in-progress customer events in real time. She can then send a message via a two-way pager or other device to a field service rep for an explanation, to her boss for advice on how to handle a touchy client situation, or to her marketing contact for up-sell suggestions.
- Wireless messaging can be invaluable when it comes to just-in-time personalized messages. These "pushed" messages—meaning they are sent unbidden but nevertheless geared to the user's stated interests, subscriptions to news services and other information providers, and even geographic location—can include broadcasting traffic bulletins en route to

---

3. The CRM Mission Statement from a network equipment manufacturer.

a client, automatic calendar updates, and daily company press releases. Personalized messaging also mitigates the "noise" accompanying the ascent of handheld communications by limiting information to only those messages the user has requested.

- Last but not least, wireless Internet access provides field staff with access to vast amounts of information, restricted only by the capacity of the device to display the data. Not only can a sales rep view external Web pages on his PDA to glean data about clients, stock prices, and business news, he can also log on to his company's intranet, thus accessing company-specific information in real time from wherever he is. An account rep on the way to a sales meeting can check inventory for a product at an airport Internet kiosk before boarding his flight. Emerging technologies such as the so-called voice browsers even allow users to navigate the Web via vocal commands over the telephone. Thus a sales rep can make a phone call during the seventh inning stretch to verify a client address, check on the status of his customers' orders, read his e-mail, and order flowers for Secretary's Day.

Various technology developments are responsible for bringing information literally into the hands of disparate business organizations and communities that nevertheless must exchange information on the go. Having emerged to great fanfare in the early 1990s, the Java programming language meant applications could run on different platforms. XML (extensible markup language) simplifies intersystem communications by encoding descriptive information about that data so it can be gathered and shared across applications and companies. For example, XML can define information about a purchase order so when a salesperson transmits it, the company's accounting system can recognize and process it.

New wireless protocols such as WAP—a set of standards for the transmission of content to different handheld units—allow information to be conveyed to a variety of devices in real time. Thus, a company's lead management system can transmit sales leads to a salesperson's cell phone for quick turnaround. Bluetooth is the new standard for short-range wireless communications (it allows laptops to communicate with tiny printers no larger than a rib eye steak, and it's the way those handheld computers buy sodas from vending machines). And emerging Web portal software provides your cell phone or PDA with a Windows-like interface. Palm recently launched its MyPalm portal, allowing users to wirelessly synchronize information on their Palm devices with information on their desktop PCs. Forgot what time the Big Meeting starts and can't get to your office to look at your online calendar? Access it right from your Palm.

Vendors are providing a variety of choices for real-time access to their centralized CRM servers with products designed for specific access devices. Many CRM vendors offer complementary products for the Web, handheld devices, and thin clients alike. Individual salespeople can select their preferred way of accessing and communicating information. For example, a salesperson might prefer accessing customer data and news reports on her cell phone while at the point of customer contact, but would rather configure products on her PDA.

Does this mean you should sell all your stock in laptop PC manufacturers? Not just yet. Challenges remain in the wireless world, such as various messaging formats, different screen sizes, assorted graphics capabilities, and emerging mobile portal options. Bandwidth limitations linger, and security issues are still

"It appears to be some kind of wireless technology."

(sometimes literally) up in the air, according to Anne Thomas Manes, Director of Market Innovation for Sun Microsystems:

> The software infrastructure required to support mobile applications is just starting to become available. For instance, many SFA tools don't provide their own document management systems, so things like making contracts and other documents available to wireless clients within SFA systems can still be impractical. Thankfully, there are tools—like Sun ONE WebTop—that allow people to maintain various files and access them from any device.

Indeed, mobile computing means new users, new devices, and new ways of doing business. Until companies get their arms around the mobile business model from both infrastructure and cultural perspectives, the laptop will live on.

Field Force Automation

Field force automation, or FFA, is sort of a hybrid. It's part customer service in that field service implies the service or repair of customer equipment on the customer's premises. Likewise, it's part sales force automation, leveraging the emerging mobile workforce management technologies being widely adopted by corporate sales organizations.

Field force automation (also known as "field service management") began in the 1980s in manufacturing companies, who regularly dispatched technicians to remote sites to test and repair equipment. The classic process of dispatching a technician involved an unwieldy, paper-intensive set of instructions that took days or weeks as various staff members became involved to register, communicate, analyze, diagnose, allocate, dispatch, monitor, close, and review the problem. Figure 4-3 shows a simplified version of how field service technicians are enlisted.

Note that each communication involved in Figure 4-3 can be performed using wireless technology, from the customer reporting the problem via his cell phone to the field service rep closing out the trouble ticket via wireless laptop. Considering that only five years ago most of these interactions took place on paper, these processes have become (and continue to become) exponentially more efficient, generating not only faster turnaround times but also higher customer satisfaction rates.

The CSR can actually enlist the support of product specialists or field service engineers by sending a message to their wireless devices. With the right analysis capabilities, the CSR can rate the severity of a customer problem and

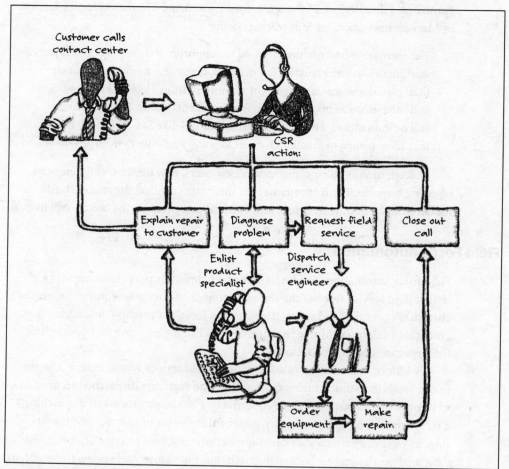

Figure 4-3: Enlisting field services

then determine whether a field service rep should be dispatched, based on either her particular skill set or her current distance from the customer's site. In this way, the CSR can dispatch the technician most likely to fix the problem the fastest.

Field technicians not only receive dispatch orders via their PDAs, pagers, and cell phones; they can even make use of these devices during the actual repair. The ability to pop a CD into a CD-ROM or insert a memory card containing installation instructions, repair guidelines, or equipment specifications provides the technician with the information he needs while at the customer site and frees him from lugging around bulky how-to manuals. The technician can use the device to order additional parts and supplies, as well. Communication software can then alert the CSR handling the trouble ticket that additional equipment is needed.

Figure 4-4 illustrates some of the features inherent in the newest wireless devices, some of which look and work more like micro-laptops than like the pagers of old.

The advanced features they provide sure beat the alternative: the technician trying to find a computer someplace so he can dial a corporate server or access the Web to order the part and enter the updated repair status—leaving the company and the customer at the mercy of a single field rep's busy schedule.

In real life, field engineers for my local telephone company send completion status of their fiber-optic installations to the company's large customer database via Motorola 2-way pagers, ensuring near real-time repair updates. No more calling the home office with their whereabouts; no more syncing of databases. Moreover, CSRs and sales reps can interact with the same data in real time.

Although current CRM products remain more sales-oriented than service-oriented, customers' field service requirements are nevertheless more

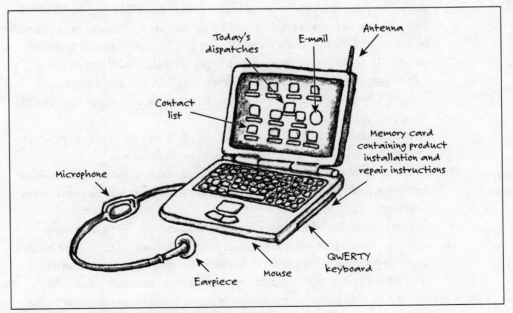

Figure 4-4: A field service wireless terminal

quantifiable—and higher-profile—than their sales needs, and much more time-critical. Additionally, FFA comprises a set of customer touchpoints that should be recorded as part of the customer's profile, so when the account rep in Scenario 1 prepares his next pitch, he has timely information at his fingertips. It's no wonder field force automation is the fastest-growing area of CRM.

An SFA Checklist for Success

That CRM programs benefit both internal and external customers is nowhere more apparent than with sales force automation. Rendering salespeople better informed and more productive increases the likelihood that they'll close more business. And this type of productivity is bound to enhance the customer relationship, not to mention the corporate bottom line. Yet a few high-profile "gotchas" have foiled many a well-meaning and badly-needed SFA program. Be sure to avoid them by adhering to the following suggestions:

- Understand how SFA will help, and enlist salesperson stakeholdership at the beginning. Throughout the CRM readiness assessments I've done, this problem recurs with stunning regularity across industries and organizations. The project team chooses a highly functional CRM tool with robust SFA features, customizes it, and notifies the sales force that the new tool will be deployed. Like most new technologies, SFA requires its users to understand its benefits before they use it. Involve sales staff at all these points:
  - *Initial requirements gathering.* By describing SFA and soliciting advice about how its capabilities would help or hinder account reps in performing their jobs.
  - *Product selection.* By including key salespeople and managers in product demo meetings and enlisting them for pilot evaluations.
  - *Rollout of the tool.* By involving sales management in defining the rollout strategy, including when and where the new software will be deployed in each phase and to whom.
- Communicate the value proposition to the sales force up front. Many— arguably most—first attempts at sales force automation fail because using the tools provides no apparent net benefit. Communicate the benefits of automating key tasks, defining repeatable processes, integrating disparate data, and knowing customers better as they pertain not only to the sales force—as in, "You no longer have to run and mail in sales reports;

management can now do it themselves!"—but to the entire company. If possible, quantify the value of these benefits in terms of potential revenue uplift or increased market share. Commit to allocating the funds recouped from the expected productivity gains into additional marketing and advertising campaigns, rendering your company's products and services more accessible.

- Invest in—and enforce—training. This is true when deploying any type of CRM, but salespeople are especially reluctant to take time out to be trained on something they aren't convinced they need. Although functionality training might be overkill for basic contact management, you should require training before distributing integrated CRM suites with a variety of features that will ultimately affect the company's customer knowledge base. (Consider combining CRM training with quarterly regional sales meetings to maximize sales staff time.) Train sales managers before training their employees, ensuring that their concerns are addressed first and separately from their staffs'. Allocate logon IDs and PDAs only upon completion of the formal training course.

- Beware of inherent sales processes packaged into SFA tools. Although standardized sales processes have been shown to result in greater efficiencies, an out-of-the-box process might not be the best one for your organization. The more complex your current sales process, the more likely you'll need to customize the default process defined by your CRM vendor. Be prepared to invest the time and resources necessary to optimize current sales processes—ideally, before you select an SFA product.

- Understand the infrastructure necessary to support wireless technologies. Adopt these technologies based on specific remote communications required by your business. And know what will work with what you have: This means ensuring your wireless service provider supports your geography and can provide dependable service.

- Let SFA use affect sales compensation. This tactic is controversial and somewhat doctrinaire, but don't those salespeople who are delivering current and timely activity data back to the corporation for growing customer knowledge deserve a bit more money than those who aren't? After all, customer data, a critical corporate asset, is at stake. Offering salespeople a bonus for maintaining customer data and sales managers further incentives for enforcing the practice is just good business. And with technology evolving the way it is, remote communication of client activities becomes consistently easier and faster; thus the benefits are more obvious than ever.

- Change hiring practices and job role descriptions to include use of CRM. Integrate CRM training with new-hire orientation. Require new account reps to use SFA as part of their formal job responsibilities, outlining the discrete functions for which they are responsible (e.g., "Maintain and transfer updated client information via product 'database update' function at least twice weekly"). Revise sales position interview guidelines and job description documentation to include SFA use as a core responsibility.

The range of customer touchpoints availed by a robust sales force automation infrastructure can mean the difference between sporadic name-and-address updates and an efficient flow of communication between account teams, their clients, and the company at large.

Case Study: Hewlett Packard

Think of Hewlett Packard as an innovator and you probably think of quality printers, high-end servers, and a crack management team. But you'd better add CRM to that list because the company is intent on delivering an industry leading customer experience. As if that weren't enough of a challenge, HP's doing it on a global scale.

Listening to Mike Overly talk about customer relationship management at Hewlett Packard is like listening to Alan Greenspan talk about the U.S. economy. As CRM Program Director at HP, Mike not only knows his stuff, he articulates it with a blend of experience and authority that makes people go out and act. And when it comes to CRM, HP is definitely taking action.

Although the company set out to improve a variety of business issues with CRM, its overarching goal is to provide an industry-leading customer experience. With customers ranging from the largest companies in the world to small mom-and-pop operations, HP has a lot of customers to satisfy. Combine this with the fact that the company is rolling out its CRM program worldwide and the program's magnitude only begins to hit home.

Mike Overly and his HP CRM team weren't naive. They knew that to deploy a global CRM solution, they needed to influence the entire organization. Having the commitment and involvement of the President of HP's Business Customer Business Unit provided the team the necessary clout and visibility to gather consensus from a range of different corporate functions, from the sales organization to marketing to the company's myriad call centers. The mantra sung by each organization is the same: To manage the total customer experience.

HP's initial CRM effort focused on the organization that touches the customer most: the sales force. Its goal was to provide the company's global sales force with an automated—and standard—way to perform contact management and account planning. Although the initial functionality was classic sales force automation, the hurdles were high. "Everyone had their own rules and guidelines about managing their customer activities," says Overly. "But what makes a customer happy is pretty universal."

The company chose a CRM solution from business partner Oracle and has deployed the Oracle Sales Online product to customer-facing employees in North America and other countries around the world. With customer activity data in an Oracle "customer master" database, HP can provide a remote salesperson with the ability to track a customer's activities across organizations. For instance, a salesperson can find out which of his customers have contacted the company's help desk or can call up information about the latest marketing campaign and its primary channels. Indeed, Overly's CRM team has made the ability to share information about customer touchpoints across organizations a key CRM success measure.

HP is gunning for even bigger improvements, such as dynamic personalization for Web visitors and automatic lead routing from marketing to the internal sales staff and HP partners. "We're in the solutions business," says Overly. "We're not just interested in solving today's problems." Over time, both headquarters and field staff will have access to a range of customer information. The goal is to enable customers to control their relationships with HP.

Standardizing CRM corporate-wide has meant phasing out numerous legacy systems. Data, business processes, and technologies that are customer-related will slowly be merged with the current CRM program, driving cost savings into the hundreds of millions of dollars. Although Overly demurs from estimating revenue generation from CRM improvements, his optimism makes it clear he expects additional revenues of similar scale as a direct result of HP's CRM solution.

THE CHALLENGES:

Overly is frank about his biggest challenge so far, and it's no surprise: deploying CRM worldwide has its trials. No matter where they are in the world, sales reps share the goal of being as productive as possible; however, every salesperson has a preferred way of getting the job done. Overly and his team have had to surmount habits and assumptions that are often not only organizationally entrenched but also cultural. "We're no longer talking about every country's having a unique personal productivity tool," he says, "but about an HP solution."

Because Oracle's CRM environment is based on portal technology, salespeople can customize their interfaces to include client information and contact activities as well as data from external news sources and the global financial markets. The company is delivering much of the training via the Web to educate staff on how to use the Oracle CRM technology and apply it to their specific job functions. Although most of the training is conducted in English, the company offers localized Web courses in native languages to several countries, including Korea and Japan.

Another challenge has been rendering ongoing management sponsorship and involvement as painless as possible for HP's busy executives. "We realized early on that we'd need to make it easy for executives to support us," claims Overly, whose team includes a CRM Change Manager. Besides establishing ongoing CRM performance measures and training, the Change Manager is chartered with developing and tracking all project communications, including internal communications across HP, such as guiding executives in communicating new customer-focused policies.

GOOD ADVICE:

From the beginning of the CRM initiative, Overly's team shrewdly steered away from the point-solution approach, preferring instead to expend the extra time, money, and internal education necessary to deploy enterprise-wide CRM. This meant organizing CRM development around so-called "vertical silos" representing corporate functions such as internal sales, marketing, and customer service.

The CRM team members for each vertical silo work with the executives in related business organization to design the future-state business processes. In addition, a horizontal design group is responsible for the cross-functional process design.

"We didn't want to build more stovepipe systems," Overly explains. "You've got to keep one eye on the big picture. Otherwise you'll end up with ten different 'best in class' CRM solutions, not to mention a huge integration issue that would impede our ability to do on-the-fly process improvements." This approach of uniting vertical design efforts with horizontal process standards not only avoids development in a vacuum; it also ensures that CRM business processes, technologies, data, and implementation methods are consistent across the company.

Overly advises others who might be deploying CRM on a similar global scale to be mindful of three success metrics:

1. Obtain sustained executive presence, meaning that executive leadership must be engaged throughout the CRM lifecycle.
2. Always keep one eye on today's problem, and the other on tomorrow's problem.
3. Ensure change leadership, with emphasis on the word leader.

Says Overly, "Every day there's a new challenge—you need someone who has a good understanding of the problem and the authority to fix it."

THE GOLDEN NUGGET:

When asked how he'll know when CRM is a success, Mike Overly quotes one of HP's co-founders, who once said, "You tell me how a person is measured, and I'll tell you how they behave." In keeping with this core cultural tenet, HP continues to establish and meet a series of CRM performance measures.

"We're putting measures in place to reinforce the behavior we're looking for," says Overly. Although HP has committed to three primary measures—increased revenue, decreased costs, and industry-leading total customer experience—measurement, like the CRM program itself, is ongoing. Measurement results might dictate a range of business changes, such as having a portion of HP executives' pay based on customer loyalty. The CRM team considers direct customer data to be a primary measurement source.

For a multidisciplinary technology conglomerate like HP, deploying a global and interdisciplinary CRM program could take years. When asked about the duration, Overly expresses his vision that CRM be adopted as a continual corporate practice with no end in sight. With such a high-visibility commitment—not to mention the complexity, executive involvement, and process changes—it's noteworthy that the initial SFA application took months, not years, to be released to its global business users.

How can a company of HP's size be so nimble, yet so visionary? Overly politely reiterates: "We're in the solutions business."

The Manager's Bottom Line

Although emerging technologies have taken sales force automation from a nice-to-have productivity tool to a competitive weapon, the company willing to establish simple and well-defined procedures for its field staff will be the big winner. Sales organizations are working better than ever with headquarters, with their customers, with each other—and with their automation. Remote teams rely less on headquarters to provide them with the information they need.

It's no longer about simply tracking account history or updating address lists. Through sales force automation and its accompanying technologies, companies are proactively helping their salespeople manage the selling process and improve it. The early adopters are finally seeing returns, witnessing how these efficiencies result in lower costs and increasing profits. And customers are experiencing these improvements in faster turnaround times and in price breaks that reflect those cost reductions. For companies, their sales staffs, and their customers, SFA has been a win-win-win.

CHAPTER FIVE

CRM in e-Business

M any of today's (and now, yesterday's) e-businesses have made the often fatal mistake of delaying customer-focused initiatives until their companies turned a profit. With pressure to gain market share, these companies have adopted the "customer at any cost" credo: in their zeal to capture market share, they assumed all customers are created equal. This meant handing free goods and services to new customers who might not return, selling products at cost or below, and spending hundreds of thousands of dollars on mass marketing campaigns with no hope of recouping their investments.

Analysts didn't help matters by proclaiming "early to' market" e-commerce companies the winners in their online categories, unless of course you were a customer expecting freebies and rock-bottom prices. Notwithstanding well-designed Web sites, slick product demos, and futuristic trade show booths, a number of e-commerce companies went belly up, and hundreds more saw their stock prices plunge at exponentially higher rates than those of their brick-and-mortar counterparts.

Many of these companies were focused more on their Web site traffic than on their profitability. They soon learned the number of visitors didn't necessarily correlate with the number of customers-those who made purchases at the site. Marketing campaigns were focused at the for-mer-visitors whose intentions were informational or who might have stumbled upon the site accidentally-and not the customers who would ultimately determine their profits. Visitor-focused campaigns and number-of-hits reports would fail to recoup the hefty investments made in these companies.

Kozmo cancelled plans to go public after the home delivery service lost over twenty-six million dollars on only $3.5 million in sales.[1] The problem? The company's average delivery costs often exceeded the costs of the products being delivered. For delivery companies like Kozmo and Webvan, the customer craving a Dove bar and a disposable razor—not the one needing regular delivery of a month's worth of groceries—was the unfortunate rule. The per-delivery losses forced these companies to expand their product offerings and slap purchase minimums on their deliveries to protect their costs—though such measures still don't guarantee profitability. In the case of Webvan, the cost-cutting and restructuring weren't enough to prevent a management shakeup, including the CEO's resignation (after constant press speculation and prolonged shareholder grumbling). For Kozmo, similar changes came too late: the company closed its doors in April 2001.

eCRM Evolving

What about the loyal Kozmo customer who spent an average of $100 per week and wanted that Dove bar without the surcharge? With the right CRM functionality, a delivery service would know when to waive the surcharge to keep the customer. In many such cases, 10 percent of a company's customers account for 90 percent of the profit. Unfortunately, dot-com companies offering commodity-based products have been investing more in their basic infrastructures—warehousing and distribution, recruiting costs, and such—and less in analysis capabilities that would tell them who their good customers are. Some would argue they have no choice. Others would maintain that without a clear view of the customers they want to attract and those they want to keep, the best logistics and the best procurement in the world won't matter.

Pure-play dot-com retailers are getting a run for their (dwindling) money these days from traditional retailers who have parlayed their existing infrastructures into a competitive edge. After all, brick-and-mortar businesses have mastered economies of scale, having learned the lesson early that a wider variety of

---

1. As reported in "How Kozmo is Getting Killed by its Customers," *The New Yorker,* September 4, 2000.

well-priced products will draw more customers, and they are expert at getting rid of nonproductive inventory. In leveraging the Internet, these brick-and-mortar firms find themselves firmly planted in the world of e-commerce, with the systems and processes in place to support them.

Multichannel CRM

Some predict that the brick-and-mortar companies will have the last laugh. After all, for every futurist proclaiming the Web will revolutionize the world, there's a pragmatist who pronounces it "just another channel." Although both might be right, it's where the Internet provides the most value that it incites the greatest change.

Companies such as high-end retailer Tiffany (www.tiffany.com) simply use their Web sites as an additional means of luring people into their stores by providing add-on customer service and product-related information on, for instance, choosing a diamond. Similarly, Levi Strauss & Co. includes a retail store locator on its Levi's (www.levi.com) and Dockers (www.dockers.com) Web sites so customers know where to go shopping. Bloomingdale's (www.bloomingdales.com), with limited physical stores across the United States, has dramatically extended both its presence and its brand through its Web site, allowing its Web shoppers to purchase their items by referencing the product's catalog item number. The Web has become a cost-effective way of increasing the corporate footprint.

Indeed, many acknowledged e-commerce best practices are retailers—like Eddie Bauer, profiled in Chapter 2—who combine powerful online features, including customer self-service such as order and shipment tracking, with an established brick-and-mortar presence, giving customers the experience they still want. The award-winning J. Crew Web site (jcrew.com) offers more than just apparel: specialized services uniquely available in cyberspace. J. Crew Web shoppers often see promotions before they make it into the catalog, but they're free to return items purchased on the Web to the company's physical stores, maximizing the customer's—not the retailer's—convenience.

The failures of Garden.com and cosmetics e-tailer Eve.com have been partially blamed on the lack of the customer's tactile experience. It's no coincidence that when Eve.com closed its virtual doors, the Web site directed customers to Sephora.com (www.sephora.com), a company that combines its successful online business with a worldwide chain of stores.

Physical storefront or no, the service orientation of e-commerce leaders aims at giving customers as many choices as possible, and—as we discussed in

Chapter 3—puts more power in the customer's hands. Web-enabled self-service allows customers to use vendor sites to change their own addresses and track their own orders, and many are providing powerful search engines and other features to keep customers on their sites and keep them coming back.

Petco (www.petco.com) offers pet lovers a community center where they can chat with animal behavior experts and access a range of articles. The site also features an online "pet yellow pages," where visitors can find a range of pet-related services available near their homes, and even provides a way to donate money to the ASPCA online. And drugstore.com (www.drugstore.com) features the ability to analyze the interactions of certain drugs, and the company's eMedAlert program provides daily information about drug product warnings and recalls.

But such value-added features motivating customers to return to the Web site, catalog, or store don't necessarily guarantee customers will buy more of a company's products. Effective marketing means more than just a slick Web site and automated campaigns. And the more companies know about how their customers prefer to interact with them, the better service they can provide.

CRM in B2B

Companies that are actually communicating with online markets have flung the doors wide open. They're constantly searching for solid information they can share with customers and prospects via Web and FTP sites, e-mail lists, phone calls, whatever it takes. They're not half as concerned with protecting their data as with how much information they can give away. That's how they stay in touch, stay competitive, keep market attention from drifting to competitors. Such companies are creating a new kind of corporate identity, based not on the repetitive advertising needed to create "brand awareness," but on substantive, personalized communications.[2]

There's no question that the Internet has streamlined business processes, providing efficiencies unmatched by traditional ways of doing business. The Web makes things happen faster. But is speed enough?

In the early days of e-business, companies built their Web sites implementing so-called storefront software that enabled them to accept a customer's credit card information and automatically check inventory. They then ensured that their systems were robust enough to allow customers 24-by-7 access. Dot-com companies had to build organizations to support inventory tracking, delivery, and returns processing, and traditional companies had to quickly incorporate the Web channel into existing business practices.

The ability to exploit multiple channels introduces a series of headaches for the IT executive charged with integrating legacy applications such as fulfillment and purchase-order systems with the Web. The better the organization's current computing power, the more effective will be integration of the new Web channel into existing operations.

Don't get me wrong. The Web shouldn't simply be shoehorned into a company's existing business unless processes are already robust. Simply put, mere automation of business processes isn't enough. Companies will be expected to provide their customers and suppliers with even more information than ever before. To do that, they need the best databases, with the highest-quality data, and the applications and processes necessary to deliver that data, not to mention a cultural willingness to share data with suppliers and customers.

Whether the company was a pure-play dot-com e-tailer or a traditional brick-and-mortar general merchandiser, key processes such as ordering, fulfillment, inventory management, and distribution all had to run at Web speed. The challenge of streamlining the supply chain to keep pace loomed ever more large. As companies adopt the mantra of "differentiate or die," they realize that manufacturing, like customer service, is an area of opportunity.

---

2. Levine, Rick, et al., *The Cluetrain Manifesto: The End of Business As Usual.* Perseus Books, 1999.

Enterprise Resource Planning

Enterprise resource planning (ERP) systems have become the heart or, more accurately, the spine of many corporate technology initiatives, having been widely adopted in the late 1990s by companies eager to streamline their operations. Goals for ERP ranged from reducing inventory levels to increasing process efficiencies across the supply chain or even integrating core business systems.

ERP systems were the focal point of new work processes across these companies. Because ERP products offer easier information-sharing across various organizations from purchasing to manufacturing to finance to human resources, corporate procedures were aligned with the way ERP products worked. Gone were the archaic general ledger systems and warehouses brimming with file cabinets full of purchase orders. ERP automated key corporate functions, and the companies buying these systems complied with their inherent business processes, including

- Order processing and fulfillment
- Production planning and scheduling
- Logistics management
- Accounting
- Human resource allocation and planning

Major ERP vendors such as PeopleSoft and SAP not only automated these and other functions; they also linked them for companies who previously had disparate systems that had never been interrelated. These companies replaced their outdated legacy systems and enabled integrated operations across the enterprise. The products themselves required hefty investments, often into the millions of dollars, and ERP implementation resources usually doubled those budgets.

The integration piece alone was a boon to companies. With ERP, salespeople could access a single system to check inventory, a purchasing agent could look up a supplier's pricing history, and a marketing product manager could track defects. Despite war stories about underestimated budgets and overestimated consultants, ERP delivered across-the-board efficiencies.

This integration had dramatic effects on downstream customer-facing business processes. Ravi Kalakota and Marcia Robinson describe Colgate's ERP success in their book *e-Business: Roadmap for Success*:

Before SAP R/3 . . . distribution planning and picking used to take up to four days; today it takes 14 hours. In total, order-to-delivery time has been cut in half.[3]

In other words, Colgate's customers—including heavy-hitter retailers such as Wal-Mart and Rite Aid—were getting products faster, which can in turn increase satisfaction rates. Companies were also reducing out-of-stock situations, an influential factor in enhancing customer loyalty.

The marriage between ERP and CRM is stronger than ever. For instance, a company's accounts receivable staff might choose not to open collections on past-due customers who have in-process trouble tickets. Likewise, CRM business users can use accounting and supply chain information to decide how to treat customers who don't meet provisioning deadlines. ERP vendors have recognized the link between tighter, more integrated operations and business customer satisfaction and are now busy releasing CRM modules that tie into their core products, rendering the customer a key link in the supply chain.

Supply Chain Management

Michael Porter's classic "five forces model," a business-school staple since the early 1980s, identified five key factors that dictate how companies fare competitively. Porter argued that suppliers and other vendors wielded a certain amount of power in their ability to raise prices or compromise product quality, and that this was a key factor in dictating how effectively a company remained competitive. Porter contended that too much power in the hands of suppliers could erode corporate profits.

Indeed, the classic supply chain itself involves costly and often manual processes that enable a company to go from raw materials to completed product to sale. Depending on supply chain efficiency, the entire cycle can take months or even years—and can make or break an entire company. In the classic supply chain environment, each link in the supply chain operates in a vacuum. At some points, production can't keep pace with orders; in others, inventory levels inflate due to misunderstandings of, or no knowledge of, customer demand.

---

3. Kalakota, Ravi and Marcia Robinson, *e-Business 2.0: Roadmap for Success.* Boston: Addison-Wesley, 2000, 183.

Forrester Research recently estimated that processing a single order costs a company an average of $107. The number of discrete people who "touched" a mortgage between the customer's initial application and the decision to approve the mortgage was widely cited as the overarching reason for the failure of dot-com high-flier Mortgage.com.

It's no wonder that supply chain management (SCM)—the automation of much of the supply chain—is top-of-mind for many executives. Reengineering the supply chain with SCM technology is particularly promising when you consider that the traditional legacy supply chain systems managed mass-production environments, not the increasingly customized, one-to-one process companies are rapidly embracing.

Here's an example: To procure car parts, an automobile manufacturer would have to decide how much inventory it needed, analyze which of its suppliers carried a given part or find new suppliers who did, make 30 or 40 phone calls, and issue a request for bids, all of which involved manual effort and paper documentation. Moreover, scores of potential suppliers could be vying for the business, requiring the company to mail an equal number of bid requests and await responses. Never mind the rest of the supply chain, the procurement process alone could take months. And as it turned out, the cost of ensuring the lowest cost could exceed the purchase!

For companies selling commodity products, such cumbersome procurement procedures triggered the adoption of "preferred suppliers," effectively limiting the number of contenders for a given bid, but at the same time decreasing competition and driving prices upward.

How do businesses anticipate inventory? Manufacturers such as Dell build products according to demand, requiring a just-in-time inventory model. Such a model was designed to prevent companies from having to anticipate customer demand by stocking huge warehouses full of parts and tying up funds in inventory rather than, say, marketing. Other manufacturers using the just-in-time model have seen the Internet deliver business-to-business efficiencies that are improving their relationships with their customers, both directly and indirectly.

Extranets—also known as private portals, accessible only to company-sanctioned partners—and e-procurement software have allowed companies to organize and monitor their purchasing processes by qualifying and communicating with suppliers over the Internet. The ability to submit purchase orders directly to the supplier's inventory system over the Web—via an extranet that allows access only to selected outsiders such as approved suppliers—has dramatically minimized waste, reduced costs, and improved supplier negotiations. Tailoring product support to certain partner or customer segments, as well as to individual customers, is also an emerging benefit of extranets.

Companies, particularly those selling commodity products, are increasingly doing away with their approved supplier lists and posting proposal requests directly on the Web, inviting all potential suppliers to bid and thereby increasing competition and lowering prices.

This tactic also removes the complex Request for Proposal (RFP) review process and contractual and legal maneuverings necessary to establish long-term supplier contracts. Companies can just post proposal requests on the Web to buy what they need at the lowest price, thus eliminating extraneous human involvement through lower-cost automation. Some forward-thinking companies have already eliminated their approved vendor lists and consider such free market bidding requests to be the beginning of the end for their corporate purchasing departments.

Combining the Internet with innovative business practices also levels the playing field by enabling smaller suppliers to bid on larger opportunities with prospective customers in a fast and inexpensive way. Suppliers can receive proposal requests, communicate product specifications, and even collect payments, using the Web as the communications channel. Suppliers can compete more effectively than ever before, and their customers have access to a larger pool of potential partners.

Supplier Relationship Management

Emerging exchange models and e-marketplaces allow companies to further improve their supply chain management by establishing alliances with "best of breed" partners, pooling both buyers and sellers worldwide to facilitate timely and less costly exchange of goods. Partners work together to streamline processes, outsource critical services, and apply automation to key areas, ultimately providing a range of products and services that might otherwise not be available. Tighter supplier collaboration via trading exchanges increases the velocity of products through the production lifecycle and enables evident improvements in customer support.

For instance, an airline in short supply of peanuts might release an urgent order to its exchange, which would have the means to route the order to the supplier most capable of filling it in the allotted time. Automating not only the order-routing but also the supplier qualification can be essential to fulfillment and is increasingly occurring in real time. Depending on the supplier's proximity to the airline, the supplier might deliver the peanuts directly.

This practice, known as collaborative commerce, or "c-commerce," involves a company's sharing its valuable customer information with its suppliers so all of the partners in the supply chain have relevant data. The Internet—extranets in particular—has been a boon in terms of process efficiencies, which over time can translate into customer satisfaction.

Collaborative commerce and trading exchanges are not only resulting in reduced costs and faster time to market, but also in the ability to nimbly tailor products and services for specific types of customers, driving critical information through the supply chain, and improvements along with them. After all, fulfilling an urgent order that might have previously been impossible to deliver can result in a satisfied airline customer, not to mention the satisfaction of its hungry customers. Figure 5-1 illustrates the supply chain's links to customers.

The supply chain increasingly relies on the communication of customer behavior data (purchase patterns, in particular) to render production scheduling more efficient and intelligent than ever.

But first, a company must culturally believe that sharing information with its suppliers is important. If it is fundamentally reluctant to reveal its sales prices to its suppliers, all the CRM in the world won't matter. After all, there might be sensitive competitive information. The company might be willing to let its supplier know how many product units have sold but nevertheless not want to give the supplier the specific sales price and risk that supplier's revealing this price to the competition. Such companies must consider that already a wealth of information is moving back and forth between themselves and their suppliers—additional information might be added over time as a means to further reduce costs and enhance productivity.

How do companies know which suppliers to select? How do they qualify the best choices? Supplier relationship management (SRM) products help companies analyze vendors based on whether they are considered strategic suppliers—those with which the company has established a mutually beneficial collaborative strategy—or commodity suppliers, which the company selects based on price.

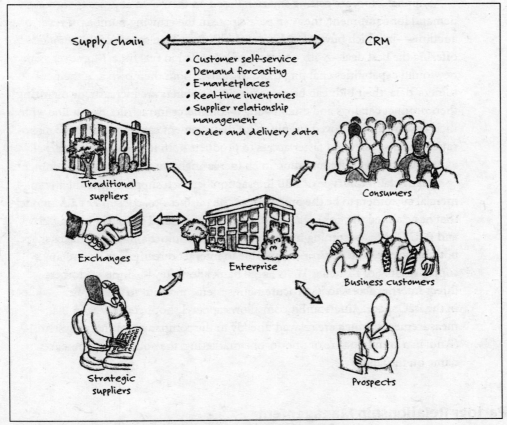

Supply chain ⟷ CRM

- Customer self-service
- Demand forcasting
- E-marketplaces
- Real-time inventories
- Supplier relationship management
- Order and delivery data

Traditional suppliers

Exchanges

Strategic suppliers

Enterprise

Consumers

Business customers

Prospects

Figure 5-1: Customers: The final link in the supply chain

Companies are leveraging the Internet more than ever to qualify, track, and monitor their supplier relationships. SRM tools such as the one from SAS allow companies to assess the relative cost, value, quality, reliability, and risk of individual suppliers, thus optimizing supplier qualification and selection.

Likewise, suppliers are motivated to improve their relationships with their business customers. In the world of e-commerce, the supplier intent on providing its customers with the equipment it needs, when it needs it, is the supplier who gets points for service as well as price. The ability to respond to—indeed, to predict—product demand means being able to intermingle forecasted orders with actual orders. Many companies have posted their current demand forecasts on private portals where suppliers can access them at will.

Suppliers, too, are getting smarter. Based on their own abilities to forecast demand for equipment, they can participate in the growing number of reverse auctions—in which buyers hold online bidding wars in search of the supplier offering the best deal—with optimal pricing, often in real time. Moreover, with newfound capabilities enabling them to analyze both their own and their customers' data, their bids can be more precise. Suppliers are increasingly digitizing their product catalogs and establishing e-commerce infrastructures in line with their customers' improved supply chain management capabilities. Such collaboration means easier and faster access to products both internally and externally, as well as supplier differentiation in an increasingly commoditized environment.

Many claim this type of B2B interaction between suppliers and their commercial customers to be the precursor of the business-to-consumer CRM model that has claimed the lion's share of the market thus far. The line between B2B and B2C CRM is becoming increasingly fine. As multichannel CRM takes shape, both businesses and consumers are able to interact directly with a company's supply chain. For instance, Wells Fargo bank allows key business customers direct Internet access to its procurement system, and thus to its suppliers, while in the B2C space, AmericanFit.com allows apparel shoppers to type in their measurements, which are relayed directly to the company's inventory system. (And, in a grand gesture of one-to-one marketing, they put the customer's name on the label!)

Partner Relationship Management

As with suppliers, companies have realized the need to foster more productive dialog between themselves and their channel partners, dealers, and resellers. As with SRM, the Web provides these partners with automated access to centralized information and support resources, enabling them to deliver more accurate product information and better services to their customers.

Partner relationship management (PRM) is a subset of CRM that allows companies to ensure partner satisfaction. This usually means providing sales partners and resellers with the tools and information they need to

- Access up-to-date product information, including release dates, defect data, and marketing materials
- Communicate with support resources and offer online assistance with products and services

- Reduce paperwork by obtaining online knowledge management resources such as pricing revisions and sales contracts
- Access a company's supply chain network to check inventory, outstanding shipments, and other order details
- Download customizable sales presentations and other product marketing literature

Some PRM products also help companies qualify and recruit new sales partners. (Prior to PRM, qualifying sales partners involved in-person meetings, philosophical discussions, and tons of paperwork.) Products like these help companies establish desirable partner attributes and allow them to assign partner categories that might limit partners to specific product assignments or sales strategies (see Figure 5-2).

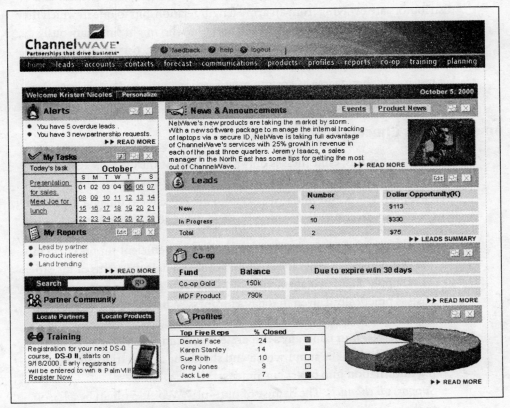

Figure 5-2: ChannelWave's PRM Product

PRM tools also provide partner profiles that enable a company not only to understand a business partner's characteristics—from their headquarters address to which competitive products the partner might be selling—but also to track the partner's overall successes and contribution. Companies can use this information to further improve their partner relationships with additional training or joint marketing activities.

Perhaps the highest-impact use of PRM is its facility for automating lead distribution to the best partner. By providing analysis and reporting capabilities, companies can match partners with key sales leads based on their skills, geography, or areas of specialty. When a company's marketing department receives a lead, it can use a PRM tool to score the lead, allocate the lead to the best partner, and subsequently track that lead through to its close.

The Internet has rendered supply chain and sales partnerships less of a guessing game and less of a waiting game. Companies and their vendors and distributors are evolving from an arm's length relationship to one in which they are all intertwined by a network of collaborators who might simultaneously cooperate and compete. The resulting efficiencies lower costs, triggering downward pricing and higher customer profitability. In addition, faster time to market means a higher degree of customer satisfaction at the end of the line.

An e-Business Checklist for Success

As important as it is, e-business is only a small part of the overall CRM picture. Indeed, with the questionable future of the pure-play dot-com business model, even the purest of eCRM initiatives needs to include a focus outside the Internet. This checklist can ensure that your e-business and CRM strategies are in synch:

- *Keep your eye on service improvements.* The most efficient supply chain in the world doesn't matter if a customer can't wrangle the status of his order. That supply chain management technologies are decreasing production costs is practically a given in today's business. What's not as apparent are the resulting improvements in service at the sales, marketing, and contact center levels. Your company's disparate organizations should all be able to view each link in the supply chain and should be able to translate the resulting information into better customer service.
- *Support all channels.* The demise of pure-play Web sites might be a lesson to those brick-and-mortar companies who might be tempted to relax. The

more available channels from which a customer can make a purchase or have a question answered, the more visible your brand. In an effort to ensure that customers in their physical stores get the merchandise they came for, Barnes & Noble is installing Internet kiosks so in-store customers in search of an out-of-stock book or CD can order the item from the company's Web site, thereby covering all potential bases.

- *Don't count out the Luddites.* There are and will always be customers who simply don't use the Web but nevertheless want to do business with you. In the flurry to integrate the Web and handheld technologies as major purchasing channels, many companies put customers who want to call or fax in an order at the back of the line, despite their potentially high value. Customers' overall data, including purchase history, revenues, profitability, and support costs—not their channel preferences alone—should dictate their value and thus their treatment.

- *Start profiling your partners now.* Even advanced technology companies suffer from the "shoemaker's children" scenario, storing sporadically gathered and often paper-based profiles of their alliance partners and resellers. Don't use the fact that you're in the throes of building a data warehouse or CRM data mart as an excuse for not profiling and tracking attributes of your partners and suppliers. When you have your customer data available, you'll need that partner information more than ever.

- *Remember business processes!* Most business integration efforts involving CRM focus much more on technology than on process, an assumption that can lead to overspending or to solving the wrong problem. (What good is building a system to provide order status to the sales staff when neither the contact center nor the customer is permitted to access it?)

Be it tighter supply chain integration, optimization of alliance partnerships, or customer self-service, understand CRM's objectives before deciding on its mechanics. (We'll see a before-and-after business process scenario in Chapter 7.)

The Manager's Bottom Line

Whatever a company's reason for starting on the road to eCRM, the destination should be competitive advantage and enhanced customer perception. Too many companies have made customer relationship blunders by assuming the Internet sales channel was the most critical, only to be confronted with new online competitors and renewed vigor from the brick-and-mortars.

Likewise, make sure your company integrates its e-business initiatives while there's still time. The flash-in-the-pan dot-coms who failed to make the process improvements necessary to keep customers happy realized their mistakes too late. The customer-at-any-cost strategy doesn't work, nor does the assumption that every transaction must be profitable. Both strategies risk alienating the frequent customer who occasionally makes small purchases but who is nevertheless valuable.

In *The Cluetrain Manifesto: The End of Business As Usual,* the authors make the point that "markets are conversations." How a company encourages and facilitates feedback from its customers, partners, and suppliers is a sound indicator of that company's nimbleness and ability to innovate.

Indeed, the innovative business plans and youthful executive teams of yesterday's pure-play dot-coms were often overshadowed by inflexible business practices and halfhearted technology integration efforts, and the results litter California's Route 101 from Menlo Park to Marin. Know your customers and partners, and differentiate them according to their value. We'll explore the means of understanding that value in the next chapter.

CHAPTER FOUR

Analytical CRM

A customers become savvier shoppers, they will continue to blend their purchasing and service habits. A busy executive who buys a video game for her child online while at the office might nevertheless check the status of her order from her Handspring palmtop while en route to the mall for a new set of golf clubs. Likewise, a customer support agent needs to understand who's at the other end when he picks up the headset or initiates a live chat. The customer calling a toll-free 800 number to make a purchase doesn't care that your systems are@t integrated-she assumes your company knows she's made past purchases on your Web site. In short, she expects you to know who she is.

The Case for Integrated Data

Take the case illustrated in Figure 6- 1, in which an e-tailer's marketing group has implemented CRM to target more effective marketing campaigns. By tracking specific purchase patterns, Marketing can segment customers and then e-mail those customers a promotion targeted to that segment's characteristics. In the case study, Marketing has already seen a 7 percent uplift in sales as a result of this strategy.

In the meantime, the e-tailer's customer service department is using another vendor's CRM tool for call center automation. information about specific calls is loaded from the call center system into a database used by

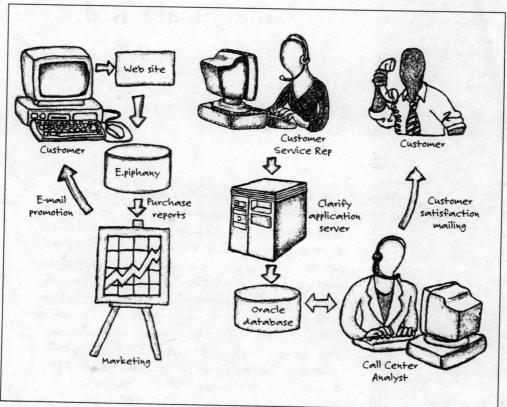

Figure 6-1: One company, two CRM systems

an analyst in the customer service department to evaluate trouble ticket resolutions. The analyst then gathers post facto customer feedback by sending customer satisfaction mailings to customers who have registered a certain type of complaint.

Although both CRM environments have resulted in improvements in their respective departments, the scenario as a whole is actually risky.

Both Marketing and Customer Support are well intentioned in their efforts to improve one-to-one communications with their respective customers. But what if the customer happens to be the same person?

The risk here is that the marketing department might not recognize when customers within its targeted segment have contacted the call center with problems about a popular product and whether those customers are currently unhappy with the company. In such a circumstance, cross-selling another product might do more harm than good. Conversely, the CSR responding to a complaint might not recognize that the customer on the telephone has made several purchases in the past week and falls into the company's "Golden Circle" segment. Failure to escalate this customer's complaint could mean losing a high-value customer. Indeed, applying the same rules to each customer is not only risky; it will put this company behind its competitors, who are striving to differentiate customers and their treatment of them.

Understanding the customer's most recent interaction, or touchpoint, with the company—whether or not it was with the call center—can help the CSR determine how to best meet that customer's needs. Even more important is the knowledge that the customer has a rich, multi-year purchase history. (Indeed, a detailed order history is critical for understanding when and how a customer buys products, whether she is regularly up-sold products, and if she responds to promotions.) Purchase history can combine with other information, such as whether the customer has recently moved, has college-age children, eats out often, and rates high on the customer value scale. Such information can be summarized as a customer profile on the CSR's screen or displayed as a "screen pop" as soon as the call center system recognizes the customer's incoming phone number.

This scenario is a growing problem for companies deploying CRM, "e" or otherwise. In their haste to adopt customer loyalty programs and increase retention rates, marketing departments are acquiring CRM tools without touching base with other areas of the company. Likewise, customer support centers—whose existing call center platforms might include supplementary CRM capabilities and who are likely to have already established customer communications procedures—might not account for the needs of their counterparts in sales or marketing before formalizing their own CRM initiatives.

This problem is often due to company politics but more often due to diverse logistical and infrastructure problems that mandate greater levels of customer knowledge, and fast. The flaw with such a "stovepipe" approach to CRM is that the relationship with the customer is understood to be based on a subset of the customer's actual interactions with the company. The company deploys CRM and bases decisions on a subset of these interactions. The resulting decisions—for instance, Marketing sending out a satisfaction survey a few weeks after the customer support survey is released—could end up alienating the customer rather than instilling loyalty.

In a recent survey by the Yankee Group, 73 percent of companies claimed to be collecting information about individual customers. However, as shown in Table 6-1, how they collected that information varied widely.

It's clear that although companies might agree they need CRM, many don't agree on the reasons why. A CRM assessment my company recently conducted represented the problem brilliantly.

So we could gauge an Internet service provider's CRM readiness, we asked to meet with several of the executives who had expressed the need for a CRM strategy. The differences in their individual interpretations of CRM, as described in Table 6-2, proved profound.

The alarming degree of disagreement in our conversations with these executives led us to believe that developing a detailed, enterprise-wide CRM strategy wouldn't garner much support. However, everyone agreed on one common denominator: the pressing need for more and better customer data.

A Single Version of the Customer Truth

The scenario illustrated in Figure 6-1, in addition to being unwieldy, is hardly cost effective. Multiple overlapping tools within a single company involve duplicate effort in technology acquisition, systems integration, installation, deployment, and training, not to mention multiple and often redundant investments. Likewise, the lack of a single CSR interface for customer data forces the CSR to access multiple systems to aggregate different information about the customer—sometimes while the customer waits.

Table 6-1: How Customer Information Is Gathered[1]

Direct Sales Interactions	60%
E-Mail	50%
Call Center Interactions	43%
Web Site Visits	40%
Surveys	28%
Focus Groups	28%
Events/Trade Shows	27%

1. (Source: The Yankee Group, 2000)

Table 6-2: Four CRM Perspectives, Four Different Executives

Executive	"Take" on CRM
VP of Marketing	"We desperately need a CRM system. We don't even know how many real customers we have! I'll pay for the darn tool, but we need it fast. I'm thinking of a customer profile dashboard. Now, when can we get started?"
VP of Sales	"Of course we need it, but we're not ready yet! I've just funded an effort to clean up all our contact data. After all, what good is customer profiling if the data makes no sense?"
VP of Customer Support	"CRM? Why, we're already doing it! Our call center system gives our service reps customer information automatically when the customer calls in. We can even see a list of products for that customer! Who says we need anything else?"
VP of Engineering	"Sure, customers are important but it's taking us 65 days to provision new services. If we don't fix that first, we're not gonna have any customers left! If we only knew how to prioritize our installations . . ."

After all, the majority of CRM products started out as so-called point solutions, designed to solve a specific business function such as sales force automation. Each of these products typically used a local database to store current customer information, hardly a flawed architecture. But the proliferation of these CRM tools around the enterprise begat assorted and mismatched customer files, all of which were critical to their respective systems, but none of which were linked:

Notice in Figure 6-2 that each database contains key customer information critical to the purpose and functionality of the CRM system. The customer data in each database is different, depending on the requirements of the organization using its data. But as in real life, some organizations need the same data about customers; thus the SFA and contact center databases both contain customer contact information as well as payment status, and the SFA and marketing databases each store sales revenue data. Though the names are the same, the contents

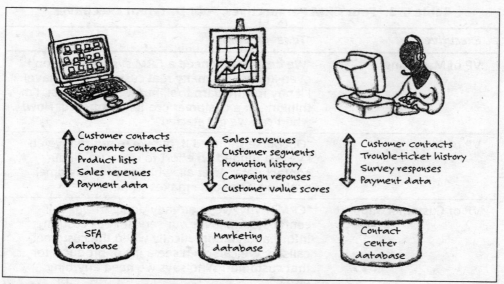

Figure 6-2: One Company, Multiple Customer Databases

and format of the data elements themselves are likely to be drastically different across systems.

Availing a complete customer profile to a range of different organizations often means storing data in a centralized, cross-functional database known as a data warehouse. Once exclusive to the realm of large companies who had a burning need for strategic decision-making as well as generous IT budgets, data warehouses have emerged over the past 15 years as the de facto platform on which companies store and analyze comprehensive data. This analysis is performed using application tools specially designed to deliver business intelligence.

Though data warehouses can be used to store a wide cross section of subjects from sales compensation data to product specifications to geographic mapping, they are particularly valuable for offering an integrated view of the customer or, in data warehousing parlance, "a single version of the truth." Information stored on data warehouses originates from various systems across the company, providing a true 360-view of activity, both current and historic. Such source systems include any of the following:

- Billing systems
- Order and provisioning systems

- Enterprise resource planning (ERP) systems
- Human resource systems
- Point of sale (POS)
- Web servers
- Marketing databases
- Call center systems
- Corporate financial packages
- External data providers[2]

The greater the number of subject sources for a data warehouse, the richer the information available to the business. Figure 6-3 shows the type of data that typically moves to and from a data warehouse to provide an integrated view of the customer.

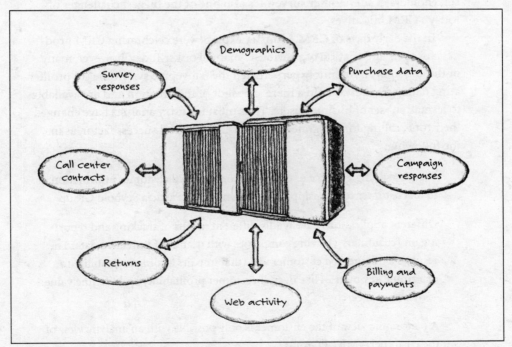

Figure 6-3: Integrated customer data on a data warehouse

2. "External data" means data coming from outside the company. This can include anything from competitive data from a market research firm to consumer change-of-address data from national data service firms.

One of the strengths of a data warehouse is in its ability to store large quantities of historical data, enabling companies to compare customer behaviors over time. For instance, by storing customer purchase history, a company can evaluate what might have attracted a customer to making a purchase or gauge whether that customer's purchases are increasing or decreasing. Comparing time-variant data can provide the company with the information it needs to deploy intelligent marketing and sales campaigns and offer customers appropriate levels of service. Storing historical customer data is the main reason for the enormous growth of data warehouses, both literally and figuratively.

Failure to integrate customer data across all touchpoints results in having only partial customer data, which can in turn cause poor decisions about how to treat customers. This is why data integration is an oft-stated goal of CRM stakeholders in survey after survey. It's also one of the biggest challenges of today's CRM initiatives.

In the early days of CRM, industry experts were celebrating CRM products for their automation of previously manual tasks. Today, however, many of these systems have simply perpetuated the "stovepipe syndrome" of proliferating databases that contain a mere snapshot of information and are available to a small subset of business users. Thus most industry analysts have changed their tune, calling for integrated data as a CRM critical success factor, as in the following:

> You need a single source of clean and consolidated customer information to do customer relationship management well. –Patricia Seybold Group

> Different applications have wildly different means of tracking and reporting on [customers], leaving companies with islands of unrelated data. The result is a fragmented customer view that impairs a company's ability to determine key metrics like overall customer profitability and lifetime value. –Forrester Research

> A panoramic view of the customer is only possible with an analytic view of the customer. –META Group

> Indeed, in a recent research study, Forrester reported that

- Only 37 percent of those surveyed knew if they shared a customer with another division in their company.

- Only 20 percent could tell if a customer had visited the company's Web site.
- Only 23 percent of CSRs could see a customer's Web activity.[3]

Clearly, integrated customer data is mandatory for a company to serve its customers well. Motivating the customer to come back—remember our definition of CRM in Chapter 1?—means understanding more than a customer's name, current address, and income level. It means knowing his preferred products, his consumption rates, values, lifestyle, life stage, and even a superset of his behaviors *outside* of his relationship with your company.

And it works the other way: customers respond better with a unified view of the company. The scenario in Figure 6-1 can deliver disastrous consequences in the all-too-common instance in which the Web shopper and the customer requesting assistance are in fact the same person. Receiving a cross-sell promotion a day after complaining about a product might irritate a customer on the brink of leaving.

"I just complained about the product and now they're trying to sell me another one . . . didn't they hear me?" is the likely refrain from the customer who's received disjointed communications from different organizations within one firm.

CRM and the Data Warehouse

The best-intentioned companies often slip up when it comes to providing data warehousing and the accompanying business intelligence capabilities to their business users. On the one hand, the IT department understands that data cannot be divorced from CRM and that the corporate data warehouse is the ideal CRM source system. On the other hand, the business community is pushing for a quick win and doesn't care where the data comes from as long as they get it fast. The business begins using its CRM application without a vision for how to drive ongoing business-process improvements.

IT scrambles to provide enterprise data to the CRM application without understanding which data will support the actions and business processes the business wants to improve. The businesspeople keep asking when it will all be finished.

So begins the slippery slope of the CRM point solution. As the data warehousing community saw with its stovepipe data marts that effectively served

---

3. "The Customer Conversation," *The Forrester Report,* June 2000.

organizational needs but were tough to link together, stovepipe CRM systems like those in Figure 6-2 represent the burgeoning reality for many companies, even those with robust, enterprise-wide data infrastructures. When the time comes to integrate disparate CRM systems, there is often more work—and more expense—than if CRM had been built around the data warehouse the first time.

At a recent conference, a well-known industry analyst proclaimed CRM to be the new data warehouse "killer app." The analyst hailed CRM as the first practical application for vast amounts of customer data and claimed it would reinvigorate many a dormant data warehouse.

Such proclamations, although quotable, aren't necessarily right. Data warehouses provide a rich source of analysis for a range of topics, customer-focused and otherwise. They contain product defect data, welfare claims, criminal records, and human gene sequences, among other information. Indeed, there are thousands of data warehouses that don't involve managing customer relationships.

CRM is not a mandate for data warehouses; it's not even a data warehousing best practice. But the inverse is true: data warehousing availing rich customer information across the enterprise is definitely a CRM best practice. Even so, data warehousing—while necessary to a successful CRM program—isn't sufficient in and of itself.

Enterprise CRM Comes Home to Roost

> Companies are quickly discovering that their customer relationship management efforts aren't worth much if they don't include analysis.
>
> *—Information Week*

As we discussed in Chapter 1, selling to existing customers is much easier and more cost effective. And the better your company understands those customers, the better it can communicate with them. The ability to leverage the data from customer-facing systems for back-office analysis has proven to be directly proportional to a company's success in enhancing customer loyalty.

Perhaps the most challenging problem posed by stovepipe CRM environments is that they prevent the company from knowing certain potentially critical facts. From the disconnected environments illustrated in Figure 6-2, it is clear that some important business questions cannot be easily answered.

- A CSR scheduling a follow-up communication with a customer cannot discern that customer's value score to determine the level of service that should be provided.

- A segment manager can't track a customer's complaint history before trying to cross-sell a product.
- The campaign staff in marketing doesn't want to solicit customers who are late paying their bills.
- An account rep has no idea whether a key business customer has responded to certain key promotions.
- A CSR can't see the full list of products a customer might have so she can determine whether a given trouble ticket applies to more than one.
- A customer support analyst tries in vain to measure complaint history against sales revenues for a given product.
- A marketing data analyst lacks the data necessary to understand the role of the company's key sales contact for customers in the segment with the highest sales revenues.
- A customer support executive can't obtain a regular report on average customer satisfaction survey scores for each customer segment.

The customer information that can provide answers to these and other business questions can drive key decisions about customer treatment, sales techniques, and upcoming promotion strategies, among others. By integrating operational CRM data with information from around the enterprise, companies can begin performing analytic CRM and, with it, make truly customer-centric business decisions.

The practice of data analysis predates even databases and transcends data warehousing and CRM. Plus, it's a varied discipline ranging from standard queries to statistical analysis to complex predictive modeling. Many CRM vendors have incorporated analysis—thus the term "analytical CRM"—into their products, thereby offering users the ability not only to perform key CRM business processes but also to apply business intelligence to these CRM functions to make them more accurate and more valuable.

For instance, E.piphany has incorporated predictive modeling into its toolset to provide lists of customers most likely to respond to a given marketing campaign. Other CRM product vendors have incorporated purchase-pattern recognition into their offerings, enabling marketing and sales staff to compare customers with like behaviors so they can position new products to an optimal audience.

The main difference between operational and analytical CRM, as introduced in Chapter 1, is that analytical CRM is the only means by which a company can maintain a progressive relationship with a customer across that customer's relationship with the company. This means being able to track a range of customer actions and events over time, using data from operational CRM systems as well as from other enterprise systems, as shown in Figure 6-4.

Analytical CRM's 360-degree view emphasizes communicating with customers across channels based on the optimization of relevant two-way and personalized interactions, be they through a new marketing campaign or from a caller's complaint history. This offers the ability to transcend more broad-brush

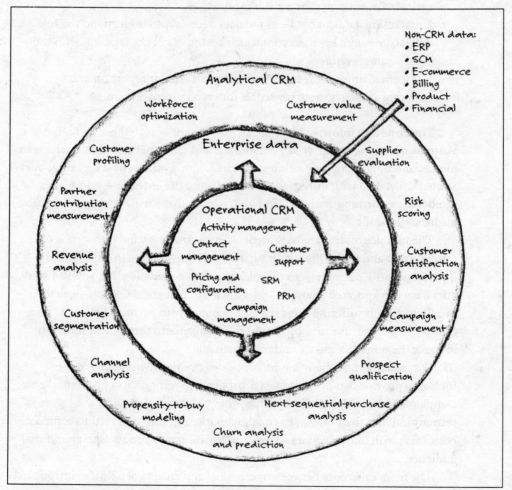

Figure 6-4: Analytical CRM: The sum of its parts

customer segmentation and deploy customer communications that are truly one-to-one. Companies with both operational and analytical CRM capabilities are changing business strategies to

- Reward customers with personalized discounts and perks for using lower-cost channels
- Proactively offer products and services that fit a given customer's needs based on what the customer has already purchased
- Increase purchase rates by dynamically personalizing content based on the Web visitor's profile
- Adjust per-customer marketing expenditures based on lifetime value scores
- Analyze combinations of touchpoints across channels to predict a customer's next likely purchase
- Relate high Web traffic to individual visitors and customer segments to better understand Web use and improve Web design
- Tailor commissions and incentive programs for sales partners based on the value of the customers they bring
- Prevent a customer from churning by offering incentives based on individual preferences
- Provide customers in the highest value tier with personal representatives who understand their history and preferences

The advent of CRM suites has taken up a lot of the slack when it comes to data integration. Until recently, companies that didn't already have established data warehouses were out of luck if they tried to integrate disparate CRM products' software, processes, and data. The job was just too difficult.

Suites—single vendor solutions offering a range of functions—by their definition tie CRM functions together with a seamless user interface so CRM users can not only share data but can actually run the same CRM modules. A marketing person can look at a customer's contact data through the same application used by the sales force. Likewise, analysts within the company can access a centralized CRM portal to view a range of customer-related data without having to change application tools.

MicroStrategy's new eCRM product provides a central portal or "cockpit" through which marketers can create and view customer segments, monitor campaigns in real time, and generate a variety of customer reports. This vendor, long known for its business intelligence software, is combining powerful analysis capabilities to interrelate CRM functions such as Web traffic analysis and marketing automation. Database powerhouse Oracle continues to enhance its integrated suite of tools, which includes everything from Web site storefront customization to customer self-service, and arch rival Siebel Systems, in addition to offering a range of service, marketing, sales force automation, and analysis capabilities, recently unveiled its Siebel Handheld organization to further its multimodal capabilities.

The Major Types of Data Analysis

As we've discussed, the integration of operational and analytical CRM applies across channels. Indeed, it excels there. But the Web is more than just a communications channel for most companies—it's a rich source of data, offering customer behavior information that has no equal in the brick-and-mortar world. A few emerging analysis techniques heavily leverage enterprise-wide data, and others rely particularly on Web-collected data.

OLAP

Despite its varied interpretations, "data mining" has acquired an almost mystical allure over the past decade. Although its widespread interpretation is as an activity associated with querying increasingly detailed data—"drill down," as it's called—in fact, data mining is a highly specialized subcategory of analysis that has specific applications from both within and outside CRM.

In fact, the term "drill down" is more appropriately applied to the practice of online analytical processing, known as OLAP. OLAP has become the most popular type of decision-support analysis, allowing the average businessperson to explore data online with the aim of focusing on detailed data at a lower and lower level of the data hierarchy. Most often, this means generating an online report, analyzing the results, and submitting a more detailed query in order to understand the result data.

OLAP generally focuses on providing a set of data attributes from a database organized around certain dimensions, such as time and location. Thus, a user can request the company's regional sales revenues for all baby care products by region or by store. He can request a report detailing regional revenues for each month within a quarter.

Although OLAP is generally lumped into the data-mining rubric—usually by software vendors eager to claim the data mining moniker—it normally relies on data that has been summarized according to particular dimensions. Data mining involves the identification of meaningful patterns and rules from detailed data, usually from large amounts of data. Thus, instead of analyzing customer segments to determine who is likely to churn, as with OLAP, data mining would examine individual customers, touching each of the millions of records in a database.

OLAP analysis requires the analyst to have a query or hypothesis in mind, but data mining can generate information to show patterns and relationships without the analyst's knowing about them. Data mining can identify clusters of customers who buy similar products—for instance, home office workers who buy PCs, power supplies, toner, printer cables, wastepaper baskets, and coffee. With an OLAP tool, the analyst would have to guess which products a home office worker would purchase and then identify customers making such a purchase. OLAP analysis typically examines category groupings such as PCs, printer cables, and toner (computer-related products), but might not recognize out-of-category purchases such as coffee and wastebaskets.

Where Theory Meets Practice: Data Mining in CRM

Data-mining tools identify patterns in data and deliver valuable new information that can increase a company's understanding of itself and its customers. Data mining is commonly used to help data analysts search for information they don't yet know to look for, often involving no hypothesis. It has helped companies uncover a diverse set of new knowledge, from a customer's next purchase to optimal store layouts to the most favorable release date for a movie in preproduction.

There are many different types of data mining algorithms, some esoteric and not easily applicable to business problems (multivariate adaptive regression splines, anyone?). Although the specific algorithms themselves might vary—decision trees and neural networks are fundamentally different but can both be used to predict behavior—the following three types of data mining are particularly germane to CRM:

1. *Prediction.* The use of historical data to determine future behaviors. Predictive modeling generates output that populates a "model" or structure to represent the results. For instance, a predictive model can indicate the next product a customer is most likely to purchase, based on historical purchases by that customer and other customers who have purchased the same products.

2. *Sequence.* Sequential analysis identifies combinations of activities that occur in a particular order. Businesses use sequential analysis to determine whether customers are doing things in a particular order. It can help a business distill behavior from events captured from various operational systems around a company to determine patterns. For instance, a bank or telephone company can learn more about a given customer or customer segment by examining patterns in the slowdown of purchases or in service cancellations.

3. *Association.* Association analysis detects groups of similar items or events. It can be used to detect items or events that occur together. The association algorithm is often applied to market-basket analysis to help businesses understand products being purchased together (peanut butter with jelly, for example). By understanding customer and product affinities, a company can make important decisions about which products to advertise or discount and which customers should be targeted for certain products.

One central difference between data mining and other types of decision-support analysis is that data mining usually involves statisticians or product specialists intimate with the use of the correct algorithms and their application to business problems, as well as with the specific data mining software. Although a businessperson rarely mines the data herself, she might use data-mining results—either represented graphically in a visualization tool or deployed to a database for general query access—to help make important decisions about managing customer relationships.

There are myriad uses for the three types of data mining just described, from targeting brand new customers by modeling existing customers' response patterns to avoiding high-risk prospects through risk prediction or forecasting a customer's lifetime value. Many companies have acquired dedicated data mining servers, onto which they load customer data records to build models and explore various customer behavior patterns. Such activities are usually processing-intensive so standalone data mining platforms avoid impacting processing on other systems. These servers are usually linked to a company's data warehouse, enabling data analysts to easily access customer data to experiment with various pricing plans, for example, or to create dynamic customer segments for testing new campaigns and performing what-if analysis.

Each type of data mining can yield findings that result in high-impact business actions. For example, an electronics retailer in London discovered that most prospects likely to buy a portable DVD player commute to work on the train, causing the retailer to reallocate much of its marketing budget from daytime television commercials to newspaper ads and billboards. The company saw sales of these players shoot up 43 percent after changing its ad media. Understanding the impending behaviors of customers and prospects is the key to data mining, and where CRM is concerned, two data-mining applications in particular stand out: *clickstream analysis* and *personalization*.

Clickstream Analysis

IT departments have become giddy over capturing clickstreams—the data that illustrates a Web visitor's footprint around the site. Clickstreams connote how the user arrived at the site, how long he stayed, what he did during his visit, and when he returned. They're the equivalent of a camera in a department store recording a shopper's every move.

Clickstream data—usually stored either as part of a company's data warehouse or in a dedicated clickstream data store sometimes called a "data webhouse"[4]—is growing hand-in-hand with corporate e-commerce activities.

One client of mine, a general merchandise retailer who has joined the e-tailing ranks, wants its Web site to be as "sticky" as possible and has begun analyzing clickstream data to surmise why customers might leave the site prematurely. The company has sharpened its analysis to determine the value of abandoned shopping carts. When a customer leaves the site in the midst of a shopping trip, whatever the reason, the company looks to see what products were in the cart. The data is then compared with similar data from other abandoned carts to examine

- How much revenue the abandoned carts represented (in other words, how much revenue was lost because of the customer's early departure)
- Whether the products in the cart were high-profit items or loss leaders
- If the same products were found in other abandoned carts

---

4. Yes, ideally a customer's clickstream data should be integrated into the enterprise data warehouse along with other customer-related data. However, much of the clickstream data collected by companies is anonymous data that needs to be mapped back to customer-specific information with the customer's permission. Furthermore, clickstream data warehouses are growing at such a rate that it is often administratively impractical to store clickstreams on the same hardware platform with other corporate data.

- The volume of products and the number of different product categories in the cart
- Whether the total bill for the abandoned carts consistently fell within a certain dollar range
- At what point during the shopping trip the cart was actually abandoned (When the customer saw the shipping charge? When the site required a personal survey before confirming the purchase?)
- How the average and total bills for abandoned carts compared with "unabandoned" carts—those that made it through the checkout process

The result of this analysis can trigger some interesting theories. For instance, perhaps none of the products in the cart was appealing enough to a particular customer to motivate her to continue shopping. Or the customer was put off by frequent inquiries asking her whether she was ready to check out. Or possibly, at a particular dollar total, the customer thought the better of the entire shopping trip and bailed. Finally, perhaps the number or mix of products in the cart reminded the customer of another site that offered a steeper discount for similar purchases.

Admittedly, some of these theories are mere guesses. But when examined regularly and with consistent metrics, clickstreams can reveal some interesting patterns. The fact is, whatever the customer's reason for leaving the site and a cart full of merchandise, the e-tailer can take a variety of actions based on both hard findings and less-then-certain extrapolations. The e-tailer can use these results to tweak the design and content of its Web site and monitor resulting improvements. Patterns might indicate product affinities, suggesting cross-selling or up-selling strategies. And when combined with customer demographics, psychographics, and past behaviors, clickstream data can bring the understanding of customer behavior to a whole new level.

The latter option is perhaps the most intriguing: rather than simply examining a customer's navigation patterns and guessing about which actions to take, the retailer can combine those patterns with more specific customer data—his previous purchases in that product category, key demographic and psychographic data, or his lifetime value score, for example—to provide a holistic view of that customer's value and interests. It might have been a one-time-only shopper who was lost, but in other cases a high-value customer might have left the site on multiple occasions. A tailored e-mail message or electronic coupon—perhaps targeting one of the products left behind on a prior trip—could make all the difference the next time that customer decides to log on.

The following scenario, based on a real-life case study, illustrates how clickstream data, when integrated with other key data from around the enterprise, enhances opportunities to personalize customer communications.

Scenario

You're a marketing manager at an up-and-coming eyewear Web site, www.glasses-r-us.com. Your company has just deployed a so-called data webhouse and for the past few days you've been looking over your data analyst's shoulder—they've just begun gathering user clickstream data.

Your data analyst, Jack, points out one session particular. You notice that the shopper arrived at your site through a banner ad posted on a partner's Web site: www.eyecare-youcare.com. After the shopper arrived at your site, he entered his prescription and began looking at various brands of glasses.

After browsing for glasses, the shopper started comparing brands of contact lenses. He finally selected a brand of contacts and placed the product in his shopping cart. He entered the order information, including his credit card number, but left the site rather than submitting his data and completing the purchase. How do you entice this shopper to return to your site and buy something?

Most marketing managers won't be looking over analysts' shoulders at individual clickstreams. But understanding a customer's navigation around a site can help a company decide how to lure him back.

You have several choices. Your company's usual tactic for all registered visitors who visit the site but don't make a purchase is to mail them a coupon for $5 off a new pair of fashion eyewear. However, this particular visitor was looking at contacts. He'd probably trash the glasses coupon as soon as it arrived in the mail.

A better choice might be to e-mail the visitor a discount code—a coupon is given a unique code so no one but the given customer can redeem it—for

$10 off a new pair of hard contacts or three pairs of disposable lenses (a predictive model could confirm this as the best course of action). Your profit on contact lenses is usually good, and the shopper seemed on the brink of making a purchase. Besides, e-mailing the offer is a lower-cost option than the U.S. postal service and would probably result in quicker turnaround time.

Along with this more personalized tactic, you could also monitor the referring Web site for other referred shoppers who have researched or purchased contact lenses. If contact lens activity is particularly high, you might consider placing a more customized banner ad on the partner's site and even provide better financial incentives for the partner when new contact lens customers click through.

With the e-mail strategy, the customer's more likely to return to the site and you're almost guaranteed a purchase. Win-win, right? Wrong.

The problem with this scenario is that even though analysis is involved, it's still dangerous. The fact that you're looking at only a single customer touchpoint can mean big problems and bad decisions. If your clickstream database contained behavior history on this shopper, things might turn out differently. You would have more information about the customer, and you'd know the following:

- This isn't the customer's first visit to your Web site.
- He has made three other purchases on three separate occasions.
- The products he has purchased have all been on sale.

In short, you would understand that your Web visitor is what's known as a "cherry picker," someone who only purchases low-margin products when they're being promoted. No cross-selling, no up-selling, no true loyalty. He'll be back again, too, when he finds the next markdown.

If you had this information, you would understand the optimal marketing tactic for this customer: Do nothing. Any further marketing to him would be a bad investment. Of course, you're perfectly happy to have this customer return to your site of his own free will. But you've already invested too much money in an unprofitable customer, and you can't afford for the next transaction not to be profitable. Each time a retailer price-subsidizes products for cherry pickers, it is losing an opportunity to sell that product to a more valuable customer. The retailer is in fact investing in an undesirable customer relationship.

Personalization and Collaborative Filtering

Chapter 2 introduced personalization, the practice of tailoring communications directly to a customer segment or, increasingly, to an individual customer. The premise of personalization is that, by collecting sufficient customer data, a company can market to an individual's unique needs, both now and in the future. Personalized communications is the principal technique via which companies can convince customers they understand them and that their information—which the company often uses thanks to the customer's explicit permission—is mutually beneficial. The goal is to deliver accurate product recommendations, content geared to individual preferences, and targeted promotions for individual Web visitors—and in real time.

When done right, personalization means not only maintaining customer loyalty, but also driving purchases higher. It leverages detailed information about individuals and can dictate some very tactical decisions. The following analysis topics from a drugstore e-tailer suggest the level of individual detail and resulting tactics personalization can provide:

- For people who have bought or expressed interest in vitamin supplements, which other products are they likely to buy?
- How likely is Customer X to buy prescription drugs online?
- What other items are likely to be in a shopper's market basket if he buys, say, decongestant?
- Which products are most similar to the Brand X eyedrops the customer chose?

Personalization can take various forms. It can involve customizing actual Web pages, including a Web site's look and feel, according to the features favored by an individual visitor. Many Web sites allow the visitor to customize the site according to her preferences, eliminating format variations and allowing her a private window into the company. Use the search function often? Move the search window to the top of the page. Like customization, so-called localization can focus site content to the visitor's particular geographic area.

Notice that the personalization examples from the drugstore e-tailer above hint at prediction? Indeed, most personalization software involves specific data mining algorithms. The two main types of personalization are rules-based personalization and adaptive personalization.

Rules-based personalization leverages established rules that dictate, for instance, which products might be purchased together or whether a certain Web page should precede or follow another. When a visitor to a software Web site buys Quicken, the site might suggest he buy *Quicken: The Official Guide* before going to the checkout screen. Rules-based personalization most often involves rules that have been hard-coded into the software. For this reason, it's often difficult to maintain and support.

The other type of personalization, adaptive personalization, learns as it goes. More commonly known as collaborative filtering, this type of personalization gets smarter as it observes customer behaviors and applies them to new circumstances. For instance, if a gardening e-tailer using collaborative filtering observes that shoppers tend to buy low-cost perennial flowers at the same time they order gardening tools, the Web site might begin suggesting a flat of pansies to all customers who buy bulb planters. Collaborative filtering uses the behavior of other "like" visitors as the basis for its recommendations. Collaborative filtering tools are often more complex, and thus more expensive, than rules-based personalization.

The most celebrated example of collaborative filtering is Amazon.com's purchase circles, in which Amazon factors in the buyer's past purchases and geography to suggest what readers who live in her neighborhood and have similar interests might be reading. The more similar shoppers buy, the smarter Amazon becomes about their preferences, and the more accurate are the site's recommendations. Several Amazon.com customers I know are cherry pickers on other booksellers' Web sites during special promotions, but they always return to Amazon because "they know me better."

Perhaps the most telling delineation in personalization is in whether or not the user knows it's happening. In the permission marketing scenario described in Chapter 2, Web visitors voluntarily provide personal information to Web sites where they believe there will be some sort of *quid pro quo:* the company will use the information to provide a value-added service such as periodic discounts or special-interest newsletters. Some sites can personalize content without making the shopper aware that the products he's seeing are different from those of fellow shoppers—who might have different profiles and preferences.

Web retailers who combine eCRM with detailed customer data and advanced personalization can customize content and screen layouts for individual visitors to increase the site's stickiness and the shopper's propensity to buy. On the other hand, companies such as Lands' End simply ask customers what they like, whether or not they make a purchase. The company's My Personal Shopper feature shows Web visitors various product combinations and solicits their feedback. This practice is different from the "inferential" personalization in which a company applies complex logic to infer a customer's preferences— "referential" personalization simply stores a customer's responses to questions or surveys, making those answers part of her profile so they can be used to cross-sell her additional products.

Although custom content seems innocuous enough—it's tantamount to reorganizing a brick-and-mortar store's layout according to the way the shopper likes to move around the store—it can also have more controversial uses.

Amazon.com was revealed to be selling the same DVD movie for different prices to different shoppers. This practice, known as dynamic pricing, turned the concept of consumer choice on its head. The Web, famous for offering shoppers the opportunity to find the best deal with a simple mouse click, was now allowing sellers the opportunity to differentiate consumers and their price sensitivity. Dynamic pricing actually leverages CRM technology and detailed customer data to let a company, say, compare a shopper's desire for the product with his perceived ability to pay for that product. For the first time, consumers are the ones competing for the best deal.

Arguments for and against dynamic pricing raise issues of consumer privacy (see Chapter 10) as well as good will. After all, the more a shopper buys on a company's Web site, the more information the site has on that buyer and the weaker the buyer's negotiating power. In the past several years, airlines were routinely accused of raising their online fares for frequent fliers—their most loyal customers—who are more likely to fly a particular carrier because of the mileage perks. And, in a now infamous public relations gaff, Coca Cola was alleged to have been considering a vending machine that raised the price of beverages when the temperature soared.

In defending dynamic pricing, e-tailers point to their brick-and-mortar counterparts who have been engaging in the practice for years. Drugstores have been known to price cold medicines higher in chillier climates, and the shortage of Sony Playstation 2 units last Christmas drove prices up sharply. (Kmart used the shortage as a way of rewarding loyal customers first, steering Playstation availability to loyal shoppers on the company's Bluelight.com Web site.) In the Web world, where consumer data can include a shopper's home address, income level, number of children, and even his resolve to purchase a product, dynamic pricing—along with a number of other personalization techniques—can be implemented more quickly and to a wider number of shoppers.

Good or bad, Amazon's dynamic pricing experiment might have gone unnoticed altogether if it hadn't been for . . . the Web. In an ironic twist, participants in an Internet chat room began comparing their movie receipts and discovered that prices seemed higher for regular customers. Amazon claimed the dynamic pricing was simply a test and denied plans to formalize the practice. But the example proves the Web has affected both business and social communications to the point where even CRM can sometimes be a double-edged sword.

An Analysis Checklist for Success

Integrating data from around the company, let alone using that data to drive sophisticated analysis that can differentiate you from your competition, is a lofty CRM objective. Even companies with billion-dollar IT budgets still grapple with the challenge. Learning from their mistakes is a good first step, including considering some of the following suggestions:

- *Don't underestimate data integration.* From this chapter we know integrated customer data can mean the difference between a decision that alienates a customer and one that triggers long-term loyalty. But even the best CRM suite products don't offer easy answers on how to integrate disparate data from around your company. Talk to vendors about their databases and their processes for systematically locating, gathering, modeling, cleansing, and loading data into a database or data warehouse. And remember: A flashy user interface is useless if the data is incorrect.

- *Beware of "dirty data."* That means data in its natural state, prior to being cleansed and formatted for use by businesspeople. Savvy business users who need customer information might be wary of it if they understand the data's origins. I once heard a user declare he would "never touch that data!" after he learned the data came from the company's archaic billing system, known to have data problems. Understanding data definitions and business rules before implementing CRM is the surest way to guarantee users will use what they're given. Conduct data definition dialogs and terminology discussions with cross-functional user groups to ensure common terminology—ideally, before CRM development begins.

- *If your company has a data warehouse, reinvest in it now.* In 1999, one of the "Big Three" U.S. automakers reportedly invested $50 million in its data warehouse infrastructure in a prescient attempt to centralize its customer data and bolster data quality before launching an enterprise CRM program. Although they had little experience with institutionalized customer management processes, managers at the auto company nevertheless understood that—due to complex interrelationships with its dealers and its drivers—its newly formed e-commerce organization would hit the wall without a single version of critical data.

- *Know who's analyzing the data.* There's a vast divide between the occasional user who points and clicks to access revenue figures at month end and the statistician who spends days trolling through data to arrive at findings that can result in strategic business shifts. Understand which users are actually performing analytical CRM, the data they're looking at, and what results from their work (see the next bullet point). Avoid the all-too-common "interesting-but-not-relevant" analysis, where users simply play in the customer-data sandbox with no identified goals or resulting actions. Categorize the continuum of end users from basic business users to so-called power users to statisticians, and consider setting up policies to dictate privacy controls, system security constraints, and appropriate analysis tools for each group.

- *Translate analysis into action.* Many companies with really big databases and really neat end-user tools nevertheless ignore what their data tells them.

Even though they have rich customer information, they continue to rely disproportionately on the appointment books of their salespeople to generate leads and on executive golf outings to nurture alliance partnerships. Know your current customer-focused initiatives and which ones could be improved with analysis. Institute ways in which that analysis can result in recommendations for improvement. Sometimes this simply means empowering the businesspeople performing the analysis to actually make decisions themselves. And sometimes it means setting up new internal processes to ensure that important findings drive tactical business improvements.

- *Consider your customer data a corporate asset.* This means not only dedicating to data the same infrastructure and budget as to other corporate assets; it also means recognizing data management as an organizational core competency. Ascertain if your company has a single architecture and standards in place to define and source the data and translate it into meaningful business knowledge. Understand the resources and budget you've dedicated to data management, not as a component of CRM but as an overarching competitive weapon.

- *Don't forget business processes.* Improvements don't start and end with the right data, and just being smart about customers isn't enough. Effectively managing and enhancing customer relationships has as much to do with work process improvements as it does with data analysis. Performing analytical CRM means understanding how your customers interact with you and using this to refine business processes to provide them with a better experience—be it on the Web or in your stores. So beware the vendor or consultant who proposes analysis as the end game. Analytical CRM should be used to improve business processes, streamline workflows, establish sound policies, and accelerate customer purchases. As we'll see in the following chapter, sound business processes are the fastest way to a CRM return on investment.

Case Study: Union Bank of Norway

Summary: In the early 1990s, Union Bank of Norway, Norway's largest savings bank, with over a million residential and commercial customers, realized it was losing touch with its customers. It needed to act fast—and this meant more than just implementing customer relationship management. It meant changing the way 3000 bank employees did their jobs.

It's a scary thing when you realize you don't know what your customers want anymore. Especially when your business is growing and you've managed to avoid the substantial losses of your European competitors in a market that, in the early 1990s, was anything but stable.

That Union Bank of Norway had managed to escape the debilitating losses sustained by some of its competitors was great news. The bank had succeeded in providing more automated ways for its customers to perform their banking. This automation led in turn to lower costs and helped the bank limit some of the losses other banks incurred.

As customers adopted this automation, starting with automated teller machines but gradually encompassing the telephone and then Web-based technologies, they grew less dependent on their local Union Bank of Norway branches for executing their transactions. This was good news: the bank had begun driving its customers to use lower-cost channels. And yet, as customers refrained from in-branch banking, the in-branch bank staff was also losing the opportunity for customer dialog. No one knew what was on customers' minds and what customers wanted.

WHAT THEY DID:

One of the big problems was all the different systems that contained customer data. Most of this information was dispersed across multiple production systems. To obtain basic information on a customer, the bank needed to find, gather, and consolidate information from all these systems—a process that could take days. One bank executive described this network of disconnected data as "an information labyrinth."

Officials at the bank reasoned that to obtain—and more important, use—pertinent customer information, the bank would need a complete view of its customers across the various systems that contained their data. Indeed, the bank realized this view extended across sales channels, customer demographics, and the bank's various products as well.

If the bank could track customer behaviors, executives realized they'd have a better shot at understanding and predicting future behaviors and customer preferences. This new information could drive cross-selling and target-marketing initiatives that promised to boost revenues and further mitigate costs. Union Bank of Norway embarked on the acquisition of a data warehouse to consolidate its disparate customer data and to provide the bank's businesspeople with a centralized analysis platform on which to determine who their customers were, what they were interested in, and what they were likely to buy. In addition to eliminating the costly, time-consuming, and pervasive practice of data gathering, the data warehouse would provide the so-called 360-degree view of the customer base that would allow the bank to get to know its customers.

Kari Opdal, Head of CRM for Union Bank of Norway, says the bank's Teradata data warehouse has become "the heart of our organization." In addition to aiding marketing functions, the data warehouse has made data available to a cross-section of the bank's organizations, from finance to accounting to auditing. "At first, only a few people were interested in using the data warehouse," Opdal admits, "but now nearly three thousand people have access." Most of the business users use the data to perform sales and financial reporting, as well as customer portfolio analysis.

But beyond the daily analysis, Union Bank of Norway can directly relate its ability to react more quickly to market opportunities with customer information to an increase in market share. For instance, Opdal and the CRM team launched a customer loyalty program focusing on the bank's most profitable customers. Customers provide personal information through a permission-based marketing campaign. The bank then uses this information to determine the optimal type of communication it should subsequently have with that customer. Overall, this program alone has resulted in a mind-boggling 70-percent response rate from customers whom the bank has obviously engaged in a dialog.

"Our customers were saying they were happy with our offerings," Opdal explains, "but they didn't feel that we had been interacting with them on a one-to-one basis." Union Bank of Norway added CRM functionality to its data warehouse infrastructure, enabling it to supplement its classic marketing programs with event-based marketing and optimize its customer communications based on relevant and timely occurrences through all its distribution channels. Customer response rates have reached 60 percent.

The bank has also used its newly robust customer data to aid in channel optimization. For instance, customers who weren't using the bill payment service best suited to them would be told, via customized promotions, how much money they could save by switching to the best payment service. Not only does this help the bank cut down on more costly services; it also instills the perception that the bank is acting as the customer's advocate.

THE CHALLENGES:

Having begun the process of building a data warehouse back in 1995, Union Bank of Norway has witnessed its evolution, in terms of both the data and the applications that provide business users with critical information. Because the bank took a requirements-driven approach to CRM, development has proved to be relatively problem-free.

The challenge was in building the organization around the data warehouse. Not having had a centralized location for key corporate data in the past, many of the skills required to develop and support the data subject areas, database, and applications were new to the bank. Job roles such as database administrator, application designer, data modeler, and others unique to a data-centric organization had to become institutionalized to support the bank's newfound business intelligence environment.

As the data and applications that helped the bank manage its customer relationships continue to grow and evolve, other areas of the bank have taken notice. More users have requested access, and more systems have been integrated to ensure the "single version of the truth" about customers. This has meant continuing growth of the development and support staff for customer data and its usage.

GOOD ADVICE:

Kari Opdal is unequivocal in her belief that CRM is more of a series of behaviors than it is an actual project. "We don't actually use the term internally a lot because there's so much hype these days," she admits. "CRM can be so easily misunderstood to be something that it's not." Opdal and her team symbolically point to the 1995–1996 period in which the data warehouse was adopted as the hub of CRM.

Opdal's advice to others beginning large-scale CRM projects focuses on the clarity of the CRM vision. "Have a clear goal of where you want to go," she counsels, "and then take it one step at a time." Almost as an afterthought, she adds what might be the best advice of all: "Think big; act small."

THE GOLDEN NUGGET:

Notwithstanding Union Bank of Norway's sophisticated customer-focused marketing strategies, Opdal insists that a two-way dialog between a company and its customers is an unending process. The bank continues to survey its customers about their products, their investment preferences, their financial goals and planning activities, and their overall satisfaction with the bank. The bank then stores the feedback in the data warehouse, maintaining ever-evolving profiles on each individual customer. For a company who admits it was losing touch with its customers, Union Bank of Norway has become very high-touch indeed.

The Manager's Bottom Line

In a recent survey of companies engaging in CRM programs, META Group and IMT Surveys found respondents intended to increase their investments in marketing analytics as a result of implementing operational CRM. Trouble is, the term "marketing analytics" could mean anything from simple list generation to dynamic product recommendations. Will these companies be ready? After all, the diversity and richness of customer-related data is directly proportional to the range of choices a company has about extending its CRM program to include analysis.

The well-worn term "360-degree view" extends beyond customer data to your entire enterprise. Using Web and non-Web data to drive improved relationships with customers and suppliers should result not only in cost savings but also in actual revenue generation. The key is in the range of data available from across your company about your customers, as well as in its accuracy. The differentiator is in how the data is used strategically.

Returning to our depictions of operational and analytic CRM in Chapter 1, we can begin to see how CRM can bring the front office together with the back office, resulting in what the analyst firms have coined a CRM "ecosystem" like the one in Figure 6-5.

The integration so widely acclaimed as a CRM imperative has as much to do with systems and business processes as it does with data. Communicating with customers not only needs to be effective and on-target, it must be seamless. Customer perception is everything, and customers should perceive that your company applies intelligent service standards regardless of the customer's preferred channel, desired product, or service request. Only you know how that intelligence translates into initiating the right message to customers.

Neither Rome nor an enterprise CRM infrastructure is built in a day. In Part 2 of the handbook, see how a series of implementation tactics and critical success factors play a critical role in CRM deployment.

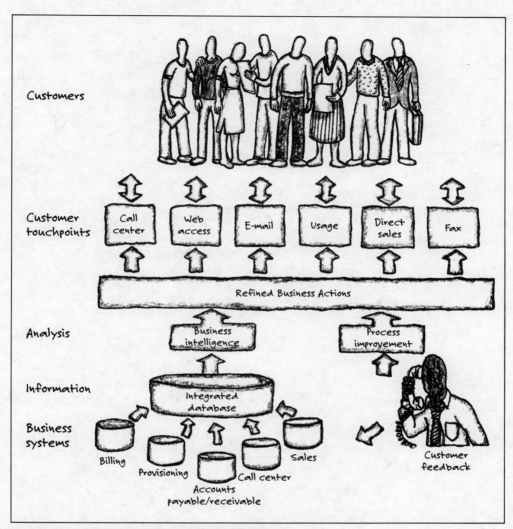

Figure 6-5: An end-to-end CRM infrastructure

PART II

Delivering CRM

Planning Your CRM Program

Planning a CRM program can be as simple as building consensus over a series of meetings with key stakeholders who all have a vested interest in keeping customers. Or it can be as complex as launching a multi-month project to gather requirements from across the company, interview stakeholders, and draft a game plan-working with staff members who might not have ever heard of CRM. Whatever its scope, planning a CRM program is rarely as straightforward as it first seems.

CRM engenders business change, and business change isn't just a by-product of CRM-it's one of the goals. Trouble is, many managers consider change to be a simple signature on a statement of work or even a mere "yes' " But change isn't just a point-in-time approval or edict; it's an ongoing sales job. There's a lot more to CRM than throwing together a project plan.

Although good planning can make or break a CRM initiative, planning involves more than simply drafting a list of action items. A CRM program requires a clear understanding of and commitment to the company's customer focus, vigilant adherence to detailed goals, commitment from both executives and line workers, and a constant awareness of the customer's viewpoint. And it usually all hinges on a crystal-clear business case. Unfortunately, many managers in charge of CRM zero in on the solution before they really get the problem.

Scenario

You're a consultant at one of those ubiquitous Web design and consulting firms. Your company's stock price has plummeted (unlike staff attrition, which has skyrocketed). Management is frantically trying to re-brand the firm from a Web design boutique into a bona fide management consulting company. A high-profile e-commerce client has recently decided to take on CRM and has come to you for help.

Chet, your company's retail partner, calls a meeting of the newly formed project team. A debate ensues about what the client means by "CRM."

"They obviously mean personalization," says Thad, a programmer with thick black glasses that label him a hip techno-geek.

"Personalization?" says Chet. "The site's not even tracking its visitors yet. We'll have to assess their e-business technology infrastructure."

"What kind of customer data do they have now?" asks a project manager as she munches on a muffin.

"I think they have a marketing data mart," says another programmer.

"They have to capture clickstreams, we know that much," comments a database expert hovering near the door.

You're new and reluctant to weigh in, but your time management ethic overrules your shyness and you ask, "What does the client want to do with CRM?"

All heads turn in your direction. Nobody speaks. The retail partner looks at you as though you've just fallen off a charm bracelet. You sink down in your chair.

It's going to be a long project.

Can your company or department answer the question: *What business value do we expect from CRM*? And if so, is the answer one that will lead to quantifiable improvements in customer retention and satisfaction? Will it generate profits?

As we've seen in Part 1 of the handbook, CRM isn't a single product or technology. It's not exclusive to marketing or customer care. And it ideally involves a cross-section of customer touchpoints. Indeed, CRM's inherent complexity renders it a risky endeavor, even for the most mature companies.

Defining CRM Success

One of the most difficult parts of launching a CRM program is defining success metrics. After all, a lot has been written about enterprise CRM (aka, ECRM) and the ability to understand customers across their various interactions with the company, meaning that the organizational boundaries of CRM should be understood up front. Indeed, the entire company—from executives to programmers—should agree on a unified CRM vision. The pressure is on for those forward-thinking managers who can articulate that vision but lack the organizational buy-in to enact a truly corporate-wide program.

The payoff of such foresight could be revolutionary—employees from across the company accessing common data about customers through a single enterprise portal and making better decisions based on that single view. Imagine: No more contradictory customer counts, interdepartmental sales revenue battles, or returned sales brochures stamped with "RECIPIENT HAS MOVED." The IT department with an acknowledged customer system of record and no longer taking months to reconcile customer data and delivering outdated information. Your entire company having finally realized a "single version of the customer truth" and using it to increase customer profitability.

Trouble is, proselytizing this ambitious objective could span an entire career. Do you really want to spend time bringing managers—many of whom have a vested interest in the status quo—around to this ideal when you could instead launch a CRM pilot project for a single department to actually prove CRM's benefits in a couple of months?

And therein lies the dilemma for most CRM proponents: should a company try to socialize an enterprise-wide vision, despite the inevitable politics and lofty education necessary, or should it try implementing a quick, functional prototype and run the risk of lack of acceptance and wasted money?

Many vendors and consultants eager to catch the brass ring and land huge CRM implementation projects continue to advocate the "just add water" approach to out-of-the-box enterprise CRM, with the accompanying elevated budgets and executive-level exposure. It's certainly a laudable goal.

Not so the CRM initiative driven by the company's IT department. Technology organizations spearheading CRM don't usually have measurable business improvements in mind. At best, they foresee implementation and process improvements that accompany centralized data and Web access. At worst, wily IT staffers envision the payoff of having the CRM acronym on their resumes. Whatever the case, far too many companies begin their CRM initiatives in IT in the hopes that eventually the rest of the company will catch on. Many of the pervasive statistics citing CRM failure rates in the 60 to 70 percent range reflect such IT-initiated projects.

The majority of successful CRM projects I've come across have started out as "stovepipe" projects in business units. They begin in a single organization—perhaps marketing—where a visionary manager recognizes the benefits early and enlists the IT organization in developing a standalone CRM system. Once deployed, the system generates efficiencies while delivering value. People in other departments gradually take notice, either because the CRM users tout their success or because the benefits get noticed. Other organizations eventually request access to the CRM system, which gradually grows horizontally with additional functionality, data, and users.

Indeed, there are good ways and better ways to implement a CRM program. Just because political or infrastructure CRM roadblocks exist—and every company has 'em—doesn't mean you shouldn't start putting the pieces in place. Table 7-1 illustrates some of the inevitable factors to evaluate before you start socializing a new CRM initiative.

Table 7-1 can assist you in gauging the relative expectations for CRM from within your company. Is there a collection of line-of-business squeaky-wheels who want CRM but can't explain its value? Is your IT department driving CRM for reasons unrelated to better customer relationships? Are there clear metrics with which to measure CRM success? Take the test included at the conclusion of this chapter to determine your CRM readiness.

The bottom line here is that, although you should be working toward eventual enterprise CRM, such a vision doesn't happen overnight and trying to force it to happen could take a lifetime. The better your view of how a finite and clearly described CRM solution can help deliver long-term benefits to the company, the more likely you are to get the support you need. A 1999 research study conducted by Yancy Oshita and Dr. Jay Prasad at the University of Dayton[1] illustrates four overarching measurements for CRM success:

1. CRM's ability to impact corporate strategy (according to 25 percent of respondents)

---

1. "Critical Success Factors in Planning, Implementing and Deploying CRM Technologies," working research paper, 2000, University of Dayton Graduate School of Business, conducted by Yancy Oshita and sponsored by Dr. Jay Prasad, Dept of MIS and Decision Sciences.

Table 7-1: Gauging the Factors of CRM Success

Factor	Ideal	Desirable	Undesirable
Initial trigger	An executive or board member reads about CRM and understands how its benefits can result in competitive advantage.	A customer support exec returns from an industry conference where a case study depicted uplift in existing sales via CRM.	A product manager sees a vendor demo and returns to the office touting functions and features.
Sponsorship	A cross-functional executive team agrees that CRM is a competitive necessity.	A business visionary sees quantifiable benefits for her organization in the short term and for the company at-large soon after.	The IT organization decides to implement CRM because an existing vendor has just substantially discounted its CRM software.
Objective definition	Increased customer loyalty, better customer service, additional sales revenues, and an overall enhancement of external perception.	To provide an organization with a greater degree of customer knowledge and improved customer interactions.	To automate existing processes—especially if they aren't costly to begin with. Or to add CRM technology to the IT portfolio.
Solution selection	Allowing corporate strategy and business drivers to dictate CRM functionality and letting required functionality dictate tool selection (see Chapter 8).	Tool delivers process efficiencies (e.g., marketing list creation) while applying additional customer intelligence via integrated data.	Selection of CRM market leader or existing software vendor with minimal research.

(continued)

Table 7-1: Gauging the Factors of CRM Success (*continued*)

Factor	Ideal	Desirable	Undesirable
Operating environment	Integration of CRM product into existing IT infrastructure, including ERP and data warehouse systems.	Introduction of dedicated CRM environment linked to corporate network and key data sources.	Standalone CRM system.
User community	Employees across the corporation at all levels, using CRM for different purposes but basing their decisions on the same customer information.	Business people from one or two departments leveraging operational and analytical CRM.	Operational CRM available to a select group of users who disperse findings from time to time to selected executives—on paper.
Efficiencies	Process efficiencies and integrated data combine to deliver strategic decisions, in turn leading to higher customer profitability, sales uplift, and customer satisfaction.	Automation leads to process efficiencies and new information that advance departmental goals and result in improved customer satisfaction.	Automation leads to process efficiencies resulting in timesavings but failing to cover CRM program expenses.
Measurement	Clear sales uplift or decreased complaints and measurable improvement in customer response rates across touchpoints.	Improved perception among existing customer base and suspected improvements in marketing campaigns, closed sales, product quality, and so on.	IT has successfully linked the CRM system to operational systems and has deployed CRM to 100 desktops.

2. Successful technology integration (23 percent)
3. Enhanced strategic partnerships (20 percent)
4. Assimilation of CRM-related technologies (18 percent)

As Figure 7-1 illustrates, companies participating in the study cited other success factors: end-user desktop workstation configurations, user skill sets, and overall technology architecture.

The point here is that companies implementing CRM understand that the means to the end doesn't matter—it's the program's ultimate strategic impact and the usefulness of the resulting tool set that affect the perception of success. If the new customer profiling system provides new details about customer behavior but can't be viewed by call center staff, it's still a flop. And even the happiest campaign managers won't bolster the dashed hopes of

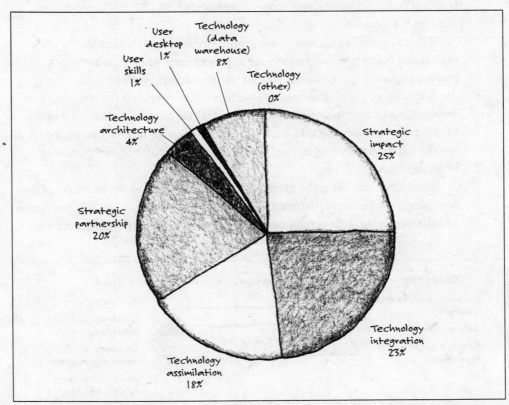

Figure 7-1: CRM Success Factors (Courtesy of University of Dayton Graduate School of Business)

executives who were expecting increased response rates corresponding to CRM deployment.

From Operational to Enterprise: An Implementation Scenario

Indeed, CRM can be both revolution and evolution. A single department can adopt a CRM program that promises value to other organizations, which—averse to starting from scratch—grab the proverbial CRM ball and run with it. The wireless phone company described in Figures 7-2 to 7-5 illustrates how CRM can evolve from a point solution to a corporate-wide program.

Because the company's customer support organization required basic information about customers and trouble tickets, it was the first department to recognize the value of combining operational CRM—the company was surveying customers at the conclusion of every Web- or telephone-based contact and tracking customer satisfaction scores—with analytical CRM to streamline its call center processes.

The call center's goal was to use survey scores to analyze customer complaints and foster product and service improvements while simultaneously putting in place a Web-based customer self-service infrastructure. Over time, the company's customers would be able to request service on the company's Web site, mitigating the need for in-person assistance, in addition to being able to order new services and add-on features such as caller-id. Customer support recognized the promise of not only cost reduction but also higher customer retention rates.

Soon after launching the project, customer support got the attention of the company's marketing department, which was interested in the satisfaction scores and their correlation to certain customer segments. Marketing convinced the

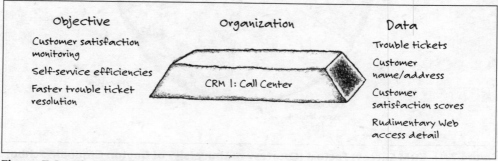

Figure 7-2: The call center adopts CRM

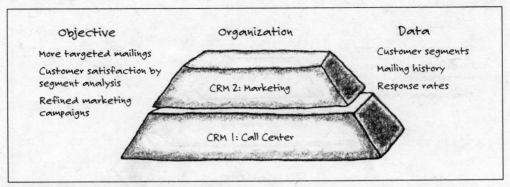

Figure 7-3: Marketing adopts CRM

call center to share its data, which existed on a server accessible by the call center transaction system. Marketing purchased an additional module from the company's CRM vendor in order to perform dynamic customer segmentation and begin more targeted customer communications and campaigns.

The advantage of this building-block approach was that marketing could leverage the CRM product, system resources, and data the call center was already using. Moreover, by supplementing the call center's database with additional data, marketing was providing call center employees richer customer information that they could in turn use to qualify higher value customers at the time of contact.

As the call center and marketing organizations became more integrated, the two departments realized they could be even more customer-focused with more data and processing power, and they lobbied upper management for budget money, citing the benefits already gained by cross-functional CRM. "We're singing out of the same customer hymn book for the first time ever!" crowed the Vice President of Marketing.

Members of the company's IT governance council—an executive committee in charge of approving information technology expenditures of over $100,000—recognized similarities between the evolving CRM system and the sales organization's recent bid for a new sales force automation system. By leveraging a centralized customer database, sales could deploy SFA across regions and territories, ensuring access to a richer base of customer data—data that already existed on what was now known as the CRM server.

The company's IT department ran a synchronization program that reconciled customer data from each salesperson with the customer data on the CRM

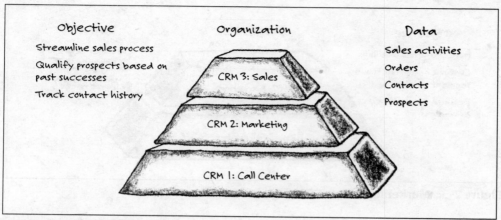

Figure 7-4: Sales adopts CRM

server. Due to new sales data added to the CRM system, sales staff in the field could now not only access centralized customer data but track outbound correspondence their customers might have received from the call center and marketing organizations. For the first time, a salesperson truly understood how his entire company—not just himself or his office—was interacting with his clients and prospects and how they were responding.

Moreover, the call center could use the new sales data to track trouble tickets on recently placed orders and could tell whether the party calling was an existing customer, a prospect, or a lapsed customer. Call center management implemented call center scripts according to the caller's customer segment and status, guiding CSRs in responding to customer contacts in a way that was tailored to each customer segment.

Marketing too was able to use the new sales information to close the loop, tracking campaign responses through to actual orders. Campaign managers could refine their campaigns now that they knew which customer segments ordered which products, and through which channels. This in turn allowed the marketing organization to establish a "segment marketing" function, wherein specific customer segments were managed and communicated with separately. With this information in hand, marketing could interact more effectively with sales and channel partners about the optimal sales plan, given a prospect's profile and characteristics.

The sales organization went public with the improvements right away. Sales managers encouraged their colleagues in field services to use the CRM server's data remotely to register and track field installations and repairs. Accordingly, field services communicated their requirements: to track historical customer outages and repair histories.

For the first time, anyone with access to the system could log on and find out whether a longstanding order had finally been provisioned or whether a repair had been made at a key customer site. Salespeople in particular were grateful that field services employees were using handheld devices to communicate remotely to the CRM server; the fast turnaround time was key to their communications with their customers.

Marketing could analyze how long repairs were taking by customer segment. Soon thereafter, marketing helped drive the modification of the field services dispatch system so high-value customer segments received higher priority for installation and repairs. In the meantime, the call center was able to correlate open trouble tickets to actual repairs, information they fed back to R&D to foster product quality improvements.

In fact, as the wireless communications company moved "up the pyramid," its CRM infrastructure—and consequently, its customer relationships—became much more robust. Not only were the planned improvements implemented successfully; there always seemed to be unforeseen uses for new CRM data and functionality.

Ten months after the call center brought CRM online, the marketing department was able to demonstrate lower customer attrition directly attributable to

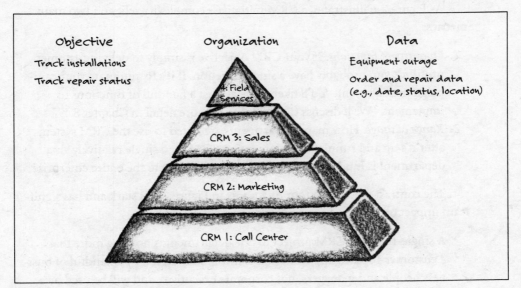

Figure 7-5: Enterprise CRM

preemptive targeted communications with at-risk customers. Marketing had never planned on stemming customer attrition, let alone quantifying the improvements. The wireless services provider continues to enrich its CRM capabilities, regularly measuring profitability gains as a result of increasing customer loyalty, and is now making information on the CRM server available to its financial and executive organizations.

Your company doesn't have to start its CRM program in the call center. Indeed, you might have an organization badly in need of CRM that doesn't appear in the above example. The point of this example is to illustrate that, far from being a "big bang," CRM at this company relied on incremental delivery of functionality over time. And with that incremental functionality came incremental value, the whole being worth way more than the sum of its parts.

Determining CRM Complexity

Unfortunately for those of us searching for that anecdotal but ultimately undependable silver bullet, there is no single cookie-cutter approach to CRM. The truth is, the more complex your ultimate CRM vision, the more complex your implementation project will be.

The key to planning your CRM initiative is in the ability to deconstruct it into manageable pieces. And to do this, you must first understand how complex it is.

As Figure 7-6 illustrates, a CRM initiative's complexity relies on two main metrics:

1. *Quantity of functions.* If your CRM objective is simply to deliver customer profiling, you probably have a single function. If it's to automate your campaign management, you'll likely have at least a handful of functions to implement. (We'll discuss functionality in more detail in Chapter 8.)
2. *Range of usage.* How many departments are slated to use the CRM system after it's up and running? Implementing CRM for a single relatively small department is much less complex than deploying it to the entire enterprise.

The contrast among the four quadrants in Figure 7-6 is stark and has significant impact on the development process, as illustrated here:

- A single-function CRM project to one department is nothing more than a customer-focused application. It is most likely driven by a handful of business people and managers, not corporate executives, and will be used by a

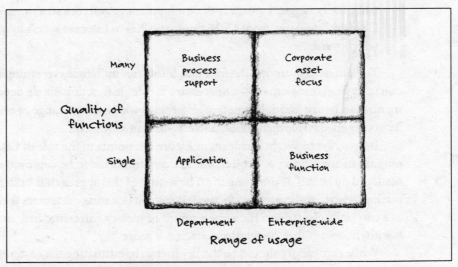

Figure 7-6: Estimating CRM complexity

single organization. You'll probably be able to leverage a series of in-house development processes and existing staff to deliver single-function CRM to the department that needs it.

- A multifunction CRM project to a single department is another story. Instituting a customer-focused contact center dictates a range of new customer-oriented business processes, not to mention new policies and end-user training. Defining and documenting business processes, as we'll show in this chapter, will give you a good idea of the CRM system's true complexity and the development resources it requires.

- Conversely, a single CRM function to be deployed across the company represents a newly institutionalized business function. If the call center, marketing, risk management, and sales organizations have each requested customer lifetime value information, a simple function takes on additional complexity because it involves multiple departments, and thus varied business requirements. This additional complexity will likely require additional development resources and longer up-front planning.

- The most complex type of CRM is multifunctional and multidepartmental or enterprise-wide. This means deploying a range of new business functions across the company to a variety of businesspeople for a variety of purposes. Requirements will be complex, as will the technology to enable CRM. The complexity suggests a variety of development resources and a range of CRM technologies, from CRM product suites to Internet access to data warehousing.

The differences among the four quadrants can influence everything from executive level involvement—unnecessary for single function/single department, mandatory for multifunction/enterprise-wide—to the range of required technologies, development skills, and end-user involvement.

Indeed, the top right quadrant of Figure 7-5 points to the role of CRM as not just an application or project, but as a *corporate asset* to be deployed and managed on behalf of the company. The nature of this approach is both information-centric and customer-focused. It suggests treating customers themselves as a corporate asset, given the same amount of money, infrastructure, and executive attention as other corporate assets, if not more.

While complexity should be the key metric in estimating the cost, resources, and development steps necessary to implement CRM, your company's size is also a factor. A large company, for instance, might have the skills and infrastructure to dedicate to a CRM project and is probably adept at handling large-scale enterprise systems development.

Small to mid-size companies, on the other hand, won't have as many organizations or the same number of stakeholders as larger firms. Though this can streamline business planning and vendor selection—fewer players simplifies consensus-building—securing funding might be more challenging for a smaller firm. Nailing down the right executive sponsor for CRM is probably also more straightforward in smaller companies.

Preparing the CRM Business Plan

Want funding for a new IT project this year? Make sure you have a really strong business case first. That's because concerns about an economic slowdown are making corporations far more selective than usual about how and where they allocate their IT budgets . . . –*Computerworld,* January 15, 2001

Whether your company is a multinational conglomerate with a structured governance process or a dot-com company with loose standards for project approval, you'll likely need to justify your CRM program to management. A CRM business plan includes several discrete components that, when combined, explain the value proposition and tactical implementation plan for CRM.

Understanding the program-approval process in your company will take you a long way toward creating a solid and useful business plan. As with the wireless company described earlier, many companies have governance committees made up of executives from various organizations. These executives decide which programs to fund and how much money to allocate to each one, based on the content of the business plan as well as a formal pitch from the program's sponsor. Funding is allocated according to a variety of factors, detailed in Table 7-2.

The business plan might also include:

- The requirement for new technologies
- The impact on existing technologies
- Ongoing support and maintenance requirements
- CRM alternatives

Even if your company doesn't have a structured program-approval process, including a discussion of each of the above considerations in your CRM business plan will ensure you've done your research and help bolster your arguments.

Defining CRM Requirements

The extent to which you can align your CRM business objectives to your company's overall strategy is proportional to the amount of funding you're likely to receive. Unfortunately, many companies don't have a set of lucid corporate strategies to which a set of CRM initiatives can align. The days of large strategic alignment projects replete with chart-building management consultants and binders overflowing with spreadsheets are mercifully behind us.

Defining the set of business requirements CRM will address is nevertheless crucial. For CRM to work, its objectives must be customer-focused and tactical in nature. The objective to "improve the supply chain," for example, could be both customer-focused and tactical—or neither—depending on the envisioned improvements. By their very definition, business requirements are specific and granular.

Requirements-gathering can be a long and complex process, but at its heart it involves listing what CRM can do for the business. For each business area, ask this question: *"What need, pain, or problem can CRM help us address?"*

The answer depends on the individual executive or the organization in need of CRM. But it also relies on understanding the complexity of the ultimate

Table 7-2: Typical CRM Approval Factors

Evaluation Factor	Explanation	Examples
The program's long-term value	Why the proposed CRM initiative will have long-term, sustainable value to the company	Marketing's CRM initiative is estimated to increase target marketing response rates by 50 percent (resulting in a 6 percent average campaign response rate), delivering annual net revenue gains of approximately $14 million.
Its adherence to company objectives	How CRM pertains to the company's stated goals or overarching strategies	An enterprise CRM program will allow us to achieve our objective of exceeding 40 percent market share through decreased attrition levels and more successful marketing campaigns.
Its ability to deliver key business objectives	How specific business goals will be met with CRM	CRM will allow the company to adopt true one-to-one relationships with our customers by delivering both personalization on our Web site and real-time customer profiling capabilities for our call center staff.
Its cost	An estimate of the cost breakdown	During the next fiscal year, the proposed CRM program is estimated to need $1.5 million in technology funding (hardware, software, networking), an additional $1 million for permanent head count, $1.5 million for consulting services, and a half million for external data acquisition.

Evaluation Factor	Explanation	Examples
Its boundaries	An explanation of the initial CRM project's resulting deliverable	The initial release of the eCRM program will include deployment of IVR self-service, Web-enabled provisioning, and Web FAQ services to alleviate demands on the contact center.
Staffing requirements	A list of necessary staff for requirements gathering, technology acquisition, development, and rollout of the CRM solution	In addition to the current CRM SWAT team, we estimate the need for • A CRM development manager (FT) • Two CRM product specialists (FT) • A CRM architect (consultant) • An additional database administrator (FT)
Risk assessment	A description of the potential risks involved in launching a CRM program at this time	We foresee the e-business organization's historical reluctance to share its data as a likely impediment to sales-department access to existing customers' Web purchase and self-service history, rendering customer history profiles incomplete and the resulting decisions potentially faulty.

CRM initiative, as illustrated in Figure 7-6. Is CRM envisioned as a corporate-wide program that will touch various business areas or as a departmental project requiring a single function, such as brochure mailing, to be addressed? Your ability to answer this question is critical to not only planning your CRM program but also to choosing your CRM products and mapping out implementation activities.

Consider the following two lists of CRM business questions taken from actual projects. The first list, from the marketing department of a cable TV company, represents a list of departmental requirements:

- Product managers must be able to define their own campaigns.
- We need to quantify the impact of hitting a customer with multiple campaigns in a year. (What is the optimal number of campaign "touches" for one individual customer versus another?)
- We need to test campaigns using purchase history.
- Our goal is to increase the number of current campaigns by 400%.
- We must begin supporting product sets across multiple campaigns.
- We need to ensure that we don't reuse targeted customers more than once every three months.
- Understanding which existing campaigns are most appropriate for a given customer is key. We need to rank current campaigns by score for their applicability to a given customer.
- We need to know which products to recommend when up-selling an existing customer.
- We need to understand the best audience for this product package.
- We need to understand the best customer for a brand new product where there is no sales history.

The next list also originated from a marketing department, this time from a large communications company. However, this list addresses cross-functional requirements:

- Our campaign managers need to know if their recent campaigns have resulted in increased customer support requests.
- Our product planners are interested in whether existing product usage rates affect new campaigns.
- We'd like to analyze whether a campaign will be more successful with customers who already spend $100 per month.
- Knowledge of whether direct sales and reseller channels influence campaign success can help both sales and marketing optimize channels and direct sales staff.
- We need to know which campaigns were more effective with resellers. With the Web and e-mail marketing. With direct sales (telemarketing).

- Sales management would like to know if campaign effectiveness is related to the length of the reseller's relationship with us.
- Sales management wants to relate the success of a given campaign with sales compensation and commission levels.

Notice how the requirements in both lists pertain to marketing improvements, but the items in the first list are exclusive to marketing and can thus be considered departmental. The cable company's marketing department has identified the areas in which it can improve campaign effectiveness and optimize customer interactions, both worthy CRM objectives.

Campaign effectiveness is important in the second list, as well; however, the communications company's requirements involve both a cross-section of users and a greater variety of data. The first requirement, for example, involves analyzing customer-support trouble tickets before launching a campaign, and the next several involve data from other systems, such as the provisioning and billing systems. The last several requirements describe how CRM will aid the sales organization.

Your CRM business plan should not only list such customer-focused requirements, but should also map them to specific applicable CRM tactics, providing management with a reconciliation of which CRM features will address which business goals. (And as we'll see in the next chapter, this also renders technology selection a whole lot easier.)

Table 7-3 illustrates the mapping between a set of cross-functional business requirements and specific CRM tactics.

The advantage of this type of matrix is that it provides a visual clue to critical CRM capabilities—notice how prominently personalization plays a role with most of the business objectives—while also presenting a good idea of what will be involved in realizing the business requirements. For instance, the "increased service and repair effectiveness" requirement ultimately warrants a series of non-CRM features to be successfully implemented, meaning CRM in field services might require more resources and take a bit longer to deliver.

To maximize the success of the first proposed CRM program, the program needs business requirements that

- Have defined boundaries
- Have a high value-to-cost ratio
- Minimize the impact to existing systems

Table 7-3: Mapping CRM Features to Business Requirements

CRM Feature / Business Objective	Web-based self service	Personalization	Contact center scripting	List generation (predictive)	Sales activity management
Greater number of Web site return visitors	○	◉	○	○	○
E-commerce efficiencies	●	●	●	◉	●
Increase in market share for core products	○	○	●	○	○
Higher customer satisfaction ratings	●	●	●	●	◉
Intelligent marketing campaigns	◉	●	◉	●	●
Increased service and repair effectiveness	●	○	●	○	◉

● = Critical path   ◉ = Related   ○ = Unknown/low impact

- Improve work efficiencies for more than one person
- Involve process change

It is the cost-to-value ratio that most confounds well-meaning managers who intuitively know CRM is the best weapon, but who need some ammunition.

Cost-Justifying CRM

When launching a visible and wide-ranging program such as CRM, it's only a matter of time before a high-ranking executive inquires, "So how much money have we spent on this CRM thing, and what have we gotten in return?" The degree to which your CRM program has been deliberately planned and executed is the degree to which you'll have a slam-dunk answer to this question.

Any CRM program has three possible financial outcomes:

1. Increased profits
2. Break-even
3. Lost revenue

Unfortunately, quantifying how much additional profit is generated or money saved via CRM is difficult. Unlike more straightforward operational systems that deliver both defined outcomes and quantifiable improvements, CRM often fosters unprecedented business practices that are by their very nature not measurable. Comparing new sales channels such as the Web to traditional channels invites apples-to-oranges debates. Furthermore, unlike its more technology-specific counterparts, CRM often delivers ROI that is both hard and soft.

From a soft return standpoint, CRM can deliver significant payback that's nevertheless difficult to quantify. Enhanced employee satisfaction, cultural and workplace improvements, perceived technology leadership, and amplified market reputation are examples. Even such concepts as customer loyalty and customer satisfaction, both crucial to business success, are difficult to measure. A March 2000 CRM study conducted by META Group/IMT revealed that 90 percent of the fifty largest CRM user companies admitted being unable to quantify a return on their CRM initiatives.

For some companies, simply knowing that, after deploying CRM, their sales figures exceeded the industry average is enough. For others, the inevitable executive questions loom large—large enough to mandate tangible benefits.

From a hard ROI perspective, CRM can result in revenue or cost savings via the following quantifiable metrics:

1. More efficient customer-focused business processes
2. Decreased customer attrition
3. Increased sales

Take the first item on the list as an example. The Director of Product Marketing at a large regional bank described it in practice:

Right now the bank can't keep track of more than 10 campaigns at a time. We want to create product offerings that are unique to specific customer segments, which could increase the number of campaigns ten- or even twenty-fold. We desperately need to manage more campaigns in order to promote more distinct offerings. Really, we'd like to move toward one-to-one, where instead of having one campaign for a million consumers, we have a hundred campaigns each focused on a group of 10,000 consumers. This strategy will increase response rates for our marketing campaigns and generate additional revenues.

In fact, every business objective you define as part of your long-term CRM planning should inherently target one of the three metrics. For example, we could map each of the objectives listed in Table 7-3 to one or more of these metrics, as we have done in Table 7-4 (where, again, "A" signifies business process efficiencies, "B" decreased customer attrition, and "C" increased sales).

The most straightforward way to calculate the financial promise of one of these business objectives is to measure how it's currently being done and what it's costing. Unfortunately, because many of these initiatives involve new corporate paradigms, there is often nothing to measure.

One client of mine understood the degree to which its call center staff was spending time on unnecessary work. The company had hired a consulting firm to measure CSR activities and determined that CSRs spent an average of 25 minutes on every trouble ticket simply gathering customer data. The company then determined that, of these 25 minutes, 15 were spent accessing and logging onto various source systems, searching for specific data, and consolidating the answer sets.

Table 7-4: Business Objectives and Financial Metrics

1. Greater number of Web site return visitors	A, C
2. E-commerce efficiencies	A, C
3. Increase in market share for core products	C
4. Higher customer-satisfaction ratings	B
5. Increased campaign response	A, B, C
6. Increased service and repair effectiveness	A, B

We used the following form as a way of measuring this company's CRM opportunity:

Problem Statement:	Our call center staff productivity has decreased dramatically as the problems become more complex. We need a means of increasing CSR productivity to improve the cost structure of the call center.
Sample problem quantification:	Everyone knows the number of trouble tickets exceeds the existing staff's ability to process them. We've recently determined that the average CSR can handle 10 tickets a day. The average amount of time spent in data-gathering (which includes accessing data from five different systems) is 25 minutes per ticket.
Improvement quote:	"A single CSR tool and screen should be able to reduce data-gathering time and allow our CSRs to address more trouble tickets in a given day." (Vice President of Customer Support)
Operational premise:	Number of CSRs = 60 Average time to gather customer information = 25 minutes Number of tickets generated for each CSR per day = 30–45
Fiscal premise:	Average yearly burdened cost of CSR = $60,000 Average tickets per CSR per day = 10 Cost per ticket = $25
CRM improvement assumptions:	A CRM system that includes dynamic customer-profile "screen pops" can reduce data-gathering time and present pertinent customer information at the point of interaction. Reducing data-gathering time will impact the overall ticketing process. (Every 15 minutes saved means a 31% improvement.) Productivity gains will reduce backlog. *(continued)*

Related applications/systems:	Customer profiling				
Quantified impact:	# of CSRs	Staff cost per year	Tickets	Time gain	$ Impact
	10	100	$600,000	31%	$186,000
	30	300	$1,800,000	31%	$558,000
	60	600	$3,600,000	31%	$1,116,000
Soft Benefits:	Reduced trouble-ticket response times Improved customer-satisfaction levels Improved employee-satisfaction levels				

In a true enterprise CRM opportunity, several such forms are completed and then compared. The highest-impact CRM opportunity inevitably rises to the top, becoming the first official CRM project within the CRM program.

Here's another CRM measurement form completed for the same company, this time for the marketing department:

In the event that several of these forms can be completed for each of your company's CRM applications, they can be collected, prioritized, and

Problem Statement:	The company's marketing process is too darn long.
Sample problem quantification:	It takes up to 6 weeks to identify a campaign target audience—using experienced data analysts. We'd like this to take days, or even hours, using marketing staff with minimal assistance from IT.
Improvement quote:	"By reducing the time needed to identify a campaign's target audience, we could double or even triple the number of campaigns we deploy, while further delimiting our target segments." (Director of Segment Marketing)
Operational premise:	Right now, for every three marketing campaign managers, we need one data analyst and one IT query support staff member to run queries.

Fiscal premise:	Each campaign manager requires two support staff members:
	Average yearly cost of 1 data analyst = $130,000
	Average yearly cost of 1 IT resource = $130,000
	Number of campaign managers in marketing = 30

CRM improvement assumptions:	• Campaign managers will migrate to using desktop CRM analysis and will need to be educated on its use
	• Campaign managers will evolve from project managers to "knowledge workers"
	• The projected cost savings will occur via the reduction of data analysis and IT support staff
	• Productivity gains will increase the number and effectiveness of campaigns by a minimum of 20 percent

Quantified impact:	# of campaign managers	# of support staff	Projected staff savings ($n * $150K$)
	10	6	$900,000
	25	16	$2,400,000
	40	26	$3,900,000

Soft Benefits:	Through the increased productivity, the company can increase the number of campaigns and thus the effectiveness of each individual campaign, in turn increasing revenues. Alternatively, the company can simply decrease the number of campaign managers but deploy the same number of campaigns.

then published in a physical or online document to serve as a living CRM roadmap.

A good example of CRM ROI is SBC Communications. According to *CIO* magazine, SBC's EASE (Easy Access Sales Environment), an online tool to help CSRs and telemarketers, cost $34.2 million. The tool helped sales reps access product information faster and pull in more comprehensive customer data, allowing an increase in call volume, a simultaneous decrease in call duration, and improved order accuracy. All told, the estimated ROI for EASE was reported to be $483.6 million.[2]

Here's an important note on ROI financials if you'll be asked to justify CRM to a Chief Financial Officer or corporate accountant: I had the pleasure of explaining CRM ROI to a finance director who asked if CRM was worth more than the "time value of money." This manager's question implied that his company would either invest in CRM or put the money into some interest-bearing checking account—which wasn't the case. In fact, cost-justifying a CRM program for most companies assumes that the allocated budget money will go either to CRM or to another proposed project of similar or higher priority. The goal is to make a case for the value of CRM versus other potential corporate programs. Although examining the time value of money might be worthwhile if your choice is either to implement CRM or to purchase real estate for a new brick-and-mortar store, the majority of companies considering CRM are going to spend their money on a project. The issue is where to get the most bang for their budget buck.

Another cost to consider when justifying CRM is the cost of delaying the decision to move forward. For instance, in one comprehensive CRM business case, one client of mine included a section citing the following opportunity costs of delaying CRM:

- The cost of lost marketing opportunities, including
  - Cost of lost customers due to competitive marketing events
  - Reduced effectiveness of new products due to lack of market understanding
  - Continued increase of marketing costs due to poorly focused campaigns and/or oversized target audiences
- Costs of continuing the support of stovepipe database systems
- Loss of staff skills and experience due to staff redeployment
- Lost IT resource and subject-matter expertise due to normal staff attrition rates
- Reduced customer loyalty and perception due to inability to enhance the customer's relationship experience

---

2. "SBC Goes Coast to Coast with EASE," *CIO* magazine, February 1, 2001.

In fact, many companies that undertake CRM are measuring their successes based not on return on investment but on *return on relationship* (ROR). Return on relationship implies the ability to compare the before-and-after effects of CRM on customer value and loyalty. Have customers in the mid-tier sector migrated upward in value? Have customers we've been "willing to lose" actually become more profitable since CRM was established? Has a low-value customer referred high-value customers to the company, thus contributing even more revenue than if she had spent that money herself?

Measuring ROR can be subjective but can provide a company with the ability to identify which components of CRM—be they changes in business processes or more targeted communications—improve customer relationships and which customers seem most responsive to new customer-focused business actions. Then the company can formalize what's working and fine-tune what's not.

A final word on CRM ROI: If your company is adopting CRM because of the cost savings it promises, beware. With the escalating complexity and pricing of many CRM products, seeing return on investment might take a few years. The real justification for CRM goes back to improving your customers' experience with your company, humanizing this experience, and making it easier to do business with you. CRM is about managing and monitoring your customer relationships and increasing their value. It's about motivating customers to tell their friends to buy your products. Yes, these too can result in revenue down the line. But when a good customer is just a mouse-click away, delaying CRM can be risky.

Understanding Business Processes

You probably already intuitively know the area in which CRM will generate the biggest return. But do you want to automate or improve an existing process? Is there even a process to begin with? Every successful CRM program involves a process improvement of some kind. What will yours be?

CRM was initially designed to help solve tactical, customer-facing business problems. (Only after the resulting data promised new strategic improvements did analytical CRM become the darling of analysts and futurists.) The common denominator of CRM-related business processes is that they should be designed around the customer's perspective with the ultimate goal of improving the customer's experience.

BPR Redux: Modeling Customer Interactions

One could argue that the days of business process reengineering (BPR), when companies redesigned their core processes to drive new levels of efficiency, are back with CRM. CRM usually begins with a definitive business question such as this one: "How should we treat valuable customers when they request a room at a hotel that's full?" The business question implies improved customer-focused processes that can in turn be automated with technology.

Such business questions were on the mind of a major hotel chain's CEO in early 2001. The CEO had recently been given several competitive reports indicating that the majority of the hotel's "overflow" guests were going to its chief competitor. Trouble was, many of these guests had stayed 100 or more nights with this chain. They were not only important; they were profitable. A query to the hotel chain's data warehouse indicated that these frequent guests accounted for only 8 percent of the company's customers but were responsible for 40 percent of its profits.

The hotel chain had heretofore been more "property-centric" than customer-centric, but it now recognized the value of ensuring that these high-value customers remained loyal. In the past this had meant giving generous room upgrades to high-value guests when they checked in and providing in-room "welcome kits" of free snacks and toiletries. However, these perks only worked when the customer had already secured a reservation.

To understand how to treat its best customers better, the hotel chain first mapped out its existing customer interaction process, which looked like the illustration in Figure 7-7.

The good news was that the hotel company was already differentiating its high-value customers—one of the main tenets of CRM. Frequent-guest card-holders had their own toll-free number directing them to call-center agents trained to take their time when dealing with high-value guests.

The bad news was that if the customer needed the room right away, he was normally unwilling to risk being wait-listed and would simply call a competing hotel chain. The company's data warehouse verified that of all frequent guests being refused reservations on their first attempt, only 24 percent agreed to be placed on a wait-list, and a mere 11 percent actually ended up staying at one of the chain's properties.

With competition in the hospitality industry heating up, the hotel chain decided to take the concept of customer differentiation a few steps further. This meant adopting new policies such as these for frequent-guest reservations:

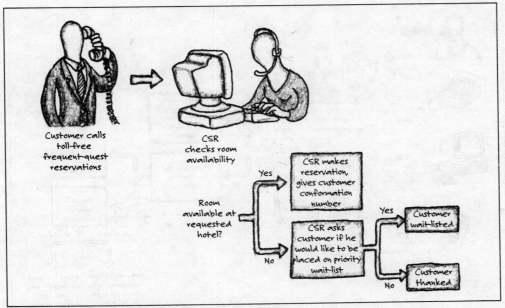

Figure 7-7: The traditional customer-facing process

- Supporting multichannel reservations, including telephone, fax, and Web
- Creating a special reservations Web site for frequent guests
- Having the system track properties in proximity to one another, so CSRs could suggest alternative hotels in the same chain
- "Advance-blocking" a greater number of rooms for valuable customers at high-demand hotels

The resulting frequent-guest reservations policies dictated a more specialized reservations process that looked like the one illustrated in Figure 7-8.

Notice that the new process has not only been rendered more involved; much of it has been automated, making it easier for the customer to communicate with the company. The rule of modeling customer interactions is that every interaction, incoming or outgoing, should have the potential to improve the customer's experience. By offering its best customers a choice of media for making reservations, the hotel effectively provided more value to the customer.

The "agent" referred to in the example might be either a human CSR in customer support or a cyberagent interacting with the hotel chain's reservation

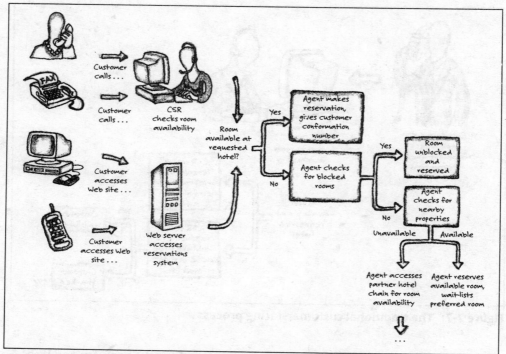

Figure 7-8: The new customer-focused business process

system as well as those of its partner hotels (who reimburse the hotel chain with a referral fee). As we discussed in Chapter 2, the use of cyberagents to automate decision-making and accelerate previously manual processes is another effective way to speed up workflow. In fact, the term "workflow" is used in CRM to refer to automated business processes. Many CRM products feature "workflow management" components automating processes such as campaign management or customer troubleshooting.

This hotel chain knew it needed to implement both operational and analytical CRM. The chain's customer support department understood the business need, and even knew where it wanted to begin. Customer support specialists and business analysts mapped out the new reservations process, focusing on the various customer touchpoints to ensure that individual interactions represented an improvement over the traditional process.

But in this case the whole was greater than the sum of its parts. It was a "soft" benefit of CRM that ultimately delivered the biggest payback: the hotel chain was also able to increase its brand loyalty. High-value customers gradually realized that when they called the chain's frequent-guest reservations line, their likelihood of getting a room, even if not in a first-choice property, was higher than before—and much higher than when calling a competing chain. Customers no longer had to waste time calling around to different hotels, because the CSR had become more than just a reservation agent: she was now a customer advocate. Customers were becoming more and more assured that, by the end of their contact with the chain, they would have a room in their requested city. The new CRM process had increased these high-value customers' brand loyalty and their likelihood of calling again.

Analyzing Your Business Processes

If you have documented internal processes already and these processes are customer-focused, you're way ahead of the game. More often than not, existing business processes need fine-tuning before they're implemented as part of a CRM program, putting a new spin on BPR, as the hotel chain in the earlier example did. Sometimes existing business processes should be entirely obliterated and a company should start from scratch. Avoid clinging to your traditional customer interactions just because they've worked in the past. (In such cases, forget the term "reengineering"; think *invention*.)

If you don't have documented processes, or if your processes need overhauling, ask the following questions for each customer-facing business activity involved in each CRM requirement:

- Is the tangible result of the process (e.g., a purchase order or return authorization number) seen or experienced by the customer?
- Is there an opportunity to gather more customer data at discrete touchpoints in the process?
- Does each interaction demonstrate value to the customer?
- Does any interaction waste the customer's time?
- Does this process improve our ability to see this customer as an individual?
- Is there an opportunity to impress the customer or personalize the interaction at discrete customer touchpoints?
- Can we include exception-handling to ensure accurate service and personalize interactions?
- Can this process be improved or even eliminated for high-value customers? What about for the mid-value tier?

If you don't know the answer to two or more of these questions, you would do well to take the time to map out new or existing processes and identify areas that can deliver an improved customer experience and tighter time frames.

In addition, try looking at your business processes from an organizational perspective. Most process planning activities neglect this step, but answers to questions like those in the following list can result in even more highly refined processes and can pinpoint opportunities to improve your overall infrastructure:

- For a given customer-facing business process, how many departments are involved?
- How many actual staff members touch in each process?
- What data is transferred between organizations, and how much?
- Does the information being shared change as it goes through the process? How often?
- Do the organizations involved in each business process agree on business rules and common terminology?

When designing and documenting new business processes, it's helpful to understand not only the customer's view of the process but its inherent complexity. A customer's potential delight at a new, Web-based order process won't matter much if the process itself is too cumbersome to program and integrate with existing systems.

Many process-design teams get caught up in modeling conventions and documentation tools. If you have such tools in-house and the expertise is handy, having an online process library enables the company to maintain a history of customer-focused improvements over time. Such a library can be part of a corporate-wide knowledge-management system and can be used for a variety of purposes. Business analysts can access outdated processes to provide CRM stakeholders with graphical illustrations of before-and-after processes during requirements gathering. Developers and programmers can use the models to ensure that the CRM system mirrors the process vision.

The main goal of business process modeling for CRM, however, is to improve traditional or broken processes and thus enhance customer interactions. If you need to initially document processes on a whiteboard rather than waiting to install the latest graphical modeling tool, do so. The convention is not as important as the result. With all process-modeling activities, the objective should be to model and refine the optimal customer experience.

Business processes that span multiple departments will not only be more difficult to document; you'll also need to build consensus, which adds time. Bite the bullet: document business processes before or in parallel with the rest of your CRM planning so when it comes time to choose a CRM product, you'll already know what tactical improvements you can expect.

Speaking of technology selection, it's important to note that the hotel chain we've been talking about had not yet chosen a CRM product. Indeed, understanding the requirements for CRM and making the business case for a comprehensive new program both need to occur before you choose any CRM product. This way, the technology is sure to match the requirements and not the other way around.

Case Study: Verizon

Summary: Intimidated by the thought of planning an ambitious enterprise CRM program? Imagine planning it for two merging Fortune 25 companies and enhancing your company's customer focus—as well as its new brand.

For someone in the throes of delivering enterprise CRM, Beth Leonard is awfully calm. A former management consultant and a telephone industry veteran, Leonard has seen her share of corporate-wide programs slated to improve the bottom line. Now Vice President of Database Marketing for Verizon Communications, Leonard might have finally found the project that puts her formidable experience to the test.

Starting just another CRM project would have been too easy for Leonard, whose first challenge was to get a grasp of the CRM-related projects already underway within the two merging companies and, moreover, to establish consensus on CRM's purpose.

WHAT THEY DID:

Wisely, Leonard banished any hopes of the two companies' disparate systems seamlessly interconnecting around a common CRM strategy. "Both GTE and Bell Atlantic had decent CRM visions," she recalls, "and each company had done a lot of self-education. Unfortunately, GTE was beholden to an outdated technology platform that wouldn't perform for the long haul." Bell Atlantic had a different set of problems, namely its surfeit of single-purpose, application-centric systems. Although most of these delivered value, there was no organized way of connecting the dots. Moreover, some executives were beginning to question the long-term value of CRM initiatives, proclaiming CRM too costly and not sustainable.

Leonard realized that for the newly formed company to launch a successful CRM program, it would have to begin at the beginning—and ground zero was the organization. This meant not only shifting from a product focus to a customer focus; it also meant instilling a new sense of cultural urgency about CRM's competitive promise. She made up her mind to craft a CRM roadmap, consciously deciding to "go for broke" and launch a bona fide, business-driven CRM program.

One of Leonard's first steps was to establish a pilot program to, as she puts it, "practice and learn." Beginning with the organization, she established a CRM Steering Committee of executives from Verizon's various business units. Buy-in was swift, as was the subsequent assignment of a CRM Core Team, a cross-functional group of managers who would help define CRM delivery capabilities. "By consciously crafting CRM job responsibilities, we were ensuring customer focus across all channels," she explains, "not only so we'd have a single view of our customers, but so they'd have a single view of us."

The CRM Core Team's first step was to understand customer interactions. A series of scenarios was developed, depicting how customers move through the organization. When the customer-focused processes were well understood, the team stepped back and made the customer the design point. This triggered changes in customer interactions at various customer touchpoints and encouraged the team to consider improvements—for instance, providing a special level of service for high-value customers.

The team also spent time ensuring that business users across the company became, as Leonard puts it, "violently aligned" around a common CRM vision. "CRM is a strategy, not a technology," Leonard maintains. Core Team members and their staffs subsequently began taking inventory of all CRM-related initiatives across Verizon, correlating them and integrating them where appropriate. "We needed to stop wasting money on duplicate yet disconnected efforts that ultimately clouded the CRM landscape," she explains. "They were keeping us off-balance in terms of focus and assessing sustainable success. And, more importantly, they were confusing our customers."

But CRM planning didn't only focus on processes. Leonard and her team realized CRM required a building-block approach to implementation, and this required a solid technology foundation. Leonard advocated the creation of a solid data foundation in the form of a corporate data warehouse, which would serve as the core CRM platform, as the evolution depicted in Figure 7-9 shows.

After the data warehouse was up and running, the company could periodically supplement its data with various data subject areas from both internal and external data sources, at each stage delivering enhanced CRM functionality.

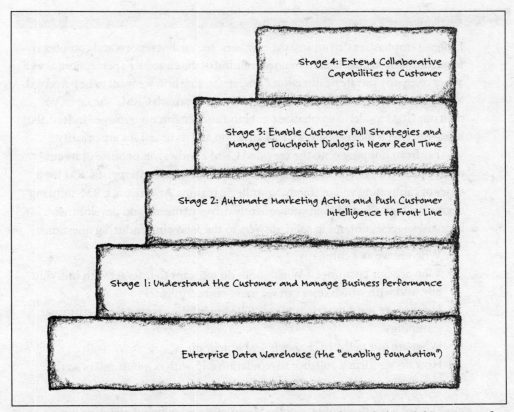

Stage 4: Extend Collaborative Capabilities to Customer

Stage 3: Enable Customer Pull Strategies and Manage Touchpoint Dialogs in Near Real Time

Stage 2: Automate Marketing Action and Push Customer Intelligence to Front Line

Stage 1: Understand the Customer and Manage Business Performance

Enterprise Data Warehouse (the "enabling foundation")

Figure 7-9: CRM at Verizon: Iterative, evolutionary, and multi-tiered. (Courtesy of Verizon Communications, Inc.)

THE CHALLENGES:

Leonard's challenges were more cultural and organizational than tactical. She cites the need for gathering consensus around CRM's value as a major hurdle—one she's gratified to have overcome. She also charges various product vendors and consultants with glibly promising unrealistic "quick wins" at the expense of the planning and rigor ultimately crucial to instilling the corporate consciousness of CRM as a true enterprise program. "CRM, if done right, is not simple," Leonard declares.

Other challenges, such as harnessing individual proclivities for building single-purpose, single-user systems, are ongoing. Moreover, the complexity of erecting enterprise CRM in a high-profile public company means unremitting pressure from the financial community with its push for immediate ROI.

GOOD ADVICE:

Leonard emphasizes that amidst the cumbersome analyst reports and complex systems comparisons, her team remained mindful of the customer's perception, as well as her company's strategic direction. "Understanding how we want to be perceived as a company has major implications on how we approach CRM," she says. "We built our CRM model to emphasize our brand and reinforce our image." Indeed, the linkage between the company's CRM direction and its brand is a top priority.

Far from hopping onto the crowded CRM bandwagon because of its current popularity, Verizon Communications has embraced enterprise CRM for a series of captivating and overarching strategic reasons. At Verizon, CRM-thinking begins strategically and then subsequently drives planning and development. Leonard suggests obtaining solid answers to the following enduring questions:

- Who are we as a company?
- Who are our customers? Which ones do we want to interact with individually, and with which ones can we mass-communicate?
- How do we want to structure our CRM portfolio around these customer groupings?
- What are our delivery channels and touchpoints?
- How do we form a collaborative relationship with our customers so the benefits exceed the risk of leaving?

"I want a portfolio of tactics that I can mix and match depending on the customer, event, situation, cost versus benefit, and availability of internal resources—as in the number of service reps who might be available to handle a new product rollout," Leonard insists. Although it supports the company's brand image, the CRM mantra at Verizon is refreshingly tactical: "Integration, reusability, and cross-functionality."

Where should a company start? Leonard's background in strategic planning has served her well, and she insists that building a CRM roadmap is an indispensable step and internal communication is crucial. When positioning CRM to her management, Leonard admits, "I told them it wasn't quick, it wasn't easy, and it wasn't cheap. I told them they couldn't go out and just 'buy CRM.'"

THE GOLDEN NUGGET:

Unlike many of her executive counterparts at other communications firms, Leonard has foregone the operational CRM solutions offered by vendors who tend to focus on discrete functionality, favoring a more deliberate and structured approach of gradual and rigorous CRM deployment. In addition to being more sustainable, Verizon's CRM program is designed around improving the customer's experience while bolstering the company's brand image. The CRM team carefully aligned its program around a key strategic requirement: a consistent customer message.

"We need to remember our brand," Leonard explains. "Is the experience we're providing our customers consistent with that brand? With our image?" Leonard cites one of Verizon's advertising slogans: *Advanced Simplicity.* "Do our tactics support this tag line?" she asks, by way of explaining how the brand image comes full circle. "Our customers receiving a different piece of mail every week from a different business unit with a different offer is not simple."

And that means more than just technology; it means a holistic approach to business change. "Technology's just an enabler," Beth Leonard asserts, adding, "Those trite little diagrams that talk about 'people, process, and technology' are actually true. CRM involves all three. And it can absolutely reinvent the entire enterprise."

A CRM Readiness Checklist for Success

Okay, so you have a vision. And you're well on your way with your CRM business plan, and you can even itemize the financial benefits CRM will deliver. But how will you know when you're ready?

Table 7-5 represents a CRM Readiness Checklist based on the one my company uses in its assessment projects. It poses a number of important questions

Table 7-5: CRM Readiness Evaluation Metrics

	Factor	Explanation
1	Targeted business users display an understanding of CRM and accompanying benefits.	Are the businesspeople slated to use CRM after it's deployed aware of its intended improvements? (A bonus: Are they enthusiastic about them?)
2	Management displays an understanding of CRM and accompanying benefits.	Not only must executives understand what CRM means; they should also understand its value proposition and be able to articulate it consistently. And they should understand which corporate objectives depend on CRM.
3	CRM application opportunities are identifiable.	The business areas most in need of CRM should be identified, along with the projected deliverables.
4	A business sponsor exists for each discrete CRM opportunity.	Staff members in the trenches, irrespective of their need for more customer intelligence, aren't enough. Someone in management should be lobbying for CRM, willing to tie his goals to CRM, and even willing to fund it.
5	Obvious stakeholdership (subject matter expertise, targeted end-users) exists for each discrete CRM opportunity.	Are there other people within each candidate business unit who will support or help deliver a CRM project? Are these people in the majority?
6	Client has expressed a need for market differentiation (or similar strategic objective).	Management should be able to tie CRM and its benefits back to the company's competitive goals and understand how CRM can help differentiate customers.
7	Communicated strategic initiatives can be supported by CRM.	If the company has a list of strategic objectives, those objectives should be customer focused and thus supported by CRM.
8	Stakeholders can articulate projected CRM benefits for each discrete opportunity.	Business sponsors or management should be able to describe the tactical business improvements that can be delivered by CRM.

	Factor	Explanation
9	Stated opportunities can be improved with customer-related data.	The CRM opportunities being discussed must be able to be supported and/or improved with clear, consolidated customer data. (In other words, process improvements aren't enough.)
10	Projected data sources are highly regarded for data accuracy and integrity.	Where will the customer profiles and segments originate? If those systems aren't trustworthy, no one will trust the ultimate CRM applications.
11	Cross-functional customer data exists in a data warehouse or centralized database.	A data warehouse containing consolidated customer information from around the company will jump-start any CRM program and will decrease the infrastructure costs.
12	Organizations currently share a cross-section of information requirements.	Has data sharing been institutionalized already with other systems? This is a positive sign, particularly if the initial CRM project evolves toward enterprise CRM.
13	The client is already engaging in some sort of customer differentiation or segmentation.	If customer segments are already being identified, there is an understanding of customer differentiation, which makes CRM much more culturally palatable. In addition, certain existing segmentation or analysis process might be leveragable.
14	Questions of data ownership across the company are either nonexistent or easily resolved.	Are specific organizations willing to share their data with the rest of the company? Is management willing to enforce this? Missing pieces of the customer puzzle could jeopardize an entire CRM program.
15	Business units and IT staff agree on CRM ownership boundaries.	The extent to which one organization wants to "own" CRM is the extent to which politics will get in the way of productivity. There should be firm boundaries for who does what.
16	Executive management has an expressed commitment to fund CRM-related activities.	Executives should understand not only that CRM involves a significant investment, but that additional funding dollars might also need to be reserved.

(continued)

Table 7-5: CRM Readiness Evaluation Metrics (*continued*)

	Factor	*Explanation*
17	Client agrees to modify business processes as a result of CRM.	Access to complete customer data should trigger business efficiencies.
18	There is willingness to sustain the organizational impact of CRM (for example, reorganization or additional staffing).	Management should be aware that, along with more data and process changes, job roles might change and new skills might be needed.
19	A general understanding of requirements-driven development exists among both business and IT stakeholders.	Successful CRM projects are "top down," meaning that they are driven by business need. Once understood, business requirements and their relative impact should drive CRM implementation priorities.
20	Management is willing to empower key customer-facing staff based on increased information and improved processes.	If employees such as salespeople and CSRs have more information, it follows that they can be more self-directed. Accountability should be maintained as employees are given more freedom, the focus being on ultimate improvements in customer satisfaction and revenues.
21	Management is willing to implement incentives or modify employee compensation to encourage CRM adoption.	Staff members who readily adopt CRM technologies and processes, and who participate in their ongoing improvement, should be rewarded. Staff members who refuse to adopt these improvements can be considered "saboteurs." Penalize them.
22	No decisions have been made about potential CRM technology solutions.	Beware the tail that wags the dog: are stakeholders communicating CRM requirements based on a product demo or sales pitch? Assumptions about specific technologies can risk overspending on CRM.

	Factor	Explanation
23	Business sponsors and stakeholders have an understanding of the differences between CRM and other programs (such as business intelligence, ERP, or data warehousing).	Even the most astute managers lump CRM together with data warehousing and other key business solutions that involve information technology. Although CRM technology might very well connect with these systems, CRM should be planned and funded separately from other initiatives.
24	IT staffing infrastructure is in place to support CRM.	Although CRM might leverage skill sets and knowledge from other IT areas, it should be planned as a discrete IT activity with dedicated implementation staff.
25	There is consensus that CRM is a process and not a one-time-only activity.	Like other large corporate initiatives, CRM is an ongoing process that grows and improves over time.
26	Business and IT stakeholders understand that CRM requires ongoing budget to support continued development and maintenance.	Because CRM is a process, it requires ongoing budget. Beware the lump sum CRM allocation . . . it probably won't cover all necessary CRM functionality.

that will allow you to score your CRM readiness and make the necessary improvements so your project can hit the ground running. Notice that many of the considerations involve culture as well as existing infrastructure.

Part of readiness assessment involves weighting to specific factors in the evaluation based on the results of the interviews conducted. (For example, if upper management is advocating an enterprise CRM initiative, the existence of cross-functional customer data would receive a higher weighting.)

Regardless of weighting, you can gauge your CRM readiness with the following rating scale:

- 4: This statement is **very descriptive** of our environment.
- 3: This statement is **largely descriptive** of our environment.

- 2: This statement is **partially descriptive** of our environment.
- 1: This statement is **not at all descriptive** of our environment.

For example, Table 7-6 shows how a specialty retail client scored on the assessment, and how to interpret its score.

Table 7-6: CRM Readiness Scoring

1	Targeted business users display an understanding of CRM and accompanying benefits.	1	**2**	3	4
2	Management displays an understanding of CRM and accompanying benefits.	1	2	**3**	4
3	CRM application opportunities are identifiable.	1	2	**3**	4
4	A business sponsor exists for each discrete CRM opportunity.	1	**2**	3	4
5	Obvious stakeholdership (subject matter expertise, targeted end-users) exists for each discrete CRM opportunity.	1	2	**3**	4
6	Client has expressed a need for market differentiation (or similar strategic objective).	1	2	3	**4**
7	Communicated strategic initiatives can be supported by CRM.	1	2	3	**4**
8	Stakeholders can articulate projected CRM benefits for each discrete opportunity.	1	2	3	**4**
9	Stated opportunities can be improved with customer-related data.	1	2	**3**	4
10	Projected data sources are highly regarded for data accuracy and integrity.	**1**	2	3	4
11	Cross-functional customer data exists in a data warehouse or centralized database.	1	2	**3**	4
12	Organizations currently share a cross-section of information requirements.	1	2	3	**4**
13	The client is already engaging in some sort of customer differentiation or segmentation.	1	2	3	**4**
14	Questions of data ownership across the company are either nonexistent or easily resolved.	**1**	2	3	4

15	Business units and IT staff agree on CRM ownership boundaries.	1	2	**3**	4
16	Executive management has an expressed commitment to fund CRM-related activities.	1	**2**	3	4
17	Client agrees to modify business processes as a result of CRM.	1	2	**3**	4
18	There is willingness to sustain the organizational impact of CRM (for example, reorganization or additional staffing).	1	2	3	**4**
19	A general understanding of requirements-driven development exists among both business and IT stakeholders.	1	2	**3**	4
20	Management is willing to empower key customer-facing staff based on increased information and improved processes.	1	2	**3**	4
21	Management is willing to implement incentives or modify employee compensation to encourage CRM adoption.	1	**2**	3	4
22	No decisions have been made about potential CRM technology solutions.	1	2	3	**4**
23	Business sponsors and stakeholders have an understanding of the differences between CRM and other programs (such as business intelligence, ERP, or data warehousing).	1	2	**3**	4
24	IT staffing infrastructure is in place to support CRM.	1	**2**	3	4
25	There is consensus that CRM is a process and not a one-time-only activity.	1	2	3	**4**
26	Business and IT stakeholders understand that CRM requires ongoing budget to support ongoing development and maintenance.	1	2	3	**4**
	Total Readiness Score:				**76**

You can now interpret the results, using the following scoring metrics:

- **104–85:** Suggests your organization is ready to begin implementing a CRM project with minimal infrastructure enhancement and confidence of a high degree of sponsorship.

- **84–73:** Suggests your organization should solidify its infrastructure, skill sets, and expectations but should expect to launch a CRM project in the near future. Planning should begin for a proof-of-concept.
- **72–50:** Suggests your organization should refrain from embarking on CRM until the technology infrastructure, data ownership, or cultural and political issues are resolved. Sponsorship should be cemented and staffing enhanced at this time.
- **49 or below:** Your organization has not expressed a firm business justification for CRM, or must perform a major overhaul of its staffing and/or systems. Another readiness assessment should occur after the identified improvements have been made.

The Manager's Bottom Line

The executive who expects CRM for its own sake to generate significant returns is the executive bargaining for disappointment—and most likely less budget money next year. A successful CRM program not only changes the way a company deals with its customers; it also changes the way customers deal with the company. The willingness to change processes and staff responsibilities is a key component of this success. A triumphant CRM program isn't so much *delivered* as it is *earned*.

Companies should be prepared for post facto organizational changes that supplement CRM. As we discussed in this chapter, CRM done right means changes in business processes. This in turn touches people's job functions and might even eliminate certain work as a result of accompanying efficiencies. For instance, the CSR who can now cross-sell products and services while the customer is on the phone is no longer just an order-taker. The field service rep who returns to the office each night to complete manual reports of the day's activities can now go directly home to dinner, having relayed that information from her handheld unit. The salesperson accustomed to darting from one meeting to another is now accountable for his customers' information. As we discussed in Chapter 4, this often means changes to compensation and bonus plans as well as job descriptions.

Establish the measurements now. Do you expect CRM to result in an uplift in cross-selling rates? Do you want to see a surge in positive customer feedback? The CRM goals you establish in the planning stage should become the CRM metrics you reevaluate after CRM has been deployed (as Chapter 9 will illustrate). Regardless of the goal, establish clear metrics for how it can be achieved and know that business requirements can be refined over time, with consequent fluid measurements. After you've established your CRM success metrics, expect to adjust and refine them as your business changes.

The CRM business sponsor is a big part of the CRM equation. After all, a lot of people will have ideas about what CRM should do, but far fewer can ensure that those ideas get executed. Not only will the CRM executive sponsor establish clear success metrics, he'll be responsible for keeping these metrics top-of-mind during development. Regardless of whether the executive sponsor is funding the CRM program, he should have the authority and breadth to see that CRM's objectives are achieved. Patricia Seybold, author of the acclaimed books *Customers.com* and *The Customer Revolution,* insists the single factor that best predicts the success of an e-business project is "a high level executive who's responsible for your branded customer experience."[3]

Have you noticed I've been using the term "program" instead of "project?" This could be a simple semantic shift in your company; then again, many companies differentiate the two. A "project" implies fixed activity with clear objectives and established beginning and end dates. A "program," on the other hand, is a complex set of goals and objectives that is institutionalized and ongoing, involving several or many projects within it. (Remember the Apollo space program?) Sometimes the differences are fuzzy. But more often than not, corporate "programs" receive a greater degree of executive support, better staff resources, larger budget allocations, and a higher level of visibility.

Here's hoping CRM is indeed a program at your company.

---

[3]Patricia B. Seybold interviewed in *CIO* magazine, November 15, 2000.

Choosing Your CRM Tool

Ever wander around the floor of a CRM trade show? You go from booth to booth, chatting with attractive vendor reps and viewing demo after demo. You fill your plastic bag with foam puzzles, rubber stress balls, and more marketing collateral than you'll ever read. At the end of the day all the products seem to run together and the pitches are identical. Everyone seems to have the same message. But are intuitive user interfaces and rapid customization features really enough to solve your CRM problem?

That contrived sales pitches and slick product packaging can persuade people to buy a software product isn't a recent phenomenon. Having adopted the ERP systems, data warehouses, and Y2K solutions of yesterday, many companies have already fallen prey to clever marketing, pervasive press releases, and the fluid buzz about market ownership. There are many ways to make a bad CRM technology decision, but only a few ways to make a good one.

Of course, technology is only a small part of CRM. Most companies who undertake CRM technology selection aren't yet ready to do so: they haven't figured out how CRM aligns to their corporate objectives, how it will impact their business processes, or how it will mandate organizational changes that will irk many a CRM stakeholder. Change is part of the CRM territory, and technology change is probably the easiest CRM change to accept-which is why many CRM business sponsors begin there. (Otherwise, this would have been Chapter 2.)

Indeed, this scenario, a true story, happens more than anyone would like to admit.

Scenario

> You're an executive at a large multinational technology company. You've recently begun reading more about the use of customer relationship management to instill customer loyalty and discourage customers from doing business with your competitors. And you've been hearing more about CRM than ever—your VP of Marketing mentions it in practically every executive staff briefing.
>
> One day she strides into your office and takes a seat. "I've just reviewed a CRM tool, and we need to get it," she says preemptively as Cheryl, your assistant, hovers at your doorway in a vain attempt to foil yet another unscheduled appointment.
>
> "What was the product?" you ask.
>
> The Marketing VP states the name of a familiar-sounding company you suspect is owned by one of your mutual funds and begins rattling off buzzwords as though she's just learned a new language. You don't know what a screen pop is, nor do you understand what she means by a "customer knowledgebase," but you let her finish. When she does, you ask what any self-respecting executive beholden to a bunch of impatient stockholders would ask:
>
> "How much?"
>
> "Three million," she says. As if it would explain everything, she adds, "A million for the base CRM platform, and another two to re-do our campaign processes and customize the code."
>
> You're still wondering why an innocent-sounding screen pop can cost three million dollars. There must be cheaper screen pops to be had. "Shouldn't we look into some alternatives?" you ask. "Maybe there's a lower-cost package that does the same thing . . . ."
>
> *"We can't wait that long!"* cries the VP. "Our customers are only a click away from one of our competitors! We have to start integrating our channels now! It costs six times as much to get a new customer as it does . . . ."
>
> You've seen it hundreds of times in your long career as a manager, and few things are as dangerous and as fearsome to behold: a businessperson who's just returned from a trade show.

> "Have Cheryl schedule a meeting with IT," you respond feebly, unsure of what else to suggest. The VP breaks into a wide grin, as if you've just handed her three million bucks to play with.
> And in a way, you have.

Falling prey to the vendor hype isn't the only way to screw up CRM technology selection. Following is a list of some of the responses I've heard to the question, "How did you go about choosing your CRM product?"

- "The salesman gave it away for free for the first year."
- "The VP of Product Planning plays golf with the software company's CFO."
- "Because the competition is doing it."
- "Our end users liked the user-interface . . . and they're footing the bill."
- "They asked us to be on their advisory committee—we're helping them plan how to integrate campaign response modeling into their product."
- "They pretty much convinced us they were 'best-of-breed . . . .'"
- "They told us the whole thing could be done in three months."
- "We already had their database product, so we thought, 'What the heck?'"

These reasons range from acceptable to dangerous. After all, who could argue with impressed users willing to fund development (even though the tool's functionality might not meet these users' needs)? And it's certain that, after they've approved the CRM business plan, executives will want to know when you'll be finished and three-month delivery could make you a hero. As for competitive pressures, it's a worthy excuse, but are you sure you know what your competitor means by CRM?

Allowing technology to drive CRM is known as the "bottom-up" approach. Usually this involves one organization, or even an individual manager, who decides to go it alone, allowing a CRM software tool or a specific functional goal to define the CRM deliverable. The justification for bottom-up CRM is usually the time required by more rigorous, requirements-driven planning.

The risks inherent in bottom-up development, however, are far more serious than the rewards:

- Limited consensus about CRM goals risks spending of money on low-priority capabilities.
- Subjective interpretation of the importance of the given functionality invites rework and wasted resources.

- Lack of integration with other technologies or CRM projects results in either throwaway work or cumbersome after-the-fact integration.
- Dependence on specific product features, which might or might not meet additional business or growth needs, jeopardizes broader CRM adoption and growth.

Although it might be tempting to espouse the well-worn aphorism "If you build it, they will come," the truth is that if you build it, they probably won't even notice. After all, how much of your company's software products have ended up as shelfware? Bottom-up CRM development means CRM in a vacuum, a project not requested by or socialized to the business.

Requirements-driven CRM, on the other hand, establishes a level of cross-functional consensus in which people participate from the beginning of the CRM program and thus feel they have a say. The fact is, when choosing your CRM technology, there's simply no substitute for allowing structured requirements to dictate your technology decision. Yes, it takes longer than the knee-jerk development with the tool du jour. But the alternative is much riskier, and examples abound of CRM systems that never delivered the goods.

Maintaining a Customer Focus: Requirements-Driven Product Selection

Although requirements-driven technology selection is definitely a CRM best practice, the way to go about it differs, depending on the type of CRM you're planning to do. Purists would argue that CRM should always be aligned to corporate strategic objectives, but rigorously planning a straightforward CRM point solution around corporate strategy might nevertheless be overkill. After all, simply deploying sales force automation to your national salespeople need not map back to your CEO's latest state-of-the-company address.

As we discussed in Chapter 7, having a vision for the breadth of your eventual CRM functionality is an important step in moving forward. Have a CRM strategy, and you'll know the answer to key development questions, such as "Will this CRM system be cross-functional—touching more than one organization—or will it be a point solution for a single department's focused needs?" As with the business case, the answer to your question will help you in understanding the right technology choice and what your company will need to do in order to implement it.

Although critical, simply having a list of business requirements is nevertheless not enough information to begin evaluating CRM technologies. Business requirements should drive a series of functional requirements. The difference between the two is that although a business requirement describes the customer-focused "need, pain, or problem" CRM must solve, a functional requirement describes how to solve it. And it is the definition of these functional requirements that will make your technology choices much clearer. Figure 8-1 shows the progression.

A customer-focused business strategy drives a series of CRM requirements (e.g., "The ability to track success of target marketing campaigns"). These requirements in turn elicit specific functional capabilities (e.g., "campaign response modeling"). And, as we'll see, when the functionality is understood, a list of products can be mapped to each specific function.

Defining CRM Functionality

As the requirements define the "what," functionality defines the "how." Interestingly enough, so does your business process. Indeed, the best way to identify your functionality is to map out your business process and identify the functions within it. Each function should map back to a business requirement.

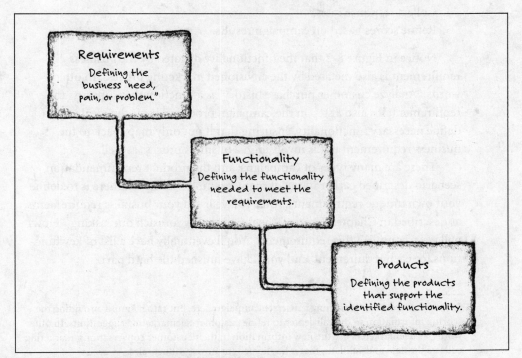

Figure 8-1: Requirements driving technology

The key question to ask when defining necessary functionality is "What aspect of our customer-focused processes do we need to support with technology?"

To illustrate how this works, consider the following example. A major bank was discovering that many of its customers did business with other financial institutions and already had the product being marketed. If the bank's customers didn't opt for the first marketed alternative, telemarketers would have the option, depending on the customer's interest level, to make subsequent recommendations. The bank decided to use CRM to generate a list of five different product recommendations for each customer, based on that customer's likelihood to buy them.

For this to work, the process had to involve these steps:

1. Analyze customer purchase history to understand the most frequently purchased products by other "like" customers.
2. Score the likelihood that a customer will buy an individual product.
3. Communicate resulting customer list and product scores to call center application system.
4. Collect response rates.[1]
5. Refine scores based on campaign results.

Notice in Figure 8-2 that the functionality dictated by the business requirement is also dictated by the envisioned marketing process. In other words, "Analyze customer purchase history" is a function that supports the requirement; it's also a step in the campaign process. This is the ideal way to define necessary functionality, ensuring that it not only maps back to the business requirement but is involved in a business process as well.

There are many types of campaigns, and the product recommendation scenario described earlier is one of many examples. The point here is to define your own unique requirements. After you've listed your business requirements, as described in Chapter 7, record the functionality for each one, asking, "How will we accomplish this requirement?" You'll eventually have a list of key functions for each requirement, and you'll have finished the hard part.

---

1. Note that we aren't launching a discrete campaign here, but rather simply providing the scoring information to the call center to refine customer telemarketing suggestions. In other words, as telemarketers use the new information in their customer conversations, marketing collects the data and validates that it has helped improve product sales.

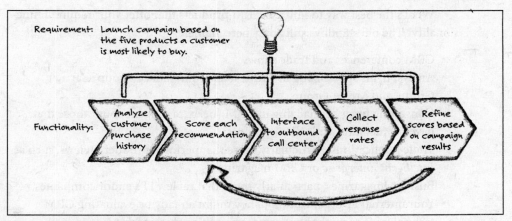

Figure 8-2: Requirements + process = Functionality

Narrowing Down the Technology Choices

When you've identified the necessary functions, you're ready to map the functions to the candidate technologies by answering the question, "Is there a CRM tool that can perform each of these core functions?"

Knowing the answer to this question is only part of the story. If indeed products offer all required functionality, is the functionality available "out of the box," or does the product require some level of customization?

Also, it's likely that whatever products best map to the necessary functionality won't all do so in the same way. For instance, one CRM product might use affinity analysis to score product recommendations, and another might use a regression algorithm. Although you might not have a preference about which data-mining algorithms are used, scoring which functions are most important to your business requirement will be helpful. This way, as you evaluate different tools, you can map their strengths and weaknesses back to the most critical functionality needs.

Another reason to score different functions is that the CRM tool might not provide all the functions you have. Can your requirement—and your process—do without a function? Are you willing to custom-build the function into the CRM package (most CRM tools support custom functions). Or, are you prepared to change your process to match the tool's explicit workflow? And what about the product's overall usability? Even if it meets *all* the functional requirements, business users should be willing to adopt it. In the past five years, companies have been grappling with similarly difficult give-and-take as they have evaluated their ERP systems and face similar dilemmas with CRM.

What's the best way to find the CRM products that offer your required functionality? The old standbys still apply here, namely:

- CRM conferences and trade shows.
- Analyst firms specializing in CRM, such as the Yankee Group, Gartner Group, and META Group.
- Consulting firms specializing in CRM (be extra diligent about those that have partnerships with CRM vendors).
- Trade publications, particularly those that perform product reviews, such as *Intelligent Enterprise* or *CRM* magazine.
- Business magazines, particularly those that review IT vendor companies.
- Your internal IT organization (They might already be evaluating CRM technologies or might have access to additional research.)
- Trade shows or other industry events.
- Vendor seminars.
- CRM Web site. (For a list of CRM publications and Web sites, see the Further Reading section at the end of the Handbook.)

When you begin assembling a short list of CRM vendors, a good idea is to get your IT department involved if you haven't already. Not only will IT staff understand product technical features and standards, but they'll also be able to offer guidance on how a given product fits into your company's systems and data management environments. And because IT provides corporate-level support, IT staff might have insight into whether products with similar capabilities have already been evaluated by another organization within the company, or whether other projects need similar CRM capabilities.

After you have finished narrowing down your product choices and have arrived at a short list of vendors, you should seriously consider formalizing IT's involvement in the project. Up until now, you might have chosen to involve key IT players, or even the CIO in CRM strategy development or planning activities. IT's participation in vendor technology discussions is now imperative. If your choice comes down to two vendors, the one that most closely aligns with your existing technology infrastructure should be declared the winner.

Defining Technical Requirements

Although functionality should be your paramount consideration in choosing a CRM tool, you should also list your technical requirements to ensure the product will work in your company's specific environment. Such requirements can be broken down into a variety of areas and even scored, based on the degree of alignment with your corporate IT infrastructure.

The following areas include examples of corresponding technical requirements, along with sample requirements to illustrate the boundaries of each:

- *Integration and connection requirements.* Ability of the tool to integrate into the company's unique technology infrastructure from a hardware, software, and networking perspective. Integration requirements might include:
  - Support of Windows 98 client OS
  - Ability of the CRM product to interact with your existing database systems (Oracle and DB2)
  - Conformance to company-sanctioned open standards (XML and CORBA)
  - Ability to interface with in-house computer telephony package to support CSR-specific call routing and Web-based live chat
  - Ability to integrate with other applications (e.g., SAP)
  - Product extensibility and customizations features
  - Inclusion of a published data model that can be customized and extended to meet business-specific data requirements
- *Processing and performance requirements.* Indicate the product's ability to support and control required operations:
  - Number of transactions the product can support (upper limit)
  - Data volumes the product can support
  - Number of concurrent users that can be supported
  - Support of data and system backups
  - Synchronization strategy and effort required
  - Ability to send and receive data to and from the data warehouse (and whether during production or after hours)
- *Security requirements.* The product's ability to limit user access:
  - Provision of usage and access reporting on a per-user basis
  - Provision of access restrictions on a per-user basis
  - Usage management at the individual, departmental, or CRM screen level
  - Password encryption
  - Ability to provide limited data access to non-company users (e.g., customers and suppliers)

- *Reporting requirements.* The product's versatility to provide company and user-requested information:
    - Ability to push pre-formatted reports to end users
    - Ability for end users to perform ad hoc reporting
    - Allowing for end-user creation of local (client-based) canned reports
    - Ability for end users to extract data for local analysis
- *Usability requirements.* Enabling end users to easily and intuitively accomplish required tasks:
    - Ability for end users to have a custom home page ("myCRM")
    - Ability for end users to seamlessly access other corporate systems through a common CRM portal
    - Ability to customize online help screens with application-specific information
    - Ability to perform screen-prints
    - Ability to display graphics, pictures, and photographs
- *Function-enabling features.* The way in which the product provides certain required functionality:
    - A workflow management capability, including the support and automation of user-defined workflows
    - An e-mail response engine able to route incoming e-mails to specific CSRs
    - Predictive modeling functionality (e.g., to apply a customer's propensity to buy to list-generation activities)
    - Support of wireless access to CRM server
- *Performance requirements.* Laying out acceptable turnaround time for CRM activities or reporting response time:
    - Ability to provide 30-second or less reporting-response time for Internet users
    - Ability to generate campaign lists, irrespective of attributes, within one hour or less
- *Availability requirements.* Indicating the acceptable level of system availability, for example:
    - Product and accompanying database both available from 8 a.m. to 8 p.m. seven days a week
    - Inclusion of self-diagnostic tools that can alert system administrators to slow response or likely downtime

- Accommodation of different time zones if your company is geographically dispersed
- Web page availability 24-by-7

After you've covered the necessary bases in terms of both functional and technical requirements, you'll be ready to have a substantive conversation with your prospective CRM vendors, not just about how great their tools are, but also about how well they correspond with your unique needs.

Talking to CRM Vendors

Anyone who has dealt with technology vendors understands that the experience can range from enlightening to embarrassing. Although it's rarely a waste of time to listen to a short vendor presentation, the time adds up when you're intent on researching as many vendors as possible in an effort to choose the best-of-breed tool.

After you understand your required CRM functionality and technical requirements, arriving at a short-list of vendors that can support them is relatively easy. The trick is to understand not only whether their CRM products can do what you need them to do, but also whether the vendor can support its toolset and advise you on the best ways to implement and deploy it.

The interview questions listed in Table 8-1 represent the core areas to evaluate when talking to a vendor. The list features examples of critical questions you can customize or supplement according to the needs of your specific environment. Having a structured set of questions will help you gauge not only whether the vendor can deliver the software code, but also whether it can be a partner for the long haul.

When you're certain the CRM product can deliver the required functionality, two reality checks remain: price and contract negotiations and reference checks. Assume that neither will be as easy as it seems.

Negotiating Price

As with a new car, few companies purchase a CRM product without a test drive. Your vendor should offer an evaluation copy of its software so your CRM team can install and use the product.[2] Such trials usually last between

---

2. Depending on the complexity of the software product and it implementation requirements, a vendor might be unwilling because of the consulting costs incurred. Some vendors will be willing to offer a proof-of-concept that allows a prospective customer to try out the software with a limited scope. Such a proof-of-concept has a price tag covering the vendor's costs, but the charges can then be applied to the product's purchase price if the proof-of-concept is successful.

Table 8-1: Questions to Ask Your CRM Vendor

The Domain	The Question to Ask	Why You Should Ask It
Vendor Expertise	What major CRM functions does your product suite provide?	The vendor should be able to provide a good description of every product or module and its relative functionality. It should be clear whether the product represents a CRM suite that provides a range of functions or whether the product is a CRM point solution.
	In cases where you don't offer certain functionality, do you partner with other companies/products?	The vendor's strategic alliances can be important clues about areas where the product might be weak. If you project needing additional functions not offered by the vendor, make sure you understand the details of its alliances with other CRM vendors.
	Can you describe how your product has evolved?	Although it probably won't change things, understanding where the CRM vendor got its start is always helpful. This doesn't mean the company that started as a call center software tool can't provide robust sales-force automation functionality, but it does suggest where the company's core competency might still lie.
Technical Functionality	Is your product Web-based, and if so, how?	As described in Chapter 4, Web-based CRM access means all relevant data is accessible via the Internet. For those with Internet access, this is definitely the most flexible and secure choice. However, for

The Domain	The Question to Ask	Why You Should Ask It
		remote users who don't always have Web access, a practical solution might be using applications on their local PCs and subsequently submitting their changes to a central CRM server. Your requirements will tell you which is right for you.
	Has your product dealt with customer data volumes similar to ours?	All the functionality in the world and a really slick user interface don't matter if you have 50 million customers and the vendor's biggest reference has 5 million.
	Has your product dealt with transaction volumes similar to ours?	You might not have projected the number of daily transactions you expect your CRM product to handle, but ask the vendor to describe the upper limit.
	Does your software work with our existing relational database or data warehouse product?	Many CRM products can still only access data one or two database products. Some even have their own proprietary databases, which means you might have to migrate data back and forth into their database.
	How do you migrate data from your product into other tools, and vice versa?	Understand how the product interfaces with other enterprise systems such as ERP or accounting packages. Does a custom program need to be written, or is a predefined utility available? Does the vendor

(continued)

Table 8-1: Questions to Ask Your CRM Vendor (*continued*)

The Domain	*The Question to Ask*	*Why You Should Ask It*
		link to other systems (e.g., SAP, Oracle, Remedy, etc.)? Is it even possible?
	Do you allow end users to extract data so they can use it locally?	Does the product let users manipulate data without being connected to the CRM server? When this is a requirement, understand whether the product has synchronization features.
	Can you provide a published data model that explains all the data?	Sometimes product vendors keep their data models confidential, requiring you to purchase additional product licenses to access their CRM data. Access to the product's underlying data model will allow you to extract the data for other uses, using software you already have.
	Is there a development toolbox that includes industry or functionally oriented templates?	Development templates speed up implementation by providing programmers with packaged software they can customize rather than writing it from scratch.
	Does the product provide data mining or other advanced analytics?	Although you might not need it now, the fact that the product offers data mining means its functionality goes deep and the vendor has spent time developing advanced functions (or money purchasing them). Either way, data mining capabilities are a good safety net.

The Domain	The Question to Ask	Why You Should Ask It
Implementation Support	What is your product's average implementation time?	The vendor might lowball this number, so beware. Also, understand the difference in time estimates for out-of-the-box configuration versus customization.
	Does your company supply implementation help, or do you rely on partners to perform the work?	Some CRM vendors are product companies, meaning they partner with systems-integration or consulting companies who implement their software for customers. Others have in-house consulting organizations that perform implementation duties. Understand who will be doing the work.
	In cases where you rely on consulting partners, who are your partner companies?	Many CRM vendors have long lists of integration partners, allowing you to select the best-qualified company. Understand the vendor's product certification process and know the skills you'll be required to invest in. And beware the vendor that has only one company experienced in customizing their product. You'll be at their mercy.
	In cases where you rely on consulting partners, where are those companies? Where would their staff originate?	With a third-party implementation company, knowing where the company's resources originate will tell you whether you need to factor "travel and expenses" into your development budget and will help you better estimate resource costs.

(continued)

Table 8-1: Questions to Ask Your CRM Vendor (*continued*)

The Domain	The Question to Ask	Why You Should Ask It
	After development begins, what do you see as your ongoing role with our project?	Does the vendor support the development process like it supports its product? If the vendor recommends an alliance partner to assist you in implementation, make sure everyone understands the vendor's ongoing role.
References	What percentage of your existing customers use the software out-of-the-box versus requiring it to be customized?	Beyond understanding whether the vendor sees its product as a plug-and-play or highly customizable, you should understand the relative usage environments between the two. (Ask the actual references the same question.)
	How many other installations of your product are there in our industry? Can you name some?	Although its ability to meet your specific functionality is more important that its experience in your industry, the vendor's penetration of your particular sector increases the likelihood its representatives understand your particular business problems—particularly valuable after implementation begins.
	Can you provide us with the names and phone numbers of three references that have used your product and have deployed some level of functionality?	Don't be shy, and don't settle for the logos on the marketing glossies. Get three names and phone numbers of customer representatives who are either managing CRM projects or using an in-production application.

three and six months to give the company considering the purchase time for the following:

- Verify that the promised functionality actually exists
- Ensure that the product works in the specific technical environment
- Gauge the product's usability
- Verify that the product works with its data

A critical point here is that verifying that the functionality exists is one thing, but discovering how the product actually offers the functionality it claims to have is another. Two products might each claim to score campaigns, for example, but one might involve significant end-user input while the other is more automated.

Likewise, ensure that the tool can work with your data. Many companies ignore this, but it can be a make-or-break proposition for a CRM program. There might be data problems such as inconsistent formatting that preclude the CRM product from working correctly. Or the product might require certain data, such as cleansed address fields or access to customer support history, that your current systems simply can't furnish. Depending on the severity of these data problems, you might want to delay the purchase of any CRM tool until they are resolved.

Even if you're not comparing different CRM tools, actually using evaluation software is a good idea in order to determine whether the per-user cost of the tool is worth the value it provides. For instance, say you're a financial services firm that has just acquired an Internet bank. You're evaluating a call center CRM product that allows seamless integration of customer data from across systems so your CSRs have a complete customer profile at the time of the customer's call. The product costs $1000 per end-user seat.

One of your evaluation goals should be to verify that the product is able to truly deliver efficiencies that equal or exceed its cost. In other words, if you have 300 CSRs across the country, will the resulting productivity gains be worth $300,000 to your company? The tool might require a CSR to perform other tasks to get the correct data, mitigating the time saved. Likewise, poor performance might slow down a CSR's ability to resolve a problem. Only by installing the product and testing it can you truly know what to expect from it.

Plan a product evaluation. If you have the time, combine the evaluation with a proof-of-concept that can deliver sample functionality, and demo the functionality to stakeholders for approval. Consider the software evaluation a separate project with metrics that mirror your expectations for the tool after it's in production. Although you won't be working with all of your data or submitting transactions on the scale you will after the tool is in use, your development team might be able to simulate workloads and extrapolate performance numbers based on more limited testing. At worst, the evaluation will save you time during the actual development project; at best, it could save you many hours and untold expense on a product that doesn't cut the mustard.

Checking References

There's always one vendor who cites nondisclosure agreements with its customers as a reason not to name names. Indeed, many CRM users consider CRM a strategic weapon and might be unwilling to go on record about what they're doing. In cases where the vendor uses this as an excuse but has cited an anonymous client, ask to have a conversation with someone on the vendor's account team who can describe the application in general terms. Whatever the case, red-flag the CRM vendor who cannot provide you with at least three on-the-record references.

The referenced customers should have experience developing a project with the tool, as well as in deploying the tool to end users. Ideally, they will be in a similar industry or be using the tool in the same capacity—for instance, specifically for eCRM—for which your company is considering it. The actual reference should be a development manager or executive who has seen the software product deliver what it promised (or not).

When you reach a reference, you could probably talk all day about CRM. If there's time, discuss what led to their decision to purchase the product in question, and ask about how the reference uses the product's key features. However you frame the reference call, remember the following five "core" questions:

1. What was the vendor's original estimate of implementation time and did your experience reflect it? Were there any surprises?
2. How many people participated in implementation (total from both IT and the line of business)?
3. What was the biggest unforeseen challenge of the implementation? (For example, data sourcing complexity? End-user training? Business process/tool conflict?)
4. What has been the vendor's (or integrator's) ongoing involvement?
5. What is your expectation for self-sufficiency with this product?

These questions are open-ended and safe. They invite interpretation, which engages the reference and encourages further explanation. And if the answer to the final question reflects a short-term expectation for self-sufficiency, you're on the right track.

Other Development Approaches

So far this chapter has assumed you'll be purchasing a software product to implement your CRM program in-house. However, not all companies approach their CRM requirements this way. Many of them choose alternative methods of developing and deploying CRM for a variety of reasons.

Homegrown CRM

Although most CRM development efforts involve some level of software customization, be it to integrate the call center CRM system with marketing's campaign management software or to change data names, they begin with a core product that provides the foundation from which to customize. However, some enterprising companies have decided to develop CRM software from scratch.

Companies develop their own homegrown CRM systems for the following four main reasons:

1. They require core CRM capabilities that didn't exist at the time they were needed.
2. They perceive retail packages as being too expensive.
3. The combination of core functions they require is too specialized for a single CRM product.
4. They want assurance of a unique solution—one competitors cannot use and vendors cannot reference.

Although you might roll your eyes at the conference presenter who claims to have been "doing CRM before CRM was even invented," many companies who have mature data warehouse and business intelligence environments have gradually evolved existing customer-focused applications into tailored CRM platforms. Such capabilities as customer profiling, campaign planning, product affinity analysis, and product recommendation engines might have been deployed to a number of organizations across the company at different times.

But because all of the data is centralized on a data warehouse, these companies have formalized their processes for integrating and deploying customer data to provide the business with a 360-degree view of its customers. An effective enterprise portal that allows businesspeople a common view of the applications and data means the applications themselves can be distributed and developed at separate times and no one need know.

It's rare, but some companies simply believe that—given CRM's strategic importance—they have no choice but to build their own CRM environments to maintain their differentiation and their confidentiality. A marketing product manager at a large wireless phone company recently explained why his company elected to build its own CRM system:

> The moment we bring in a vendor to customize its software to support our campaigns is the moment that we release our secrets to the competition. Simply put, we sell a commodity product. Our company's *only* differentiator is in our campaign strategies. Call me paranoid, but I've seen it too many times. I can't help but expect a CRM vendor to tell our competitors what we're doing so they can sell to them too, and to use us as a reference. This defeats the entire purpose of automating campaign management, which we're doing to thwart our competitors—not to clue them in.

You might not share this manager's degree of paranoia, or your CRM initiative might not be as mission-critical. If you don't plan to build your CRM solution from scratch, at least gauge your vendor's willingness to sign a nondisclosure agreement barring written and verbal discussion of your company's activities without your permission. And when your CRM program is a smashing success, be willing to serve as a reference yourself.

Using an ASP

Up until now, this chapter has assumed CRM at your company will be an "on premise" solution, that is, built and maintained in-house—as most CRM systems still are. This decision relies on the existence of core infrastructure components, including sufficient hardware and software, networking or Internet capabilities, specific skill sets in both the business and technology areas, and a development process robust enough to deliver a requirements-driven program. This is easier said than done for many companies who lack the infrastructure but desperately need to support their customer loyalty or retention programs. They need CRM fast, faster than the time it will take to hire the necessary staff and install the necessary technology. And application services providers (ASPs) are an increasingly popular alternative.

"ASP" is often used as a synonym for outsourcing, but ASPs develop, deliver, and maintain packaged software applications on behalf of their client companies, using the Web as the primary deployment mechanism. Although the traditional outsourcing companies specialized in running their customers' "commodity" systems—billing and human resources being two classically out-sourced systems—nowadays ASPs are bidding on more strategic technology solutions.

There are two principal types of ASPs:

1. Web-hosting firms providing customers Internet access plus a range of services, not to mention a robust technology infrastructure.
2. Application providers offering customers access to specific products and product packages.

Many pioneering ASPs began as small specialty shops focusing on specific technologies, most of which are complex enough to warrant specialized support. However, big guys like EDS and Oracle have jumped into the ASP game, offering everything from Internet service to accounts receivable to campaign management. Moreover, the CRM vendors are busy bolstering their own data centers so they can hang out the ASP shingle themselves.

Why the rush to become an ASP? Web delivery capabilities, for one, are making outsourcing a more realistic choice. End users accessing CRM from a browser interface need not know whether the customer knowledge is originating downstairs in the data center or three states away at a company they've never heard of.

And CRM is the darling of the ASP community. The Gartner Group has forecast that ASPs will deliver 40 percent of all applications by 2003. Likewise, Forrester Research has estimated that 64 percent of all ASP revenues come from CRM applications. With the CRM adoption rate growing exponentially, CRM outsourcing is here to stay.

The reasons companies elect to outsource their CRM implementation to ASPs include

- *Robust technology infrastructure*: Companies defining themselves as ASPs must develop mature technology infrastructures that include robust servers, wide-area networking, operations and database software, application development technologies, and wireless client support for quick and thorough delivery of multiple software packages.

- *Speed of implementation*: Most CRM ASPs usually specialize in one or a handful of product packages; thus delivery processes are repeatable across customers, and customization occurs more quickly.
- *Expertise*: ASPs hire and train their staffs to become experts on specific CRM products. Because these staff members apply a CRM product to multiple user environments, they see the product's strengths and weaknesses and thus possess an intimacy with the product set that your IT department would struggle to replicate.
- *Service-level agreements (SLAs)*: Such contractual agreements establish clear reliability and availability requirements to which the ASP must adhere. (Many argue ASPs are more likely to stick with SLA terms than are internal IT organizations.)
- *Critical mass*: Not only is the product expertise more solid, but ASPs also have bench strength, meaning the likelihood of CRM specialist availability is higher. This is especially valuable for application maintenance and support—no more months spent searching for maintenance programmers—freeing your internal technical resources.
- *Scalability*: Need to add another 50 users to your CRM system? What about another half million customers to the database? Any systems programmer understands the technology ramifications of increased workloads or growing data volumes. Justifying, procuring, and installing new disk drives to a database server or new processors to your mainframe could take you weeks, or even months. With an ASP, you simply let the company know of your new requirement and then work together to schedule the enhancements. The ASP does the hard work, which is what you pay them for.
- *Economies of scale*: Many small to mid-size firms have legitimate need for costly products provided by the CRM and ERP vendors but simply cannot afford to purchase these products. The ASP buys the software and licenses it out to its customers, who effectively become end users. The cost is a fraction of what the customer might otherwise pay in software license and upgrade fees. Companies who could never fund a data center, let alone some of the key technologies necessary to enable CRM, allow ASPs to fill the often significant void. The ASP absorbs the high cost of systems administration and maintenance as well as the staff resources and skills necessary to keep the technical environment humming.
- *Complexity*: The best ASPs are greater than the sum of their parts. They transcend the collection of UNIX and NT servers, database products, and

CRM tools installed in their data centers and become solutions providers. These companies not only deploy and maintain your CRM program, they also provide critical data maintenance, system security, end-user support, Web access, and a variety of other nuts-and-bolts services that, when added up, do more than solve your business problem: They save you money.

But choosing an ASP is hardly a slam-dunk. Each ASP has its own technology specialty, rules of engagement, service levels, and risks. Table 8-2 lists some questions you should be prepared to ask the ASPs you're considering for CRM.

Table 8-2: Questions to Ask Your ASP

The Domain	The Question to Ask	Why You Should Ask It
ASP Expertise	Do you offer both packaged CRM suites and standalone CRM modules?	Often, companies need a subset of CRM functionality. Many ASPs require their customers to adopt an entire CRM suite. Other ASPs, offering standalone customer support, sales force automation, and contract management modules, allow their customers menu-based services.
	How many different CRM products do you offer?	ASPs specializing in CRM might offer a myriad of choices, whereas more general Web-hosting firms might offer only one or two. This is a double-edged sword: On the one hand, the more CRM products a company offers, the more choices you have. However, the ASP offering a dozen different packages might also be expecting too much from its staff in terms of skill sets and availability.

(continued)

Table 8-2: Questions to Ask Your ASP (*continued*)

The Domain	The Question to Ask	Why You Should Ask It
	What experience do you have in our specific industry?	The ASP that understands your business is the ASP that can understand customer data hierarchies, for instance, or customer-focused business processes unique to your sector.
	What are the boundaries of your services?	Many ASPs are simply nuts-and-bolts technology providers. If the ASP offers professional services staff, it can provide you with the full system lifecycle, from requirements gathering to end-user support.
	How solid is your company financially?	The financial health of an ASP is a lot more critical than that of your company's other suppliers. Find out how the ASP is funded and for how long.
Technical Functionality	How will you integrate your CRM environment with our legacy systems?	Understand not only how data propagation back and forth from the legacy systems will happen and how timely it will be. (Daily? Weekly?) Also understand the lag time between data provisioning and availability.
	Can we extract certain data back to our local server?	The ASP might not have the tools or processes that allow the manipulation or transfer of data outside of the services they provide.

The Domain	The Question to Ask	Why You Should Ask It
	What type of query and reporting functionality do you provide?	Although most ASPs provide some sort of canned reports, fewer provide actual ad hoc reporting capabilities. If this is a requirement, make sure the ASP understands that.
	Are there data capacity limitations?	Find out the ASP's data volume maximums. Is data capacity limited to a certain number of customers or products? Is there an upper limit to the amount of history the ASP can keep?
Application Support	What measures do you have in place to ensure the security of our data?	Although the risk of someone's blatantly sharing customer data with your rivals or other unauthorized parties is minimal, there should be written agreements in place to penalize the ASP for doing so.
	What type of reliability guarantee do you offer?	System up-time is critical in CRM environments, where delays can spell missed opportunities and lost revenues. Will the ASP provide 24-by-7 support? When the data is being loaded, will other data be available or will there be outages scheduled?
References	Can we speak to a few companies who have had similar customization needs with the products we're considering?	Try to talk to a few customers for whom the ASP has provided customization services to assess staff expertise as well as timely delivery.

Why build CRM yourself if an ASP can do it all for you? Companies fore-going the ASP route cite several valid reasons:

- *Frequently changing requirements.* Many companies who have deployed CRM are continually fine-tuning it and have set up schemes for ongoing end-user input. A constant stream of new requirements resulting in an updated system might be too much for an ASP who has defined certain standard functionality across its CRM systems and customer base.

- *Complexity and timeliness.* Indeed, by the time a company can translate its specific needs to an ASP, it might have been able to customize its CRM tool and have it deployed. So too, many companies insist on being able to test and run marketing campaigns "on the fly," whenever they want—a tall order for many resource-bound ASPs.

- *Integration with existing systems.* The number and complexity of a company's systems—both legacy systems and emerging technologies—can render data gathering and provision too complex and cumbersome for some ASPs.

- *Hostage-taking.* After a strategic CRM system is in the hands of an ASP, the balance of power shifts. Scary stories proliferate of outsourcers trying to change contract terms while in possession of mission-critical data. One good "hole" in the contract, and both you and your customers could be at the mercy of an unscrupulous hosting service.

- *Fear.* With all the efficiencies and speed that accompany the ASP model, some companies are still nervous about relinquishing their precious customer data into the hands of an outside company, no matter how strident the security policy. Plus, many companies who embraced ASPs early fear training the ASP, who can then repeat the development process for a competitor at a lower cost.

The best ASPs offer true solutions hosting, combining operational support, change management, and problem resolution for a range of software products gathered into an integrated technology architecture that aligns to your business needs. The problem resolution is so timely and end-user support so seamless your business can't tell the difference between the CRM provider and your internal IT department. They give you and your CIO peace of mind. And, most important, they free up your business to concentrate less on technology deployment issues and more on your customers.

A CRM Tool Selection Checklist for Success

When deciding on your CRM product, here are several things to keep in mind to ensure you're not wasting talent, money, and time:

- *Consider the team selecting the product.* As we'll discuss in Chapter 9, the diversity of the team evaluating CRM products against CRM requirements should be directly proportional to how cross-functional the CRM program will be. A group of managers choosing the tool based on its purchase price (versus its total cost of ownership) is as shortsighted as the programmers voting for one product over another because it uses Java beans. Everyone has a bias. Make sure your product selection team represents a variety of business requirements and functional preferences.

- *Be crystal clear about the requirements you would expect an ASP to fulfill and the services you would expect it to provide.* Draft your ideal service-level agreement first, and compare it to those of the ASPs you're considering. And don't be shy about proposing an incentive-based contract. So-called value-based pricing means the ASP receives a competitive rate, plus an incentive for offering unique functionality or improving business processes. If such a pricing scheme isn't established, the ASP's prices will rise but service levels remain the same. A pay-for-performance plan ensures the ASP will work hard to fulfill your requirements and be rewarded when they do.

- *If you are considering an ASP, consider why you're unwilling to invest the money instead into your IT department.* After all, although the ASP will surely provide business value, the money might be better spent shoring up a lagging IT infrastructure that can support CRM more cost effectively for the long-term.

- *Choose from the customer's viewpoint.* As you consider various tools and how they'll be used in the service of your customer-focused programs, examine particular product features and continually ask the question, "How will this capability enhance the customer's perception of us?" The tool generates call center scripts? *The customer will think we really know her!* It can dynamically route a high-priority trouble ticket to a field service agent? *Customers will appreciate our fast response time!* If a series of answers emerges for one product above all others, you've probably found your solution.

- *Avoid religion about consultants, either yours or the vendor's.* Many CRM vendors have established consulting partnerships, the advantage of which is that the consultants have likely been thoroughly trained on implementing the vendor's product. Don't assume these partner firms are your only choice. Many of the larger consulting firms train otherwise unqualified junior staff on technology development without context. Conversely, boutique consulting firms might lack the critical mass you need for speed. The evaluation methods you used to choose your ERP or Y2K consulting firm will be different for CRM: Take the time to interview a selection of firms based on a clear set of success metrics.

- *Don't rely on CRM technologies alone to address business improvements.* By its very definition, CRM is a solution that includes processes, data, technologies, skill sets, and strategy. If any of these is shaky, your CRM program might be at risk. After all, CRM is about changing business processes and ensuring happier customers, not about software. Expecting one product to solve all your problems can lead to failure.

Case Study: Harrah's Entertainment

Summary: Some people like gambling at those sprawling mega-casinos featuring frolicking dolphins, mile-high revolving restaurants, and pirates skirmishing outside the lobby. Others prefer doing their gaming where the staff greets them by name. There are no almost-extinct white tigers or rumbling volcanoes at Harrah's casinos, but there's something just as unique: true customer intimacy.

You check into your favorite Vegas hotel and decide to play a couple hands of blackjack before heading up to your room. You fish around in your wallet for fifty bucks and your frequent-player card. You hand both to a friendly dealer. Five minutes and a couple of good hands later, a "host" appears and hands you another room key and a pair of tickets. When you're ready, the host explains, he'll show you to your upgraded suite—which, by the way, is on the house, along with the tickets to the hottest show in town and a comp dinner at Napa, the restaurant with the best wine list in the state, if not the region.

A dream come true? Not for elite members of Harrah's Total Rewards program who gamble at the Rio. But Harrah's Entertainment, Inc. has gone beyond offering its high-value customers special perks and has institutionalized customer relationship management across its broad base of customers. Rejecting the flashy lures of its gaming competitors, Harrah's has instead embraced a customer loyalty program that's made it the envy of the industry.

WHAT THEY DID:

In the 1990s Harrah's began an expansion and acquisition strategy that included the Showboat casinos and the upscale Rio, expanding its market offerings in both the hotel and gaming businesses and more than tripling the number of its properties. As the company reached across different cities and markets—there are 21 Harrah's locations across the United States, from Las Vegas to Atlantic City and from Joliet, Illinois, to Tunica, Mississippi—it made the same assumption its competitors made: that each customer patronized a single casino. A little market research commissioned by senior management suggested Harrah's might not know all it needed to know about its growing customer base.

In 1994, Harrah's began building its Winners Information Network (WINet), with a business portal providing "seamless recognition" of customers across all Harrah's properties. The new technology initiative included the company's online Patron database as well as its marketing workbench, a Teradata system from NCR that ultimately provided an analysis platform for over 20 million guest accounts. Tools from Cognos and SAS provided a rich set of decision-support and data-mining capabilities. A seminal customer relationship management application, Offers, was built from scratch.

Its WINet system in place, Harrah's subsequently introduced a frequent-player card, announcing its Total Gold program in 1997. Indeed, the mix of database and application technologies earned Harrah's several patents—not to mention an escalating industry buzz.

The gathered data revealed significant findings about customers and their preferences. For one thing, Harrah's confirmed the suspicion that its most valuable guests often frequented several different properties, triggering the upgrade from Total Gold—specific to the Harrah's chain—to the Total Rewards program, encompassing Rio and Showboat properties. Total Rewards introduced Platinum and Diamond player levels, offering players incentives to consolidate their gaming and remain loyal customers.

Harrah's now knew what property a guest last visited, what events he attended, and what games he preferred on the casino floor. The company was able to differentiate "one-trip wonders"—gamblers who were valuable within a single casino visit—and conclude that guests who returned for a third visit were more likely to become loyal for life. In fact, the company found it was precisely the customers who visited multiple Harrah's properties who were the most loyal of all. Since the launch of Total Gold in April 1997, the number of customers visiting more than one Harrah's property has shot up 72 percent.

Such detailed customer knowledge has helped Harrah's refine its marketing processes. The company analyzes data in order to create special offers to discrete customer segments most likely to respond to them—for instance: play slots for one hour and get a 5 percent rebate. It can also predict a guest's adjusted trip value and project the profitability of her visits, allowing for more targeted mailings. After the company began customizing its offers, it witnessed an increase in the average customer's visit frequency in their Central Division from 1.2 to 1.9 times per month (see Figure 8-3).

The company also uses its data to determine additional services customers might prefer, often deciding to promote their hotel offerings to so-called non-lodgers so customers who routinely *play* at Harrah's might also *stay* at Harrah's.

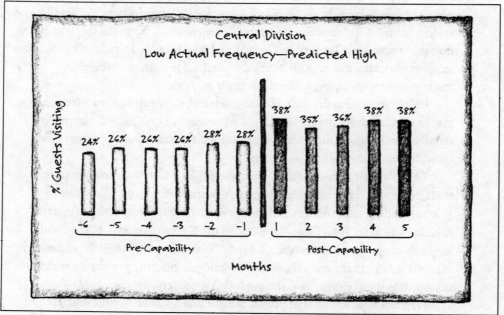

Figure 8-3: Increased frequency of visits after CRM (Courtesy of Harrah's Entertainment, Inc.)

THE CHALLENGES:

Notwithstanding a fortified IT infrastructure and advanced data analysis capabilities, Harrah's biggest challenge was convincing individual properties to believe in the newfound customer information enough to use it. At first they were reluctant. After all, since 1937, property management and casino staff had worn as a badge of honor their ability to remember regular customers' names and treat them well.

Harrah's corporate marketing department, however, convinced individual casinos that customer knowledge was in fact an extension of the customer service philosophy they were so proud of practicing. Over time, actual data proved to properties which of their customers were the most valuable and which product mixes (including games on the casino floor as well as hotel stays, entertainment events such as New Year's Eve shows, and player events such as poker tournaments) generated the most activity, and even helped them track the uplift in same-store sales. In effect, receiving regular customer-activity reports let casino staff be more customer-focused than ever.

GOOD ADVICE:

Same-store sales? Product mix? Profitability-per-visit? Harrah's managers sound more like a bunch of retailers than gaming industry execs. Indeed, Harrah's has exploited the data in their data warehouse not only to better understand the company's customers but also to understand overall corporate performance. The company has recently used customer-behavior and financial data from existing properties to plan product mixes and property configurations for newly announced locations, from where to position the buffet to how many and which types of slot machines will be on the casino floor.

Among other new findings, Harrah's has used data to determine specific configurations of new properties before they're even constructed. "The data warehouse has changed the way Harrah's considers its capital," says Monica Tyson, Harrah's Director of IT Development for data warehousing. "We're building a hotel twice as big as we'd planned, based on comparing current properties and their demographics."

THE GOLDEN NUGGET:

"We realized our core competency was in the relationships we create with our customers, and we wanted to expand that competency using automated tools," Harrah's CEO Phil Satre told *CIO* magazine by way of explaining technology as a strategic enabler. Harrah's continues to analyze customer information to drive new levels of detail, helping deliver one-to-one customer interactions with casino and hotel customers alike. The company's "Slots" project will allow it to analyze a player's "card in" and "card out" transactions at a slot machine, helping it understand customer behaviors in more detail. The company's Gold, Platinum, and Diamond player levels offer frequent players additional rewards for their loyalty. Evolving customer behaviors—and the ability to continue analyzing them—will help Harrah's further refine its product mixes, not to mention its customer interactions.

When a customer calls these days, a Harrah's customer service rep can identify who that customer is, his relative segment value, his last visit, and the promotion he's inquiring about, all while helping him reserve a hotel room. Not only has such CRM functionality increased customer loyalty and helped boost lower-tier customers' value, it has shortened the time the CSR spends on the phone with the customer, thus allowing the rep to handle a greater number of inquiries.

Indeed, Harrah's—winner of The Data Warehousing Institute's CRM Leadership Award and CIO's Enterprise Value Award—has kept its focus not on the vicissitudes of the database or even on CRM markets, but on its customers. "Our CRM system is really a holistic approach to our business," says Monica Tyson. "We didn't start out with the idea of building CRM—the business just drove the need for customer information."

As we've mentioned, such customer differentiation is at the heart of customer relationship management, and Harrah's had the foresight to harness best-of-breed technologies to make it happen. The catch? Harrah's began building its "Offers" CRM capability as part of its WINet program back in 1994, before the term even came into vogue. The company's management explains its foresight with characteristic customer focus: "Yes, it's home-grown," explains Tyson, "but in 1994 there was nothing out there called CRM that we could really use. We had no choice but to build it ourselves." A gamble, to be sure, but for Harrah's, being a CRM pioneer has paid off big time.

The Manager's Bottom Line

It's a tragedy in CRM when a company sanguine about its business requirements nevertheless skimps on CRM technology. The fact is, if your CRM program is a complex and multidepartmental customer-loyalty initiative, buying the cheapest CRM product on the market might not be the optimal choice.

More tragic, however, is the company that skipped the requirements piece altogether and went straight for the tool. One of the biggest business missteps is technology for technology's sake, and the tendency has become even greater to see everything through the rose-colored lens of the Internet. Although it's easy to assume this won't happen in your organization—after all, you have a pressing business need for CRM—technology-driven requirements are often the path of least resistance when it comes to demonstrating CRM's benefits and nabbing that all-important development budget. And wouldn't it be easy to get the vendor to help define the need?

Conduct individual interviews, hold informational luncheons, or get yourself on the agenda of the customer steering committee, but do what you must to encourage business people and subject matter experts to tell you what they need. Make sure executives are on the same page, and if they're not, be willing to educate them. Beware of using CRM as the proverbial "hammer looking for a nail," and focus on the real need, pain, or problem CRM can help remedy. Most important, keep your customer as the selection point every step of the way, from requirements definition through detailed product functionality and the implementation process, which we'll cover in the following chapter.

CHAPTER NINE

Managing Your CRM Project

hese days it's practically routine to pick up an industry
Ttrade magazine featuring a CRM case study on page 1.
Somewhere amidst the paragraph about the company's new
customer loyalty program and the part about sales uplift
increasing 200 percent, you'll find a sentence or two describing implementation.

No, CRM development isn't sexy, and yes, it's fraught
with hazards from technology glitches to hiring freezes, but
it's the hub in the CRM wheel when it comes to ensuring a
smooth rollout. The snazziest end-user interface and most
enthusiastic marketing staff will never compensate for the
CRM system that doesn't do what it's supposed to. Not to'
put too fine a point on it, the implementation project is a
critical piece of the CRM puzzle.

A Pre-Implementation Checklist

I spend most of my time these days evaluating how prepared companies are to launch their CRM programs, be
they departmental or enterprise-wide, single or multifunction. Sometimes this occurs at the requirements definition
stage, where there is uncertainty about the perceived need
and its implementation viability. Other times it involves
evaluating a company's existing infrastructure just prior
to implementation. What I do most is quiz key CRM
stakeholders about their existing environment from
both business and technology perspectives.

My company calls such evaluations CRM Readiness Assessment engage-
ments, but I like to consider them "premortems." After all, what's more valuable
than fixing problems before they occur? The best way to do this is to envision
possible outcomes based on current circumstances, using experiences gleaned
from successful CRM deployments. It's good old risk management, come home
to roost.

Table 9-1 lists a series of considerations to be aware of before moving
forward with CRM development. Make sure each of these items has been at
least considered at your company, and the more complex your intended CRM
program, per Table 9-1, the more mandatory it is that you resolve the issue
prior to beginning development.

Table 9-1: CRM Pre-Implementation Checklist

Evaluation Question	Explanation	Considered?
Have you prepared a CRM business plan?	We discussed CRM business planning in Chapter 7. Regardless of whether management requires such a document, it's a very good idea to have one that represents CRM's baseline.	✔
Do you know who your executive sponsor is and what she expects?	By the time you're ready to launch development, the CRM executive sponsor should be crystal clear. Moreover, her role in defining and validating requirements, managing executive expectations, and helping define success metrics should be well understood by all stakeholders.	
Have high-level business requirements been defined?	In CRM this activity should be separate from the formal development project for two reasons: business requirements will dictate whether the CRM program moves forward, and they require involvement from stakeholders who might not be available during implementation.	

Evaluation Question	Explanation	Considered?
Have success metrics been established?	How will you know if your CRM program has been a success? Although many companies don't require success metrics—like those we discussed in Chapter 7—to be implemented, they're an effective safety net for after the system is deployed.	
Has the project been funded?	No use planning an entire CRM program if only a mere proof-of-concept has been approved.	
Is there agreement on desired customer behaviors? Are the business functions slated to support these desired behaviors apparent?	Depending on the scope of your CRM program, you might include a description of desired customer behavior in your CRM business plan. Either way, building consensus on how you want customers to behave differently is important. For instance, if sales staff will be using CRM to manage the sales pipeline, it should establish the ideal response to an information mailing.	
Does each organization agree on a common definition of "customer"?	The marketing department of an automobile company might consider a "customer" to be a dealer, but the call center might consider it to be a driver. Have consensus on this and other key definitions before you begin.	
Can you map the desired functionality to data requirements?	Customer data is complex more often than it's straightforward. This usually means defining data requirements along with business requirements. At some point you'll need to know whether customer data is necessary and from what system it will originate. A firm	

(continued)

Table 9-1: CRM Pre-Implementation Checklist (*continued*)

Evaluation Question	*Explanation*	*Considered?*
	understanding of the level of customer data—account, household[1]—is also critical.	
Do you suspect that external data will be necessary?	Purchasing data from an external source such as Dun & Bradstreet, Axciom, Data Quick, or Experian might not initially be a high priority, but it can supplement customer profiles with such indicators as number of family members, estimated income, household-level psychographics, ZIP code breakdowns, real estate information, and other attributes that can reveal customer behaviors and preferences.	
For customization, does the current workstation development environment support the CRM product?	What type of workstation configurations does your CRM tool's development environment require? Additional development tools (e.g., Microsoft's Visual Studio) or hardware (e.g., database servers) might be necessary to correctly customize the CRM environment.	
Have you identified the other applications or systems with which the CRM product must integrate?	There should be an up-front understanding of the impact of CRM on other corporate systems and of how the data will move between systems effectively. In addition, staff members whose systems will be touched by CRM should be notified of the pending integration requirements.	

---

1. The practice of "householding" organizes individual consumers into the households in which they live. Although the term normally applies to the residential market, business householding groups various organizations of a business customer into a common hierarchy. The challenge of householding is getting everyone to agree on the definition of a household.

Evaluation Question	Explanation	Considered?
Have the organizational or political barriers to rolling out CRM been identified? Have they been resolved?	Yes, it's a loaded question. (See the end of this chapter.) No, it's not meant to point fingers, but to establish up-front what the tactics will be when questions of ownership or disagreements about functional priorities rear their heads. An influential executive sponsor might be able to resolve such issues before they arise.	
Have you truly defined your privacy policy?	Regardless of whether your CRM program will be Web-based, understand your company's boundaries for using data about your customers. CRM must not only adhere to a corporate privacy policy; it should also be the flagship example of the company's *behavior* around customer data. See Chapter 10 for more about handling privacy.	

The most valuable feature of a "premortem" exercise is that it's a lot easier to give bad news before disaster strikes than to say "I told you so" after the fact—and after the money has been spent. CRM assessment findings can alert the business sponsor to potential roadblocks. Such findings allow CRM team members to fix problems proactively rather than pointing fingers after the CRM project has failed, as 70 percent of all CRM projects allegedly do.

Ideally, the answer to each of the above questions will be "yes," with consensus on how each issue will be handled when it's encountered. At the very least, the CRM team should be aware of each issue and prepared to deal with it when it inevitably comes up.

The CRM Development Team

CRM is big. It has captured the attention and imagination of corporate executives. Marketing VPs are betting their jobs on it, CIOs are asking their staffs to formulate CRM policies, and CEOs are creating job roles such as "Chief Customer Officer" that not only embrace CRM but depend on it.

Hopefully by now your company has adopted a customer-focused strategy and is putting in place the inevitable customer-focused programs and accompanying organizations. This often means organizational change: product managers have become "segment managers," spearheading customer segments irrespective of the products and services within them, and CSR job definitions are being continually modified as companies better understand customer channel usage and interaction preferences.

In addition to the broader organizational and cultural changes that accompany an evolving customer focus, CRM calls for specific implementation roles and responsibilities. In many cases, these job roles are new; in others, existing functions play key parts in CRM development.

Table 9-2 lists the core job functions within a CRM development team. Make sure you've accounted for each of these roles before embarking on a development project, and understand the skills from both inside and outside the company might be necessary to fill these positions.

Table 9-2: Core CRM Development Roles

Job Role	Description
Business Sponsor:	The business sponsor might serve across a single CRM project or across the entire program. His main role is to establish the vision, articulate overall goals and objectives, set the tone for the project team, and serve as a tiebreaker for implementation issues. The business sponsor often funds the initial CRM application. The more departments CRM spans, the greater the level of authority the sponsor should have.
CRM Steering Committee:	For cross-functional or enterprise CRM initiatives where implementation must be prioritized, a committee of decision-makers familiar with the "pain points" CRM can address should convene on a regular basis to provide new requirements, prioritize proposed improvements, and communicate key corporate initiatives.

Job Role	Description
Implementation Project Manager:	This person's job is to ensure that the requirements defined by the business sponsor and steering committee dictate the functionality to be implemented. The implementation project manager oversees the day-to-day implementation activities, tracks status, and updates the business sponsor on current issues.
Lead Developer:	The lead developer should manage the technical development and customization of the CRM product as it relates to the requirements. She should participate in CRM technology selection (see Chapter 8) and hire the appropriate developers to implement the CRM toolset.
Database Developer (and team):	The database developer should lead the necessary data integration, regardless of whether it is operational or analytical CRM. Often this means working with the company's data warehouse and its development team. In other cases, an understanding of key company source systems and how to capture their data is mandatory, requiring a separate team of database administrators and data "extraction" experts.
Front-end Developer (and team):	Depending on the chosen CRM product, programming is needed to develop or customize the end-user interface.
Subject matter experts (SMEs):	Critical to CRM success are subject matter experts—usually businesspeople from the department slated to use the CRM system after it's in production (for instance, a CSR or a sales manager). SMEs usually have strong ideas of what CRM should and shouldn't provide and should participate regularly in the development and testing of a CRM product.

Depending on the breadth and complexity of your CRM program, the job roles listed in Table 9-3 can also participate in CRM development.

Table 9-3: Optional CRM Development Roles

Optional Job Role	Description
Director of e-Business:	Your company might have a separate division dedicated to e-business that—despite the goals of CRM—must be involved to ensure the integration of, for instance, Web-based customer services with new CRM functionality.
Director of Data Warehousing:	If your company already has a data warehouse, you're ahead of the game. Existing data, development processes, source system knowledge, and metadata can all be used to get a jump-start on CRM development. Development teams might consider sharing resources in order to integrate the data warehouse as the de facto CRM analysis platform.
Chief Information Officer (CIO):	Due to the strategic nature of many CRM initiatives, it's politically if not technically wise to get approval and visibility from the CIO, who can usually facilitate activity with the IT department to ensure the appropriate systems and data resources. The CIO can also help socialize CRM as a corporate information resource.
Vice President of Strategic Planning:	In large companies, where this position exists, the Vice President of Strategic Planning should be able to share with the CRM team new business areas or product offerings the company expects to move toward, acquisition and partnership strategies, or existing products and services the company expects to abandon.
Chief Privacy Officer:	A new position in most companies, the Chief Privacy Officer should be able to provide details on corporate or regulatory policies regarding the use of customer data.

Each of these job roles can play an important part in CRM success, but simply understanding available skill sets can take you a long way in ensuring you can supplement your CRM team with outside help if necessary. Of course, such responsibilities as executive sponsor and the CRM steering committee should be filled by staff members having history with the CRM-related need, pain, or problem, as well as the authority to make decisions.

There are roles in CRM, however, particularly in technology implementation areas, where external experts should be leveraged. Consider the following questions as you decide whether to beef up your current staff with outside help:

- *How well do we know the CRM vendor's development environment?* It might serve you well to bring in an expert from the vendor's professional services staff or from a partner-integrator to provide knowledge transfer as development gets underway.
- *Are there critical one-time-only tasks that need completion?* For work that isn't likely to be repeated, such as configuring the data, a good consultant can shave days or even weeks off a project.
- *Are we comfortable that our requirements are well defined?* Sometimes an objective third party can find the "holes" in your requirements definition. This can help you avoid false starts—which could be a bargain at twice the price.
- *Can we get started with our existing staff?* It's often true that by the time you hire and train a full-time resource, a consultant could have jump-started a critical task and the entire project could be that much farther along. Everyone would rather hire permanent staff members who have skin in the game, but don't let principle usurp progress. Be willing to focus on the value of time to the business, and invest accordingly. This might mean hiring consultants who can hit the ground running.

Another important consideration in CRM staffing is the existence of a corporate program management office (PMO). First made popular by the aerospace industry, where complex projects were the norm, the PMO deconstructed a multifaceted system into manageable chunks involving repeatable tasks such as requirements definition, software coding, design, testing, validation, and software packaging. Each project chunk had its own project manager, goals, budget, and deliverable. Usually stationed in the IT organization, the PMO is dedicated to running corporate programs such as CRM so project teams can concentrate on succinct deliverables while the PMO ties them all together.

CRM programs are business integration projects whose scope is often corporate-wide (similar to enterprise ERP or supply chain management initiatives). Because CRM is driven by business requirements and involves the integration of business processes with technology and data, its complexity and organizational reach is usually greater than the straightforward application. The PMO formalizes tried-and-true practices that can be applied to CRM implementation. This not only ensures consistency across projects in a program but can also provide consolidated status reporting, often to executives, affording a level of visibility CRM could never otherwise generate.

CRM Implementation

As we discussed at the end of Chapter 7, CRM is usually a corporate program made up of many projects. For CRM point solutions that deliver finite functionality, one well-run project might be enough. Each CRM project should focus on implementing at least one defined requirement. Whatever the complexity, CRM development should be evolutionary and multi-tiered. Figure 9-1 describes a departmental CRM program and its associated requirements.

Understanding the complexity of your CRM program is critical to planning your CRM project. For instance, if CRM is an enterprise initiative, there could be dozens or even hundreds of discrete requirements across the corporation, rendering project-planning orders vastly more complex. If, as in Figure 9-1, the program is departmental, each requirement will eventually be deconstructed into a number of different functions, revealing its inherent complexity and the development resources it will require.

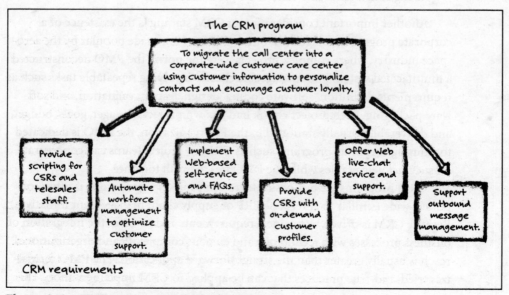

Figure 9-1: CRM program and requirements

Scoping and Prioritizing CRM Projects

Biting off all the requirements listed in Figure 9-1 would not only be dangerous; it could sabotage a company's entire CRM initiative. After you list your CRM requirements and have a good idea of their required functionality, the CRM business sponsor or steering committee can actually cast them into discrete projects.

Surprisingly, many CRM sponsors and project leaders forget this step and move straight toward trying to deliver the sum of all listed requirements in one fell swoop. Without scoping and prioritizing CRM projects, project managers lack overarching direction for prioritizing development activities, and application developers are free to arbitrarily add and change functionality during development. The results are usually disastrous. A scoping activity ensures that CRM projects are defined based on discrete requirements and are circumscribed around delivery expectations.

Requirements can evolve into individual projects based on demand urgency or perceived value or based on implementation complexity.

In the case of demand urgency, the customer support department might be overburdened. Thus the requirements pictured in Figure 9-1 might be prioritized in the following way:

1. Implement Web-based self-service and FAQs.
2. Offer Web live-chat service and support.
3. Support outbound message management.
4. Automate workforce management to optimize customer support.
5. Provide CSRs with on-demand customer profiles using existing data.
6. Provide scripting for CSRs and telesales staff.

If, on the other hand, implementation complexity is an issue, and the company needs a CRM "quick win," the following prioritization might make more sense:

1. Provide CSRs with on-demand customer profiles using existing data.
2. Automate workforce management to optimize customer support.
3. Provide scripting for CSRs and telesales staff.
4. Implement Web-based self-service and FAQs.
5. Support outbound message management.
6. Offer Web live-chat service and support.

Of course, politics figures into the decision on how to prioritize CRM projects. After all, if your customer-support vice president and call-center director are fighting over whether external data is necessary for really understanding customers, you might want to steer clear of providing CSRs with customer profiles until the issue is resolved—no matter how happy it would make the CSRs. Although formally rating the political landmines of every project could be overkill—not to mention highly subjective—knowing the political baggage that accompanies each potential project can serve as a tiebreaker.

When prioritized, a CRM requirement—or specific sets of related requirements—can be defined as an individual CRM project as shown in Figure 9-2.

Notice that in Figure 9-2 the Web-related development has been grouped into one project. This decision was based on practical reasons—specifically, the ongoing challenge of finding available Web-development staff within the company—as well as the estimated development complexity. Projects 1, 2, and 3 are all minimally related and can each leverage existing technologies and skill sets within the company.

Who should scope a CRM project? Ideally, business representatives and development staff should discuss each requirement and estimate its value-to-complexity ratio—the higher the value and the lower the complexity, the better—with the goal of prioritizing delivery on an ongoing basis. Most CRM scoping activities focus on delivering initial applications in order to hand over

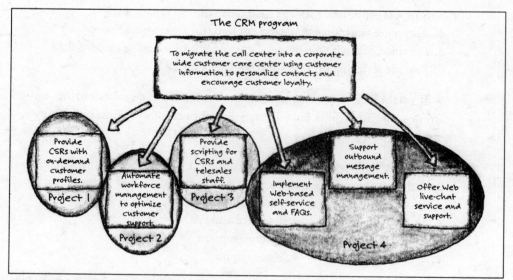

Figure 9-2: Delineating CRM projects

a "quick win" to the business. Applications with a high value-to-complexity ratio should rise to the top, and others can be prioritized accordingly.

The complexity metrics will vary according to the availability of your company's existing technology and staff resources. For instance, companies that already have robust customer databases won't rate customer profiling to be as complex as those who must start from scratch.

To correctly scope a project, simply rating its functional complexity is not enough. Ideally, you should understand the following:

- Specific technologies that will be involved in implementation
- Necessary skills to implement the project
- Number of staff members projected to work on the project
- Number of consultants needed to supplement in-house skills
- Realistic time frame necessary to deliver the first release
- Organizational boundaries and potential political issues

Scoping a CRM project prior to launching development mitigates the risks. For one thing, it's much easier to develop an accurate project plan that reflects realistic resource requirements, tasks, and time frames. Justifying headcount requests to management based on the project's true scope is also easier. Finally, hiring becomes more straightforward, because the true skills necessary to develop the CRM system are clearer than they would have been if you had simply gone straight to implementation. In fact, failure to thoroughly scope IT projects is one of the principal reasons behind many of their failures.

A CRM Implementation Roadmap

Even with the most straightforward CRM products, there's no such thing as cookie-cutter CRM. Development approaches can differ according to a company's approved development lifecycle, staff expertise, and IT standards.

Despite the possible differences in CRM implementation techniques, the following proven CRM development success metrics should define every CRM development project:

- *Incremental development.* Incremental or "building block" development means the company receives a defined amount of new CRM functionality on a regular basis. This is due not only to the inherent complexity of most CRM projects but also to the cultural issues surrounding its deployment (few organizations can absorb multiple major functional and process changes at once). Incremental CRM "releases" create a perception among business stakeholders and management of ongoing value. The alternative to incremental development is the "big-bang" approach of delivering a major new system and accompanying business changes all at once. The big-bang scenario almost always includes unpleasant surprises.

- *Requirements-driven development.* This means developers who are creating or customizing CRM functionality have an understanding of the overarching business requirements driving CRM, as well as the necessary functionality. Developing against requirements eliminates the notorious phenomenon of "scope creep" and ensures that users get what they're expecting.

- *Continuous user involvement.* Many CRM teams fall into the trap of involving business users at the beginning and end of CRM but rarely in the middle—during its development—where it's often critical. This means end users evaluating proofs of concept, validating data and business rules, weighing in on the contents of CRM training, and reviewing new screens or functionality prior to CRM deployment. It also means establishing regular communications between development, the business stakeholders, and the CRM business sponsor.

- *Implementation process rigor.* Even with other CRM best practices in place, such as comprehensive requirements and an enthusiastic business sponsor, CRM development must be planned and executed around a structured development process. This is to ensure that the PMO and project managers can anticipate and accurately scope various development activities. A sound development roadmap also ensures that programmers focus less on the implementation process and more on the actual delivery of valuable CRM functionality.

Figure 9-3 illustrates a CRM development roadmap that applies some of this structure.

Within the three main project phases—planning, construction, and deployment—the CRM roadmap features steps that contain a number of fixed and variable tasks:

Business Planning

CRM business planning involves many of the steps we discussed in Chapter 7. The most critical activity at the planning stage is defining CRM's overall

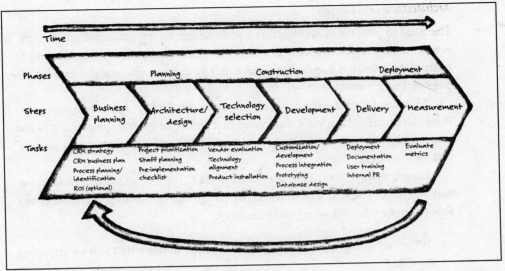

Figure 9-3: A CRM implementation roadmap

objectives—be they at the department or enterprise level—and delineating the requirements of each one. At the enterprise level, CRM business planning can involve the documentation of a corporate CRM strategy and the definition of the corresponding programs within it. At the department level, it can simply mean establishing the boundaries of a new CRM application.

At minimum, the business-planning phase should include the documentation of high-level CRM business goals in the form of a strategy document or business plan. This document will be leveraged at CRM's inception to gain executive consensus and sponsorship. It will be useful as a focal point for requirements-driven development and—after the CRM project has deployed an application—as a way to measure its results.

As Chapter 7 illustrated in the hotel reservation system discussion, part of business planning should identify the critical customer-focused business processes CRM will impact. Where they are straightforward, you might decide to redesign these processes as part of the planning activity. More often than not, companies planning their CRM projects realize that rather than simply automating existing business processes, they are defining those processes for the first time.

Depending on funding and sponsorship requirements, CRM business planning might optionally include ROI estimation or cost-savings projections.

Architecture and Design

The need to plan CRM architecture and to design an implementation strategy is what makes business sponsors and project leaders shudder and go straight to technology selection hoping for a miracle. The architecture and design step is painful, but it's worth it.

This step identifies the business processes the CRM product will support. It involves listing the specific functions that will need to be implemented—and how—ultimately giving you a good idea of CRM's impact on the organization and various technologies.

Inventorying the range of corporate areas CRM will affect, as well as those that will affect CRM, is a critical activity. At the end of this step you should be able to answer the following two questions:

1. What technologies and processes do we have in place that will be impacted by CRM?
2. What do we need that we don't have today in order for CRM to work?

Relative to existing technologies, try to project CRM's impact on your current systems. Your IT organization should be willing to do this—and in return it won't be blindsided by CRM after it's been developed. Impact analysis can mean listing current systems—for instance, you might need to know a bit about your company's existing call center operational system before you can understand how candidate CRM technologies will link to it. Indeed, a range of existing technologies, from ERP systems to current marketing automation technologies to handheld computers, are likely to be touched by CRM.

After the system impact of CRM is well understood, an IT architect can draft a CRM architecture illustrating the appropriate linkages. Integrating corporate systems that exchange data—even if the data isn't formatted consistently—is known as enterprise application integration (EAI). It's a truism of business that different corporate systems store and use data in different formats. The term EAI denotes the integration of often disparate corporate systems that routinely exchange or share data. This means moving data between systems, as well as transforming that data so these systems can understand it.

The letter depicted in Figure 9-4 is from an online retailer that is doing neither CRM nor EAI.

This letter was included in a product delivery and represents a veritable smorgasbord of CRM don'ts. The first one is that the company's online ordering

.com

Dear Valued Customer,

Thank you for your order. We hope that you are satisfied with the merchandise you have just received. Unfortunately, one or more of the items you have ordered are out of stock. Since we do not hold backorders, this order is now closed and you will only be billed for what you have received.

Please call our Customer Service Department at 1-800-000-0000 for the item availability and up-to-date stock information during our regular business hours of 8:30am – 5:30pm EST Monday through Friday.

We apologize for any inconvenience this may have caused and look forward to serving you again.

Thank you,

.com

Figure 9-4: Neither CRM nor EAI

system is obviously not linked to its inventory system. (The fact that the company happens to be a high-profile dot-com with an edgy Web site and slick e-mail marketing campaigns is not evident in its post-sales customer support.) The customer should have been notified of the out-of-stock items at the time of the order, not upon delivery of the remaining items.

The company might believe that, had the customer known that not all of the items she ordered would be in stock, she would not have placed the order at all. Perhaps some of the out-of-stock items the customer wanted were in some way related to the items that showed up on her doorstep. Or perhaps the company intends to link its various operational systems together but hasn't had the time. Either way, this company has successfully achieved these detrimental outcomes:

- Sending its "valued customer" a form letter and thus not differentiating her
- Putting the onus on the customer to follow up on the desired items
- Failing to provide similar levels of sales and service. (Notice the company's customer service hours. If the customer lives on the west coast, she only has around 5 available hours to contact the company by phone—but she can still shop on the Web at any hour!)
- Losing a "valued" customer

EAI is important to CRM because, no matter how successful a new marketing campaign or how polite the (albeit mass) marketing message, if internal systems cannot share data, vital business knowledge could be lost and customer service undermined. If the company truly had EAI, its inventory system could alert its customer support system when the desired items came back in stock, allowing a CSR to notify the customer and make a sale. It is for this reason that many companies undertake EAI as a preparatory step toward CRM.

For new CRM functionality, you'll also need to understand what data to consider. For each business requirement, one or more data requirements will result. For instance, if survey data is to be incorporated into customer profiles, which specific data elements should be collected? Will you need to collect external data such as third-party householding information or competitive intelligence data? Of the data collected, what should be displayed to CSRs? To marketing staff? And what systems will deliver that data?

A significant part of defining data requirements involves addressing the actual meaning of certain data definitions. Is there consensus across the business that the term "revenue" means booked revenue, or might it imply billed revenue? Does a "new customer" have the same attributes in the sales organization as in customer support? To many in IT, documenting data definitions smacks of cumbersome metadata management and documentation projects. However, it's more about simply gathering consensus and enforcing consistent business terminology, whatever form that takes. If information is indeed a corporate asset, as we discussed in Chapter 7, consistent and sustainable data definitions are essential.

When you've completed an impact analysis, you can begin prioritizing projects according to business requirements and staffing your development projects, as we discussed earlier in this chapter.

Technology Selection

As Chapter 8 explained, CRM technology selection can be as simple as choosing an off-the-shelf product or as complex as a comprehensive evaluation of various CRM systems integrators or ASPs. If you've bitten the bullet during architecture and implementation design, understanding CRM's impact on existing systems and its requirements for new functionality, you should be in good shape to align any candidate CRM product to your existing IT environment.

Development

Development involves the construction and customization of the CRM product, using specific product features. But CRM development is more than programmers assuming center stage and writing code; it involves the integration of business processes with the chosen CRM product.

By this time, you will have already identified the key CRM business processes. Process integration means that CRM technology you've just selected integrates into these business processes. (The converse—merging business processes into the CRM product's features—forces the product to in effect define or change those processes, thereby diluting them until they are no longer optimized.)

Process integration involves ensuring that identified business processes are tested with users to ensure not only that the business processes work, but also that technology features can be leveraged in order to refine them. In other words, technological capabilities should improve, not compromise, customer-focused business processes. For instance, a campaign management product allows segment managers the opportunity to refine a mailing list before the campaign is launched—something they've never been able to do—thus refining the existing process. The same product might also allow a campaign director to monitor a campaign's success rate as it's being executed. If the first thousand prospects have been unresponsive, the manager can cancel the campaign rather than allowing it to proceed, adding another valuable option to the campaign execution process.

Refining business processes during development means iterative prototyping: from time to time programmers demonstrate interim functionality to business users. Thus business users can monitor product development and test CRM functionality during—not after—implementation. End-user feedback about CRM functionality and desired changes can be flagged and incorporated into the CRM deliverable to ensure that resulting functionality conforms to requirements and meets user expectations.

Of course, development mostly involves technical work and thus might also include such tasks as database design, data cleansing and integration, and integration with other corporate systems. The integration step can easily be underestimated, because the CRM system might need to feed data to and pull data from other systems, such as call-routing systems or existing sales force automation (SFA) tools.

Delivery

The delivery step is often overlooked or lumped into development. Basically it means leveraging the corporation's IT infrastructure to dispatch the resulting CRM software to the business users who need it. In the case of a new Web-based sales-force automation tool, the application might be announced via an e-mail message that contains a link to the new CRM Web site. If the CRM system is client-server based, it will need to be installed on individual workstations.

Often, new CRM functionality simply supplements an existing operational system and is not considered a new standalone system. For instance, a contact center representative might now see a "screen pop" displaying a customer profile when the customer calls in. In such cases, business users might not even be aware of the new feature before it appears.

In both cases, user training is paramount. Before a salesperson begins using a new SFA package to schedule meetings or a CSR tries interpreting a customer's profile, she should be trained not only in using the new functionality but also in changing the way they work so they can take maximum advantage of it. Often, a customer-facing representative having new or improved customer knowledge can alter the way she interacts with the customer. For this reason,

CRM training should incorporate introductions to new business processes as well as new technology.

CRM delivery can also include user guides, job aids, and other documentation, as well as online or Web-based help to encourage users to make the most of the new CRM functionality.

Some companies go so far as having CRM sharing meetings to introduce the business at large to a new or pending system, and CRM business sponsors hold periodic update meetings, filling in various organizations and key staff members on CRM's progress.

Measurement

The measurement step brings the CRM roadmap full-circle as it evaluates CRM usage in order to refine CRM requirements. Many companies forego ongoing CRM measurement; such companies are confident they won't have to answer for their CRM expenditures. But can you truly claim your CRM program is a success if no measurements are in place to prove it?

In most cases management expects regular updates on programs in which they've invested heavily, and CRM is expensive. Savvy business sponsors define CRM success metrics as a result of the initial justification of CRM, and measure the successes after CRM has been deployed. For instance, if your new CRM system automates workflow to communicate widget defects to your R&D department, you might consider tracking the decrease in product defects and a corresponding increase in customer satisfaction for customers who have widgets. This measurement can include value quantification—such as lower support costs due to fewer support requests—and thus prove return on investment.

Another way to measure CRM's success is to evaluate how well it has solved existing business problems. If you established success metrics when you created your CRM business plan, supplement them over time by correlating them to actual results. Documenting success metrics along with their actual measured improvements is a valuable way to track and quantify tangible CRM business benefits, as illustrated in Table 9-4.

Improvement is usually gradual as users become familiar with new technology and business processes. An effective CRM program delivers ongoing improvements as it's adopted more widely throughout the company. The 12-month measured improvement column represents the rate of improvement since the launch of the CRM program and illustrates this incremental gain.

Table 9-4: CRM Success Measurement

CRM Success Metric	Desired Improvement	Measured Improvement (6 months)	Measured Improvement (12 months)
Reduction in the time required to generate customer name-and-address lists for targeted mailings.	Campaign list generation to take 1 day or less.	Campaign list generation takes 3–5 hours.	Campaign list generation takes 1–4 hours.
Ability to make product recommendations to customers during support request (online or phone-based).	Recommendations result in cross-selling improvement rates of 8 percent or higher.	Customer support cross-selling increase of 6 percent.	Customer support cross-selling increase of 10 percent.
Electronic distribution of customer sales reports to sales management.	Elimination of sales staff responsibility to produce weekly and monthly reports, generating a productivity increase of 5–10 percent.	11 percent increase in sales productivity and reduction of one full-time administrative position.	12 percent increase in sales productivity.
Reduction in time spent analyzing data to correct contradictory customer data from sales and provisioning systems.	Elimination of need for data correlation by implementing centralized customer database.	None—database pending.	Elimination of data correlation, resulting in redeployment of two full-time data analysts.

Measurement also includes the incorporation of user feedback to improve CRM usability and business effectiveness. As the CRM implementation roadmap shown in Figure 9-3 illustrates, CRM measurement loops back around to further CRM business planning, allowing the company and its lines of business to continually refine CRM requirements and identify new CRM opportunities at the same time. If you incorporate measurement and feedback into the planning cycle, CRM will deliver new and better functionality, resulting in small victories that add up to improved customer value.

Putting the Projects Together

After you've identified your CRM projects, your PMO or project managers can agree on an overall CRM timeline that will be enhanced and supplemented as the business uses CRM and customers begin experiencing the benefits. The projects identified in Figure 9-2 can become components of an overall CRM program timeline, as shown in Figure 9-5.

The solid boxes at the beginning of each project connote the fixed amount of time allotted for the business-planning phase. This phase includes project scoping; thus project durations might change after business planning is completed. Each project will have its own development-project plan reflecting more specific tasks and resources.

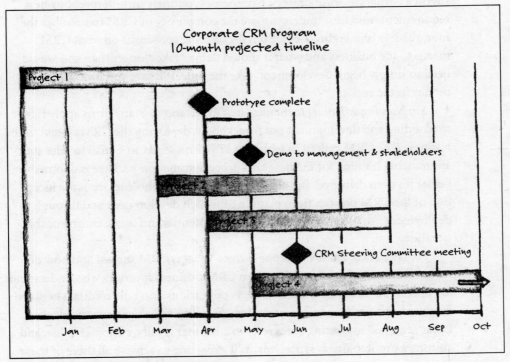

Figure 9-5: CRM program timeline

A visual timeline like the one in Figure 9-5 is not only effective in managing expectations about each project's forecasted delivery time frame; it can also become the basis for a CRM program document in which the project manager or development team leader can include individual project plans, requirements documentation, and specific CRM functions and features, either as a physical document or as part of your company's web-based knowledge management infrastructure. Thus managers and stakeholders can access up-to-date information about current CRM activities.

A CRM Implementation Checklist . . . for Failure

From the CRM projects I've worked on, evaluated, proposed, and completed, I've seen a handful of common denominators for failure. I call these "The Seven Deadly Sins of CRM." Consider the sins a checklist of what not to do if you want to enter the pearly gates of CRM nirvana.

Sin Number 1: Failure to define a CRM strategy. Simply defining what CRM means to your company is difficult enough without gathering consensus on a corporate-wide strategy. Companies routinely misinterpret business requirements and thus underestimate the complexity of CRM (remember the four quadrants in Figure 7-6?). Even if gathering consensus on what CRM means to the business and what it should deliver takes longer than you would need to simply begin development, take the time. It'll save you time and money in the end.

Sin Number 2: Failing to manage staff expectations. Many firms apply rigor to planning and development but forget about deploying the CRM system to the business. The CRM rollout in which an IT liaison sends an e-mail to sales staff announcing training for the new sales-force automation package is doomed before it's even delivered. Business users must be stakeholders from the inception of the CRM project, from planning through development and through to deployment. Anything else risks alienating potential end users, an irrevocable situation.

Sin Number 3: Failure to define success. What is CRM success and how do we know when we've achieved it? Even CRM business sponsors who understand the differences between CRM's various applications don't differentiate between increased cross-selling and improved profitability. I'm always surprised when I hear seasoned marketing execs refer to customer loyalty, customer value, and customer profitability as synonyms, as if expecting to achieve all three of these objectives with the first CRM release made sense. Define discrete success metrics—they'll be different for increasing customer profitability than for improving customer satisfaction—and then measure against them. If you don't, there could actually be business successes that aren't rightfully attributed to CRM.

Sin Number 4: Hasty ASP decisions. Companies haven't yet sorted out the advantages and disadvantages of the ASP model. Large companies assume ASPs serve only small markets and dot-coms that lack significant IT infrastructures. Small to mid-size firms assume ASPs are too costly, despite potential cost savings. Many companies are even underestimating their in-house resources and skill sets and jumping blindly onto the ASP bandwagon. Don't be one of them. Understand the pros and cons of the ASP model, and make a decision based on your business and functional requirements.

Sin Number 5: Failure to improve business processes. The proverbial mistake of "paving the cowpath" applies here: CRM should not simply overlay archaic corporate policies. It should instead formalize and automate nimble, customer-focused business processes. Be willing to drastically modify and continue to refine your business processes, and make sure your CRM technology incorporates these process modifications. And don't fall into the trap of hoping your new CRM tool will do this work for you. Processes should be defined from the customer's perspective, not the technology's.

Sin Number 6: Lack of data integration. Chapter 6 painted the picture of stovepipe CRM systems and the danger they can lead to if allowed to perpetuate. Effective customer-focused decision-making means understanding each customer across her various touchpoints and beyond your immediate knowledge of her age, income, preferred channel, or sales territory. The difficult truth is that customer data exists in multiple systems on a variety of technology platforms across your company. Finding, gathering, and consolidating this data isn't easy, but it's absolutely crucial.

Sin Number 7: Failure to continue socializing CRM to the enterprise at large. Companies who have delivered nothing less than revolutionary customer-facing improvements via CRM often rest on their laurels. CRM is an ongoing process, and success breeds success. Consider establishing an "internal PR" job function to communicate with executives and decision-makers who might determine ongoing funding, as well as to the various lines of business who might leverage the functionality and data to further their own customer focuses. Proselytizing CRM successes should not only be practiced but should be formalized and updated via regular newsletters, status meetings, or an internal Web site. Don't be shy about initially promoting CRM. If your customers experience improved service and your sales and marketing staffs generate more effective leads, it won't be long before CRM starts promoting itself.

The Manager's Bottom Line

Just because you've bought the tool doesn't mean the spending is over. After you start adding up the time needed for customization, the labor necessary to integrate CRM with your other corporate systems, the cost of external specialists needed to make it work, the time required from business users, and the new staff you'll have to hire to deliver the system on time, you'll be tempted to reconsider reengineering those old legacy systems to become more customer-centric. CRM development costs are routinely underestimated.

As is CRM complexity. Most CIOs are familiar with traditional waterfall development methodologies: projects that are linear, with a defined beginning and ending. They're accustomed to measuring system success based on the new system's number of transactions or number of users. But CRM success revolves around staff efficiency gains and process improvements, so such advances as higher productivity and enhanced customer satisfaction will be more difficult to measure. Likewise, traditional systems development means laying out requirements in concrete terms once and for all. Given that CRM stresses improving customer-focused processes, requirements-gathering should be iterative. Indeed, gathering and refining business requirements is an ongoing process, much like the CRM program itself.

Moreover, depending on the skill sets of the customary in-house business analysts, they might need some extra help. CRM business sponsors might find individuals trained in corporate quality programs to be more effective in CRM requirements definition. Quality-knowledgeable individuals have learned to focus on how people do their jobs and how the inputs and outputs relate to the overall process.

For enterprise CRM, it's essential for customer information to flow freely throughout your organization. If you are to provide the proverbial 360-degree customer view, users must be able to access that data whenever they need it. This often means staff members from elsewhere in the company need to be involved to connect important corporate systems with CRM. Such involvement can render even the simplest CRM application an enterprise-wide effort. Although the

PMO can ease the communications challenges of such potentially complex collaboration, strong management is a definite prerequisite.

Know what you already have that you can leverage. Many talented IT departments have short-changed themselves by not advertising the data warehouses and marketing databases they've so painstakingly built. The data source system inventories, extraction and transformation processes, metadata repositories, and other infrastructure components of these databases are invaluable assets to any CRM system. Find them, and use them.

Head reeling yet? Do you wonder whether CRM development might be too complex or costly? Consider the alternative. The Internet and the pressures of e-business have weakened the barriers to competition, and your customers are getting smarter. It's not a question of *if* you launch CRM but the scale to which you launch it. Don't be afraid to start small, implementing one requirement or one set of business functions at a time. Have a clear view of what's ahead, and understand the potential impact CRM can have on your customers, their immediate satisfaction, and their long-term loyalty. Where customer relationship management projects are concerned, it could very well be now or never.

CHAPTER TEN

Your CRM Future

The big news in business these days isn't the Internet, e-marketplaces, or even astronomical executive compensation packages. It's that even at good companies with solid business plans and promising products, things can go terribly wrong. Troubles at Firestone-and by default, Ford Motor Company-the late Montgomery Ward, Daimler-Chrysler, and a slew of Internet has-beens too numerous to mention have proven that bad things happen to good businesses and to their customers. And not even the best CRM program in the world can prevent them.

But it can make a big difference. Imagine being in charge of Southern California Edison's customer contact center during the California energy crisis, or in Ford's marketing department. With the right customer response infrastructure in place and a bit of nimble employee training, such challenges can become opportunities.

Making the Pitch: Selling CRM Internally

Perhaps you've read this book intent on gathering ammunition to help you pitch CRM to your management or board of directors. Maybe you're preparing a presentation that outlines why CRM is needed. Here are a few do's and don'ts to prepare you for battle:

Do:

• Do gather high-level business requirements before you introduce CRM. Ideally these requirements will originate in different areas of the company, bolstering your justification argument.

- Do run the content by your peers before presenting it.
- Do discuss the "need, pain, or problem," CRM will solve. The more visible the problem and the greater the extent to which upper management feels it too, the better.
- Do communicate the business actions and changes CRM will drive.
- Do make sure your presentation quantifies the return on investment (or return on relationship) you expect from CRM. It's an executive's job to ask, "What will this buy us?" Be prepared with an answer.
- Do discuss how CRM has helped another company in your industry.
- Do have a realistic idea of budget requirements.

Don't:

- Don't focus on specific products, diagram technology architecture, or bring a vendor.
- Don't evade discussions about "what's under the hood." You need to appear educated and perfectly able to indulge the detailed questions of the CIO or financial director who's throwing you curve balls. Touch on some specific organizational, technology, or business process impacts of CRM.
- Don't be cynical when organizational or political issues are raised. Executive buy-in can preempt turf battles and gradually establish a customer-focused business culture. Your presentation might spark that seminal customer-focused moment with the right executive and change everything.
- Don't give the impression that CRM is a finite project with a beginning and ending.
- Don't dwell on cumbersome statistics or analyst reports.
- Don't quote theory or explain philosophies.
- Don't sugarcoat the risks.

It's unlikely that any executive will be ready to sign on the bottom line after simply hearing about CRM for the first time. As with everything else, selling CRM internally is a process, and the first step's always the hardest. Be prepared to educate people and, at worst, to begin chipping away at some closely held paradigms. In many companies, advocating a newfound customer focus is tantamount to heresy. Some people will need time to evolve from roadblocks into hardcore CRM constituents.

CRM Roadblocks

Speaking of roadblocks, there are lots of them on the journey to CRM success. Some obstruct the beginning of the project during the business planning or requirements gathering that allows a CRM team time to set things right. Most CRM roadblocks aren't single events, however, but processes that gradually erode a CRM effort until the ultimate system becomes a mere shadow of its intended vision.

The Four Ps

A good CRM project can go bad for many reasons. But the principal factors—I call them the Four Ps—are Process, Perception, Privacy, and Politics.

Process

One of the failures I encounter most often in my CRM fieldwork is with companies that are slow or unwilling to modify their business processes to support better customer relationships. Some are simply unwilling to acknowledge that their business processes warrant improvement. As we discussed in Chapter 7, the weaknesses of existing business processes, such as accepting a hotel reservation from a frequent guest, should be clearly understood and refined prior to implementing CRM technology.

Many companies make the mistake of purchasing a CRM tool that supports repeatable processes only to discover that their business processes aren't defined well enough to be repeatable. Scribbling a back-of-the-napkin process for each new campaign doesn't mean it's fit for CRM prime time.

Where business processes are concerned, internal processes—or the lack of them—can also jeopardize a CRM project. The CIO for an automobile accessories company once gave me free reign to conduct interviews for a CRM assessment. "Except," he said, "don't talk to the business users." (See Politics, later in the chapter.)

Often the company won't have generated the internal support it needs for new CRM processes to become established. In such cases, staff members will simply stay in their comfort zones, claiming to prefer "the old way of doing things." Tentative or hands-off executive sponsorship results in few changes, and

CRM eventually takes a back seat to more tactical projects, such as new product development. It's a slippery slope.

Perception

Indeed, end users need to see CRM as a job enabler, not as the latest in a series of doctrinaire corporate policies. As we discussed in Chapter 4, CRM as corporate edict rarely works. After CRM has been deployed, businesspeople should be able to accomplish the same work in less time or be able to perform new tasks that ultimately make their jobs easier and at the same time enhance customer relationships.

And customer perception. After all, a customer's perception of the company is the basis for whether she will return to your Web site or store. CRM can either deliver or destroy a customer's high opinion of your company and its offerings.

Privacy

Lately every U.S. firm with a handful of customer records and a Web site seems to be steeling itself for the inevitability of Internet regulation by the Federal Trade Commission. Stories of unauthorized peddling of customer names and addresses—the late Toysmart.com was cited by the FTC after trying to cover debt by selling its customer lists, which included members' children's names and ages—and the ubiquitous cookies and spam pervading the hard drives of even infrequent Web denizens are now commonplace. A recent *Newsweek* article asked, "Is It Software or Spyware?," declaring that "While engaging in seemingly benign Internet activity, most users have no idea that they're beaming out stuff they'd prefer to leave on their desktops."[1] The press was almost gleeful in its account of Travelocity's slip-up in early 2001, in which the names and e-mail addresses of 44,000 people were inadvertently posted on the company's live Web site. Such instances, despite their often lackluster repercussions, are scaring regulators and consumer organizations alike.

Whether or not they differentiate the overblown scare tactics from the legitimate threats, the vast majority of Web surfers favor punishing companies—and even top executives—for privacy violations.[2] While the debate rages, what

---

1. Levy, Steven, "Is It Software or Spyware?" *Newsweek*, February 19, 2001.

2. According to a report in TheStandard.com (August 23, 2000) citing a Pew Internet and American Life Project study, 94 percent of Web surfers surveyed are proponents of punishing companies and their top executives for privacy violations.

can you do to ensure that pending privacy regulations don't foil your CRM program?

- Understand the *quid pro quo:* consumers are more likely to share their personal information with your company if they receive something valuable in return. (For instance, travelers reserving their flights on Expedia.com are e-mailed weather reports for their destinations a few days before they fly.) Incorporate this into your CRM planning to ensure that customers are sufficiently motivated to continue interacting with you at every touchpoint.
- Post your privacy policy conspicuously on your Web site, as well as in print ads and other customer communications.
- Understand permission marketing and the trade-offs between asking customers to opt in versus opt out. Decide which approach is best for each discrete marketing channel and, if practical, for every customer.
- Consider giving your customers full access to all the information you have about them. Although admittedly risky, this tack makes the customer a participant in managing his information, potentially enhancing his perception of your company as a partner. For instance, Allstate customers can log on to a secure Web site and actually change their own profiles, benefiting both parties.
- Request every customer's privacy preference. Ensure that this preference becomes part of each customer's profile. Make heeding these preferences part of the job descriptions of departmental executives.
- Make sure your business users are categorized based on their authority to view and use specific data. Support a policy where the de facto rule is "access as needed" rather than "access for everyone."
- Appoint a Chief Privacy Officer (CPO) or Chief Customer Officer (CCO) to enforce corporate privacy policies and communicate them both internally and externally.
- Follow the FTC's fair information practices of "notice, choice, access, and control." See www.ftc.gov/privacy. (And note the very conspicuous privacy policy on the commission's home page.)

Like CRM, privacy is big business. Online marketing companies such as MatchLogic and DoubleClick (whose stock price tumbled when it revealed plans to identify individual consumers) base their operations on tracking anonymous clickstreams that have been cleansed of their consumer-specific data. Large consulting firms are offering privacy audits—often at hundreds of thousands of dollars a pop. And a rash of legal firms specializing in online privacy law have sprung up virtually overnight.

Consumer watchdog groups such as the Electronic Privacy Information Center (www.epic.org) and Junkbusters (www.junkbusters.com) aren't letting up; they continue to publish consumer alerts and push for stricter regulatory measures. And www.privacy.org, whose slogan reads "Privacy is a Right, Not a Preference," regularly features corporate privacy breaches in its headlines.

In the meantime, businesses with a stake in consumer data are rapidly forming alliances to ease consumer fears while warding off the threat of governmental regulation. The Responsible Electronic Communications Alliance (www.responsibleemail.org) recently created a set of self-regulatory guidelines for e-mail–based marketing campaigns, and The Personalization Consortium (www.personalization.org) is a business advocacy group dedicated to illuminating the path toward responsible one-to-one marketing practices. And not a second too soon—visionary companies who once proudly heralded their one-to-one marketing capabilities and detailed customer databases are increasingly clamming up for fear of another privacy backlash. But marketing strategy in the back room instead of in the boardroom will do little to comfort wary consumers. Circumspect and deliberate planning of customer interactions and data-gathering will do a whole lot more.

Politics

My company has a long-term relationship with a major U.S. financial institution, a client whom we've accompanied on the CRM journey from planning through execution and measurement and back to planning. I know the struggles the company has had and how it has effectively worked through solutions to deliver CRM to a hungry group of private bankers whose compensation is based on a customer retention and satisfaction scorecard.

From time to time I attend conferences featuring presentations from representatives of this firm. Some of the presenters I know; others are strangers. Often they discuss CRM projects I've never heard of, deployed to lines of business who weren't involved in the sanctioned, corporate-wide CRM program our team helped deliver.

After sitting through diverse and often unrelated CRM presentations from various employees of this client, I know one thing for sure: lurking in the farthest reaches of the headquarters campus are "skunkworks" CRM projects—projects that are quietly being developed, using leftover budget money or developers unaccounted for on other projects. Skunkworks CRM projects are usually a sign of urgent business needs combined with a high degree of cynicism about delivering CRM via the appropriate channels (e.g., the IT department). They can also mean that certain organizations or individuals in need of CRM functionality might be unaware of CRM activities occurring elsewhere in the company.

More insidiously, skunkworks projects can sometimes indicate nasty politics. From time to time a rogue manager, unhappy about the way the legitimate CRM program is playing out or disillusioned with the project team's leadership, might decide to go it alone and build her own CRM environment. She meets with CRM vendors, several of whom lost their bids for the sanctioned CRM activity, and hoards an exclusive set of analyst research reports. Although excuses range from "I need to use the budget money or I'll lose it," to "It's not really CRM; it just uses the same data," the potential to dilute the value of the company-endorsed CRM program is real.

Another frequent political scenario involves the development of a data warehouse or other CRM-related technology solution and labeling it CRM without defining a clear CRM strategy, planned process improvements, organizational changes, or business participation. Declaring an activity or technology project to be CRM doesn't make it so and risks tempering the high-impact business message of any bona fide CRM project awaiting approval.

CRM in a vacuum simply doesn't work long-term and can actually delay or destroy an entire program. (I once listened to a corporate executive admonish a handful of his managers to "figure out who owns this CRM project and get back to me!" No one did either.) If you're considering launching a CRM initiative, raise the flag and inquire about related projects elsewhere in the company. Understand that CRM is a team effort that requires participation from a range of players across the business. Ensure that projects aren't already underway with technology, data, or business processes that fit your requirements—even if that means you have to follow rather than lead. Rebellion is an honorable course, but it's also usually short-lived, and a truly effective CRM effort rarely involves revolution.

Other CRM Saboteurs

Although the Four Ps remain the major threats to CRM success, here are a few more barriers that can stall or thwart a CRM program.

Lack of CRM Integration

In a recent survey of Global 2000 companies, META Group found that few had tight communications between online and traditional CRM initiatives.

The implication is that many companies are aware they have multiple CRM programs underway. Perhaps establishing an enterprise-wide CRM vision proved too unwieldy. Perhaps different organizations began projects that evolved organically into CRM. Or maybe there are valid departmental business goals that are minimally related. Whatever the reason, the result is sporadic customer-interaction information, presumably impeding these companies from understanding a single customer's range of possible behaviors and improving customer satisfaction in the bargain. As we discussed in Chapter 6, this approach can deliver tactical improvements to specific organizations, but a true, single version of the customer truth will probably remain out of reach.

Poor Organizational Planning

If you've launched a CRM project and staff members continue to ask questions about who's doing what, something's wrong. Because CRM is relatively new, development roles aren't often well understood. Moreover, confusion about whether CRM is a business initiative or an IT effort exacerbates confusion about ownership and authority. Some of this can be chalked up to politics-as-usual, but questions about skill-set delineation and organizational boundaries often have complex answers.

The CRM business sponsor should work with the project manager to define the necessary roles for the project (remember Tables 9-2 and 9-3 for a list of business and IT job roles) and then think in terms of What, How, and Who. After you've gathered your CRM requirements and have scoped and prioritized the projects, delineate the tasks within them (the What). Next, take time to understand the skills necessary to complete the tasks (the How), and then—and only then—decide Who has the appropriate skills to perform them.

Also, if you're the CRM project manager, be prepared to make some hard staffing decisions. Lots of people step up to the CRM plate, but not everyone has the batting average necessary to play. Call on the business sponsor for support in choosing the best people to participate in requirements definition, development, and rollout. And don't be afraid to hire consultants, particularly for those major hurdles—strategy planning, requirements definition, and process refinement among them—that are best done by using structured methods and must be crossed before you can move forward.

In my experience, these are the most frequent staffing mistakes committed on CRM projects:

- The CRM project manager is viewed as an administrator rather than a liaison between IT and the business, tracking development progress against requirements and success metrics. This puts more work in the lap of the business sponsor, who can quickly become disillusioned.
- Business analysts (hired to define requirements) do their jobs and leave. Instead, they should participate in CRM development through implementation and deployment, ensuring conformance to requirements every step of the way.
- The business sponsor sees himself as a lead visionary, happy to preach the doctrine of customer loyalty but nevertheless reluctant to take charge. Proselytizing a vision is usually accompanied by the less pleasant responsibilities of conflict resolution during development and tiebreaker duties for feature prioritization and data questions. The business sponsor in the ivory tower will sooner or later fall out.
- Everything's relinquished to the selected consulting firm or ASP. In their rush to deliver a CRM quick win, many companies hand over the entire store to a consulting firm or ASP that develops the CRM system without the necessary business relationships or conversations, often from the bottom up. Even when CRM is outsourced, it mandates frequent business participation and IT checkpoints by internal company staff.

Demanding Customers

It's not your fault. You were trying to capture market share. So now your repeat customers have come to expect $20 off on every $50 purchase. What do you do now?

It might be too late, at least for that seminal group that first found your Web site and continues to respond to e-mail promotions and cherry-pick at every turn. But it's not too late for the next batch, who might buy from you again because your site is easy to navigate and your customer support friendly and timely. If you're considering offering great deals to rope in customers, realize that attracting them doesn't mean keeping them.

Understand how to identify your negative-value customers, and avoid enticing them with money-losing deals. Understand who they are when they do show up, and offer them opportunities to become profitable. But also know your high-value customers and differentiate how you treat them, whether they're entering your store or your storefront.

Customer Service That's Really Bad

One ornery call center rep who drones on about company policy and won't try any workarounds on behalf of a flummoxed customer can effectively eradicate, in 90 seconds, the toil and cost of an entire CRM initiative. Chapter 3 discussed the deservedly high profile of the customer contact center and its ability to make or break customer loyalty.

Poor customer service comes in many guises. It's the employee at the home improvement warehouse whose answer is "No" before you even finish your question, the salesperson who is unable to take your order because of system problems, and the fourth consecutive "Server is down" message displayed when you try to access an e-tailer's Web site.

But poor customer service can also mean aggressive telesales staff, chronically late suppliers, or a sales rep too busy to take your call now that you've placed your order. It can also mean the well-meaning employee who has taken the customer relationship management strategy to heart, as in the cartoon.

"I'm warning you—I'm going to call the police if you don't stop touching base with me."

Whatever the problem, implement a series of new customer service guidelines for every customer-facing department in your company. Make these guidelines part of staff members' performance evaluations and compensation packages. In short, foster ownership of customer satisfaction. It'll be money well spent.

Looking Toward the Future

Keeping pace with today's technology is difficult enough. As most companies look forward to improving customer service and increasing sales uplift through better customer understanding, they're also looking backward: retrofitting existing technologies, investing in new hardware and software, and hiring management consultants to bolster their strategies in preparation for a revolution in customer loyalty.

So, after you've deployed a successful CRM program comprising several projects that have all delivered measurable improvements, what's on the horizon? A few predictions follow.

The Customer as SME

It's already happening, and it will happen more and more: Companies are asking their customers how to plan their CRM strategies, rendering these customers not mere CRM stakeholders but subject matter experts.

Although the process isn't that straightforward, company executives are realizing that for their companies to migrate from a product focus to a customer focus, customers should have a say in the improvements to be made and in what the priorities should be. It's not unheard of for a CEO or Chief Customer Officer to pay customers periodic visits to discover where the company is excelling and where it might be falling behind.

Customers are being asked to participate in strategic planning sessions to lay out CRM plans as well as new product proposals and customer support improvements. Sales managers from a $50-billion telephone equipment firm recently spent a week with their customers to understand how they were actually using the high-end line of switches the company was selling.

When asked about this novel and somewhat risky approach to gathering customer feedback, the computer manufacturer's VP of sales replied, "It's not enough anymore to simply understand your customer. You need to see your company through their eyes. We're working on thinking less like salespeople and more like our customers." CEOs like Michael Dell and Tom Siebel spend a large part of their time visiting their customers in person.

Contrary to replacing this high-profile contact between companies and their customers, CRM programs complement such relationship-building by leveraging customer input to improve business processes and recording the feedback of customers who have taken the time to participate. The customer *quid pro quo*? Better products and services (and sometimes a few generous purchase credits thrown in).

The Rise of Intermediaries

Consumers are more connected than ever and busier than ever. So they're using the Web more than ever.

Web sites such as CNET.com, part of technology news provider CNET Networks, and MySimon.com act as consumer clearinghouses for product purchase information. Why browse a handful of well-known Web sites when you can go to an intermediary and examine a range of retailer and information sources that understand the product you have in mind? Web shops at Yahoo and MSN.com take the guesswork out of finding a toaster with thick bagel-supportable slots. Intermediaries act to simplify the purchase process by acting as one-stop information resources.

The studies referenced in Chapter 3 about eroding customer service and plummeting customer satisfaction rates suggest that customers are complaining more than ever. But not without help. There has been a steady rise in the use of customer service intermediaries—individuals and corporations who take on companies on behalf of unhappy customers. For instance, Travelproblems.com charges a $30 fee for lodging a passenger's complaint with an airline and tracking its resolution. Such intermediaries work like class-action attorneys, representing both individuals and groups of people who are unhappy with a company, whatever the reason.

Some of these individuals might be looking for compensation. Others are content simply to contribute to the bad publicity the company is suffering because of its poor service. And this is where the CRM waters get muddy. As companies try to keep pace with their customers' purchases and feedback, intermediaries triangulate what might have been a two-way interaction between company and customer. Companies must become diligent about how they receive and register customer complaints and should consider being able to identify the use of intermediaries for both purchases and feedback as part of a customer's overall profile.

Digital and Broadband Revolutionize Advertising

E*Trade's clever TV ad during Superbowl 34 concluded with the question, "We've just wasted 2 million bucks. What are you doing with your money?" Indeed, the astronomical advertising prices charged by the networks are the personification of spray-and-pray mass marketing that broadcasts a single message to millions of consumers.

The combination of broadband, digital cable, and database technologies might soon change all that. Digital cable and broadband will soon enable advertisers to send personalized commercials to households that fit a certain desired profile, allowing companies to target-market television audiences in real time. The consumer's set-top box is essentially a two-way device, allowing a consumer to communicate in real time with the advertiser and even order a product as it's being pitched.

For example, two different households are watching the same football game. Through its database, a beer advertiser, knowing that one household contains a mother, father, and two adult sons, broadcasts a commercial for its most popular brand of beer. In the second household, a quarter of a mile away from a college campus, are six adult residents, only two of whom are over 21. In this case, the beer company advertises its line of snack foods, including a contest for a free NFL video game.

The point here is that companies are working on target-marketing straight into the living room of millions of households. As these households respond to the advertisements, advertisers can refine their understanding of customer purchase preferences. If the first household doesn't purchase the advertised brand of beer, the beer company might decide to market its premium beer the next time around. Likewise, in markets where beer sales don't increase, the cable company can reduce the company's ad cost.

The vision is custom advertising and immediate consumer feedback on a per-household basis, similar to the way banner-ad bidding occurs on the Web today. Advertisers can develop custom commercials for households, based on household purchase histories and viewing trends. This mass customization cultivates audiences for specific advertisers who are subsets of the television show's audience but are nevertheless targeted for a specific message.

The Threat and Promise of Customer Communities

You've heard the analogy by now. You know, the one that compares the Web to the medieval street market or the corner coffee shop? Everyone meets there and people know each other. They discuss current events and buy and sell things. They might share a cup of coffee or, in the case of the medieval market, a flask of grog.

With the Web, the zeitgeist can be formed in minutes and can last for years. As we discussed in Chapter 1, viral marketing can either call attention to a fantastic new product or kill it before it ever hits the stores.

In *The Cluetrain Manifesto,* the authors submit that such consumer communities are not only here to stay; they also represent a fantastic opportunity for corporations to listen to their prospects and customers. And they represent the potential undoing of company executives who've rested on their huge compensation packages and assumptions about traditional hierarchical organizations and marketing practices. In short, the Web has the power to tell companies *how* to change or die. The chat room has moved next door to the boardroom.

The same is true in the B2B world. After all, communities are about unrestricted access to different online parties. A purchasing agent might decide to enter a vertical industry chat room before putting his opportunity out for bid on the Web, just to see who's working with whom. In the same situation, a candidate supplier might ask other suppliers whether a manufacturer pays on time. Exchanges and e-marketplaces represent more than just streamlined supply chains; they are virtual meeting places where both buyers and sellers can come together, exchange information, and conduct business.

To be community-oriented, your company should be customer-oriented. Your CRM initiative can incorporate community insight by regularly scanning various community Web sites for feedback. You might also consider having your Web site feature its own chat room, so customers can share no-holds-barred opinions about their experiences with you. This not only provides you with firsthand feedback, but also gives you a forum for communicating improvements and fixes. And it will foster the notion that, far from being a passive observer, your company is enthusiastic about providing the medium for dialog. (See Perception, earlier in this chapter.)

CRM Goes Global

Up until now, CRM vendors have concentrated on the United States and western European markets, but this can't last. As mergers and acquisitions continue, companies are more likely than ever to be multinational and to serve a growing base of international customers. CRM vendors and users alike will need to account for the requirements of their international customers.

Global CRM usually doesn't apply to sales-force automation or to marketing—these types of CRM are normally executed locally. (A sales manager in Argentina probably doesn't care about a French salesman's contact list.) Instead, global CRM focuses on customer support processes.

The technology considerations of global CRM can be positively daunting. For instance, do your remote locations have access to your centralized customer database, or does each country track its own customers? Is there worldwide access so that support and field personnel can monitor customer issues? Does your CRM call center software offer multi-language support? What about non-English character sets? And is the vendor capable of supporting the product, irrespective of where it's being used? What about the wireless devices that are more pervasive abroad?

This introduces a number of new considerations that aren't part of the typical country-specific CRM strategy. For instance, European privacy rules are more strident than in the United States and might differ from one country to another; thus, collecting customer data might be illegal. Some countries actually forbid a company from giving incentives to consumers to do business with a partner company, as with car-rental frequent flier miles. In some Asian countries, a direct-mail communication will be summarily discarded unless it has been preceded by a personal contact. And many countries still shun credit cards in favor of cash.

Considering going global with your CRM initiative? Don't do it until you have a good grasp of the difference in business processes across countries and are certain that the need for data exchange outweighs the likely but potentially complex infrastructure requirements. Such differences could render a CRM system unwieldy, expensive, and ultimately best left to the individual country office to deliver.

The Coming CRM Backlash?

A 2000 study by Cap Gemini Ernst & Young asked a group of CEOs about their top priorities. The majority—42 percent—stated their top priority was to "launch new and extended [product] offerings." This response contrasted starkly with the 21 percent who claimed "improve customer experience" as a priority.[3]

----

3. From "Business Defined: Connecting Content, Applications, and Customers," *E&Y Cap Gemini*, 2000.

Are these CEOs latecomers, new to the message that the customer experience is everything? Or have they already soured on customer loyalty, preferring to differentiate themselves instead with marketing and selling new products in the traditional way?

The privacy debate has been partly responsible for a growing backlash against all forms of database marketing, however innocuous. Privacy groups are admonishing consumers to enter wrong data each time they fill in an online profile or enter a direct-mail sweepstakes, thereby foiling companies' efforts to use their personal information (if for nothing more than to understand who they are). And because multiple family members usually share one household PC and your daughter has just bought her third Marilyn Manson CD from an online music retailer, just how accurate are the preferences being captured by those ubiquitous cookies?

If a CRM backlash happens, it probably won't begin in the home offices of wary Web users but in the executive suites of major corporations. Expectations for what CRM can deliver are ever more lofty as software vendors make grandiose claims and CRM press releases make news. In June of 1999, Forrester Research published the provocatively titled research paper "The Demise of CRM," doubtless targeted at vulnerable executives who had begun questioning whether CRM was really worth it.

Increasing expectations for CRM invite the possibility that its cost could outweigh its ultimate value to an organization. By the time you've realized CRM's promise, determined which organizations can benefit from it, convinced them to work together, determined the data requirements, loaded the database, integrated disparate applications, and customized the software, CRM could be costing you millions. And this is before it's even been deployed.

A noted outdoor gear retailer with both an established brick-and-mortar presence and an acclaimed Web site recently told an IT journal that it has only two customer segments—one for "professional shoppers" (people who like to shop for multiple items and coordinate outfits) and another for shoppers who know exactly what they want to buy. The company maintained that understanding these two segments gave it the necessary information to craft effective marketing messages. This company is not an upstart but an established retail presence with a loyal customer base. It's regularly lauded for offering the latest outdoor apparel at a fair price for a broad range of consumers. If I were a CRM salesperson, I wouldn't want them in my territory.

If your company sells a commodity-based product, the ability to gain additional market share through CRM might not be worth the investment. There might be better ways to acquire customers, such as dropping prices, hiring additional salespeople, or adopting additional channels to gain market share. For these types of businesses, CRM might not be able to deliver the process efficiencies necessary to drive increased customer satisfaction or revenues.

And if you work for a growth company that frequently acquires other companies and undergoes regular reorganizations, go easy on CRM, at least for now. Let's say your Canada sales territory has traditionally belonged to the Americas region but is now being combined with Europe to form a single international region. Although the Canadian sales organization has traditionally followed the sales and marketing processes set up in the United States, it must now conform to the international organization's business processes and pricing guidelines. If your CRM system can't easily reflect these changes in short order, it could be rendered useless.

Although CRM successes are steadily increasing, statistics of its failure remain high. Executives continue to grill their staffs and vendors about CRM's cost/benefit ratio and payback. It's critical that you respond to such inquiries—and they'll continue—with either a promising vision or measurable proof.

The Manager's Bottom Line

An old Chinese proverb says: Give a hundred-year lease on a desert, and it will become a garden; give a one-year lease on a garden, and it will become a desert.

The point is that ownership and long-term commitment make a difference when it comes to undertaking important tasks, and building customer relationships is a big deal. After all, look how far we've come: from product marketing to mass marketing to segment marketing and all the way to the total customer experience. Customer relationship management promises a wave of change in worldwide business.

Are you ready? Are your company's executives committed to shifting from a product focus to a customer focus? Have you identified the process gains and customer perception improvements CRM can help deliver? Can you envision a way to drive product improvements from customer feedback? Do you have a single, integrated view of your customers? Do you have what it takes to differentiate them? To differentiate yourself? The worst insult in corporate America is to accuse a company of being "mainstream."

If you have doubts about CRM, don't invest until you've consulted some experts, assessed your current environment, and talked to managers about the viability of the organizational and process changes that accompany effective CRM. Know whether you and your colleagues can agree on success metrics. Understand whether enterprise CRM is feasible, and consider the value a more tactical, departmental CRM project could deliver. If it's delivered well, departmental CRM can light the fuse for a broader enterprise-CRM strategy.

When discussing CRM with the experts, beware the emphasis on quantitative methods over business value. Grill the marketing analyst whose only focus is profitability *or* customer lifetime value *or* customer loyalty. Don't trust the vendor promising a "complete hardware and software solution." Check the references of management consultants who claim to have implemented CRM "at companies just like yours."

The best CRM system in the world won't solve the problem of the airline flight attendant who behaves like an android, the record store clerk who sneers at someone's CD selection, the barista who turns out a wimpy cappuccino and a bad attitude, or the bank ATM that denies a customer's existence for the third time in as many days. Automation or no automation, the customer's experience is paramount. Humans being the social animals we are, technology will never take us to the point where we never leave our homes. The human touch will continue to play a major role in the customer experience.

Whether you've read this entire book or focused on certain chapters, you've probably concluded that CRM isn't easy. "Just follow the pizza man mantra, and deliver!" advises a client who's deployed CRM, his tongue firmly planted in his cheek. The good news and the bad news are the same: CRM failure rates are climbing at a slower rate than ever before.

At the time of this writing, CRM vendor stocks are in freefall. Earnings reports for CRM and business intelligence firms are bleak, and testy CEOs interviewed on CNBC feebly attempt spin control. Acquisitions are going south. Several representatives of vendors to be featured in this book have not returned phone calls amid organizational reshuffling or uncertainty about the future or facing the truth that their customers won't back them up. Some high-profile CRM products aren't ready for prime time. A book called *No Logo*—subtitled *Money, Marketing, and the Growing Anti-Corporate Movement*—warns of the menacing tactics of corporate marketing organizations and is an international bestseller. The term "service recovery" is getting as much airplay as the term "customer service." And consumer advocacy groups' cries for privacy laws have reached a fever pitch as opt-in legislation looms ever larger.

But despite the continued questions about whether it's "do-able" or even worth it, CRM is here to stay. As the case studies in this book testify, it's driving revenues and profitability. It's motivating customers to buy additional products and to spend more. It's raising customer satisfaction scores and helping companies understand which customers they should focus on and which channels they should invest in. What must underlie successful CRM in the end is the communal resolve that change is a continual campaign that heralds improvement. In short, despite the cost and risk, the uncertainty and the noise, CRM is valuable, viable, and real, and it's not going back in the box.

Further Reading

Following is a list of resources for you to supplement your knowledge of CRM and its various components. I've broken down the material into three categories: books, magazines and journals, and Web sites.

Books

These books cover a range of CRM and CRM-related topics.

Adriaans, Pieter, and Dolf Zantinge. Data Mining. Reading, MA: Addison-Wesley, 1996.

Barlow, Janelle, and Dianna Maul. Emotional Value: Creating Strong Bonds with Your Customers. San Francisco: Berrett-Koehler, 2000.

Berry, Michael J. A., and Gordon Linhoff Data Mining Techniques: For Marketing, Sales, and Customer Support. New York: John Wiley& Sons, 1997.

Brown, Stanley A. Customer Relationship Management. A Strategic Imperative in the World ofE-Business. New York: John Wiley & Sons, 2000.

Dyché, Jill. e-Data: TurningData into Information with Data Warehousing. Boston: Addison-Wesley, 2000.

Gladwell, Malcolm. The TippingPoint.- How Little Things Can Make a Big Difference. Boston: Little, Brown, 2000.
Godin, Seth. Permission Marketing.- Turning Strangers into Friends and Friends into Customers. New York: Simon & Schuster, 1999.

Gordon, Ian. *Relationship Marketing: New Strategies, Techniques, and Technologies to Win the Customers You Want and Keep Them Forever.* New York: John Wiley & Sons, 1998.

Hughes, Arthur. *Strategic Database Marketing.* Second edition. New York: McGraw-Hill, 2000.

Imhoff, Claudia, Lisa Loftis, and Jonathan G. Geiger. *Building the Customer-Centric Enterprise: Data Warehousing Techniques for Supporting Customer Relationship Management.* New York: John Wiley & Sons, 2001.

Inmon, William H. *Building the Data Warehouse.* New York: John Wiley & Sons, 1996.

Inmon, William H., and Richard D. Hackathorn. *Using the Data Warehouse.* New York: John Wiley & Sons, 1994.

Kalakota, Ravi, and Marcia Robinson. *E-Business 2.0: Roadmap for Success.* Boston: Addison-Wesley, 2001.

Kimball, Ralph, Laura Reeves, Margy Ross, and Warren Thornthwaite. *The Data Warehouse Lifecycle Toolkit: Expert Methods for Designing, Developing, and Deploying Data Warehouses.* New York: John Wiley & Sons, 1998.

Levine, Rick, Christopher Locke, Doc Searls, and David Weinberger. *The Cluetrain Manifesto: The End of Business As Usual.* Cambridge, MA: Perseus Publishing, 1999.

Linthicum, David S. *B2B Application Integration: e-Business—Enable Your Enterprise.* Boston: Addison-Wesley, 2001.

Martin, Chuck. *Net Future: The 7 Cybertrends that Will Drive Your Business, Create New Wealth, and Define Your Future.* New York: McGraw-Hill, 1999.

Newell, Frederick. *Loyalty.com: Customer Relationship Management in the New Era of Internet Marketing.* New York: McGraw-Hill, 2000.

Peppers, Don, and Martha Rogers. *The One to One Future: Building Relationships One Customer at a Time.* New York: Currency Doubleday, 1993.

_____. *Enterprise One to One: Tools for Competing in the Interactive Age.* New York: Currency Doubleday, 1997.

_____. *The One to One Manager: An Executive's Guide to Customer Relationship Management.* New York: Random House, 1999.

Pine, Joseph, and James Gilmore. *The Experience Economy.* Boston: Harvard Business School Press, 1999.

Reichheld, Frederick F. *The Loyalty Effect: The Hidden Force Behind Growth, Profits, and Lasting Value.* Boston: Harvard Business School Press, 1996.

Seybold, Patricia B. *Customers.com: How to Create a Profitable Business Strategy for the Internet and Beyond.* New York: Random House, 1998.

Seybold, Patricia B. *The Customer Revolution: How to Thrive When Customers Are in Control.* New York: Crown Business, 2001.

Siebel, Thomas M., and Pat House. *Cyber Rules: Strategies for Excelling at E-Business*. New York: Currency Doubleday, 1999.

Sindell, Kathleen. *Loyalty Marketing for the Internet Age*. Chicago: Dearborn Trade, 2000.

Sterne, Jim. *Customer Service on the Internet: Building Relationships, Increasing Loyalty, and Staying Competitive*. Second edition. New York: John Wiley & Sons, 2000.

Sterne, Jim, and Anthony Priore. *Email Marketing: Using Email to Reach Your Target Audience and Build Customer Relationships*. New York: John Wiley & Sons, 2000.

Sviokla, John J., and Benson P. Shapiro. *Keeping Customers*. Boston: Harvard Business School Press, 1993.

Swift, Ronald S. *Accelerating Customer Relationships: Using CRM and Relationship Technologies*. Upper Saddle River, NJ: Prentice Hall PTR, 2001.

Thorp, John. *The Information Paradox: Realizing the Business Benefits of Information Technology*. New York: McGraw-Hill, 1998.

Tiwana, Amrit. *The Essential Guide to Knowledge Management: E-Business and CRM Applications*. Upper Saddle River, NJ: Prentice Hall PTR, 2001.

Trout, Jack, and Steve Rivkin. *Differentiate or Die: Survival in Our Era of Killer Competition*. New York: John Wiley & Sons, 2000.

Unruh, James A. *Customers Mean Business: Six Steps to Building Relationships that Last*. Reading, MA: Addison-Wesley, 1996.

Wacker, Watts, and Jim Taylor. *The Visionary's Handbook: Nine Paradoxes that Will Shape the Future of Your Business*. New York: Harper Business, 2000.

Magazines and Journals

Rather than simply list a litany of business publications, I've chosen some that offer regular features on relationship marketing, customer service, data warehousing, and CRM.

Business 2.0 (www.business2.com): Print magazine includes regular features on marketing, personalization, and eCRM. On-line version has an entire track dedicated to digital marketing.

ComputerWorld (www.computerworld.com): Timely stories about CRM failures as well as successes.

CIO Magazine (www.cio.com): Regular coverage of CRM and its periphery, including supply chain management, knowledge management, data warehousing, and enterprise resource planning.

Customer Relationship Management (www.crmmagazine.com): Valuable overall CRM resource; contains several more-focused supplements throughout the year.

Particularly geared toward sales force automation and call center topics, but seems to be branching out to enterprise CRM. Also covers CRM vendor alliances and acquisitions.

DM Review (www.dmreview.com): Both the magazine and its Web site focus on the area of data management, but there are often CRM-related articles focusing on the design, administration, and use of customer data.

EWeek (www.eweek.com): Regular CRM features and product reviews.

Fast Company (www.fastcompany.com): Geared toward so-called "free agents." An often-irreverent compendium of business trends and executive profiles. Regularly illustrates creative marketing approaches and features out-of-the-box thinkers.

Information Week (www.informationweek.com): For IT managers; a staple in the areas of information management concepts and trends.

Intelligent Enterprise (www.intelligententerprise.com): More technical than the others here; offers insights into CRM and data warehouse management and implementation for practitioners. See also the magazine's CRM Web page: *www.intelligentCRM.com*.

1to1 Magazine (www.1to1.com): Affiliated with Peppers and Rogers Group, focuses on marketing trends. Offers articles on CRM development as well as case studies. Publisher recently added a journal offering, "1to1 Quarterly."

Web Sites

More and more CRM-related Web sites are popping up every day. I focus here on those that are heavy on content and light on advertising and vendor sponsorships. However, with any Web site that markets itself as a repository of information, especially with those that offer product reviews, you would always do well to note the sponsors who are footing the bill as you review products, read vendor case studies, and choose CRM conferences and workshops.

Having said that, don't dismiss the Web sites of CRM product vendors. Many feature white papers and CRM news releases along with information on their specific CRM solutions.

www.crmcommunity.com: Offers a range of CRM resources. Provides an especially thorough compendium of white papers on all topics. The "consultants corner" that allows visitors to ask questions of CRM experts and a chat room are good places to monitor current CRM vendor and product buzz.

www.crm2001online.com: A virtual CRM conference, this clever site lets visitors attend seminars and wander through a virtual trade show. Booths feature vendor presentations and provide links to CRM vendor Web sites. Visitors can even collect brochures in their virtual shopping bags.

Cyberatlas.internet.com: For the latest news on e-commerce companies. The place to go when you want to see who's bought whom.

www.destinationcrm.com: CRM product reviews, analyst reports, and surveys. Covers everything from ASP reviews to wireless technology trends to vendor coverage.

www.dsstar.com: News and editorials about business intelligence, data warehousing, and data mining.

www.dwinfocenter.org: Provides information on a range of data warehousing and business intelligence topics. Objectively lists data warehouse vendors and consultants, breaking them down according to their focus. Also has links to various publications featuring data warehouse news and editorials.

www.dw-institute.com: The Data Warehousing Institute's Web site, featuring articles, white papers, case studies, and resource guides, as well as updates about its conferences. TDWI is the only conference that does not cull speakers from its list of exhibitors, thus bestowing real-world experiences in data warehousing and business intelligence.

www.ecrmguide.com: A repository for CRM news and vendor press releases, updated several times a day.

www.epic.org: Grassroots lobbying effort for U.S.-based privacy legislation, this site has even proffered editorial viewpoints on various politicians' privacy track records. Accompanying subscriber newsletter broadcasts regular briefings on privacy developments.

www.ittoolbox.com: A knowledge center for all things IT. Offers a "toolbox" for both a CRM and Business Intelligence (among other areas), allowing visitors to review product features and read case studies about their applications. The site also offers subscriptions to free newsletters for managers and practitioners. The site's CRM area does a particularly thorough job of deconstructing CRM into its various components.

ipw.internet.com: Run by Internet Product Watch, a comprehensive clearinghouse for e-business vendors and products.

www.junkbusters.com: Web epicenter of privacy legislation and protection. Includes frequent updates on legislative measures in the United States and follows privacy-related lawsuits. Provides downloadable software and e-mail addresses for blocking the use of cookies and other methods for data gathering.

www.openitx.com: "Open IT Exchange" offers insight into a range of e-business areas, from knowledge management to operating systems to data management. The site also offers a weekly newsletter to subscribers.

www.personalization.org: The name belies this site's purpose, which is to discourage privacy legislation in favor of corporate responsibility. Also offers news and press releases on the personalization and relationship marketing industries.

www.privacy.org: Offers articles, news releases, and links to other Web sites with the aim of pushing privacy legislation in the United States. Has been known to publicize companies selling or sharing customer data externally.

www.searchcrm.com: Presents a variety of CRM resources under one virtual roof. Includes an introduction to CRM basics as well as a host of features for visitors looking for product comparisons, book reviews, current articles, and white papers (both original and gleaned from other publications and Web sites). Includes a CRM job board.

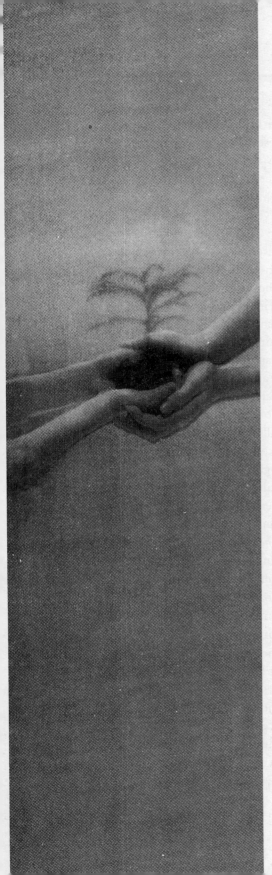

Glossary

Abandoned shopping cart: Set of products a customer intended to buy, but did not ultimately purchase. Although possible in a brick-and-mortar store, the term more accurately applies to a Web site where a visitor collected one or more items in his virtual basket but never made it as far as checkout.

Affinity analysis: Detecting sets of products or services purchased together. Example: Tortilla chips and salsa.

Analytical CRM: Use of data originating through front-office or operational CRM to enhance customer relationships. Combined with other organizational or external data to evaluate key business measures such as customer satisfaction, customer profitability, or customer loyalty to support business decisions.

Application services provider (ASP): Company whose business is outsourcing application services for its client companies. Such applications can include both tactical systems, such as billing systems, and strategic solutions, such as CRM. (CRM ASPs currently account for over half of the ASP market.)

Attrition: Customer leaving to go do business with a competitor. See also Churn.

Automated workflow: Enabling work processes to "flow" through a company without human intervention. Workflow systems usually involve moving data through a process, such as order and fulfillment, that reaches across various systems and departments.

Automatic call distribution: Ability for call center telephony software to balance incoming calls across agents, thereby optimizing agent productivity and minimizing customer wait times.

B2B: Common abbreviation for "business-to-business."

B2C: Common abbreviation for "business-to-consumer."

Back-office CRM: The area of CRM that involves analysis to optimize customer-facing business processes and revenues. See also *Analytical CRM*.

Brick-and-mortar business: A physical storefront or branch. Brick-and-mortar can be a company's core business or simply one of several sales channels.

Business intelligence: Normally describes the result of in-depth analysis of detailed business data. Includes database and application technologies, as well as analysis practices. Sometimes used synonymously with "decision support," though business intelligence is technically much broader, potentially encompassing knowledge management, enterprise resource planning, and data mining, among other practices.

Business process reengineering (BPR): Redesigning core business processes to drive organizational and technological efficiencies. Term made popular by Michael Hammer and James Champy in their 1993 book *Reengineering the Corporation*.

Business sponsor: Manager or executive who acts as visionary for the CRM program and can articulate how CRM can drive business improvements. This person establishes the "need, pain, or problem" CRM will solve, serves as a tiebreaker for issues during the project, and might actually fund some or all of CRM development.

Call center: Organization in charge of direct customer support interactions. The term "call center" refers to the classic telephone support infrastructure and is being replaced by "contact center" or "customer care center," both of which imply more technological sophistication and multichannel support.

Call center automation: Use of technology to facilitate communications to, within, and out of a call center. Automatic routing of calls to specific CSRs is one example of call center automation.

Call routing: Directing customer calls to a specific agent based on a specific parameter such as that agent's expertise, geographical location, subsidiary affiliation, or other characteristic.

Call scripting: See *Scripting*.

Campaign management: Analyzing data for purposes of launching a marketing campaign and then monitoring that campaign and tracking its results to determine the campaign's value. Can also refer to the technology that automates the campaign management function.

C-commerce: See *Collaborative commerce*.

Channel: Means and media by which a customer prefers to communicate with the company (the "inbound" channel) or to receive communications (the "outbound" channel).

Channel optimization: Determining the best channels by which to communicate with and sell to customers, especially when they have not made these preferences clear, and making these channels available to the right customers. For example, a company might choose to use resellers to sell a product in order to minimize its costs.

Churn: Customers leaving your business to go to a competitor. Implies the customer might or might not return. "Churn reduction" is another way of saying customer retention and is a major goal of CRM. Churn is most often used in conjunction with highly competitive commodity product businesses such as communications companies, utilities, and airlines.

Clickstream: Series of page visits and associated clicks executed by a Web site visitor while navigating through the site. Analysis of clickstream data can help a company understand which products, Web site content, or screens were of most interest to a given customer.

Closed-loop campaign management: Using the results of past campaigns to refine future campaigns, the goal of which is to hone customer knowledge while improving campaign response rates over time.

Collaborative commerce: Known as "c-commerce," reflects the ability of various partners within a supply chain to share important data about products, inventory levels, and orders.

Collaborative CRM: Specific functionality that enables a two-way dialog between a company and its customers, through a variety of channels, to facilitate and improve the quality of customer interactions.

Computer telephony integration (CTI): Combining telephone systems with computer technology such as software applications and databases to automate functions. Example: Using caller-id to provide customer information when distributing calls to CSRs.

Configuration support: Usually a component of sales force automation. Automates the estimation process for sizing and pricing a product, using prospect or client data as input. Companies selling complex custom products, such as computer equipment, are the main users of configuration support tools.

Configurator: Common name for tool that performs configuration support. Also the brand name for Siebel's configuration support tool.

Contact center: A more sophisticated version of the classic call center, which was staffed by telephone operators. Contact center suggests a greater degree of technological sophistication, including multimodal customer support, outbound telemarketing, and customer self-service.

Contact management: Area of sales force automation that allows salespeople to record key customer information such as names and addresses, as well as organization charts and account activities. Prevents salespeople from having to remember who's who at each of their accounts.

Control group: Group of customers, usually randomly selected, whose responses to a campaign are compared to those of a specially selected customer group that is more systematically chosen. Evaluating customer responses to a specially designed communication with the responses of a control group can indicate the effectiveness of a target marketing campaign.

Cookie: Unit of text placed on someone's computer when he accesses a Web site, intended to serve as a permanent way for the site to recognize that customer when he returns. Allows the site to track various pieces of information the customer submits to the site across multiple visits.

Cross-functional: Description for a technology that serves more than one business function (e.g., financial analysis and sales analysis) or organization (e.g., Human Resources and Accounts Receivable). CRM point solutions, by their definition, are not cross-functional, whereas CRM suites might be.

Cross-selling: Selling a customer a product or service based on her past behav-iors or purchase history. Best done when a company understands the relationship between two products and identifies which product might "pull" another.

Customer interaction center (CIC): Evolution of the operational call center into the locus of all inbound and outbound customer communications, with special focus on customer satisfaction and multimodal customer access.

Customer relationship management (CRM): Infrastructure that enables delineation of and increase in customer value and the correct means by which to increase customer value and motivate valuable customers to remain loyal—indeed, to buy again.

Customer segmentation: See *Segmentation.*

Customer service representative (CSR): Member of the company's customer support staff (or a third-party call center agency) who takes phone calls and participates in Internet live-chat sessions to answer customer questions, lodge complaints, record trouble tickets, or instruct customers on product use.

Customization: Customer's ability to tailor Web site content to her specific needs, interests, and usage preferences. See also *Personalization.*

Cyberagent: Software program that can guide a user's decisions and recommend potential action. Cyberagents can help customers navigate a Web site, answer frequently asked questions, and suggest next steps, and their capabilities are growing all the time. Some cyberagents are animated to appear human.

Data mining: Advanced analysis used to determine certain patterns within data. Most often associated with predictive analysis.

Data mart: Usually refers to a physical platform on which summarized data is stored for decision support. Data marts are commonly used for specific analysis purposes by a single organization or user group.

Data warehouse: Collection of integrated data used for decision-making. Normally the system of record for detailed customer data from heterogeneous systems across the company to provide a consistent view of the business.

Decision support: Data analysis with the purpose of fueling accurate and effective business decisions. Known by the abbreviation "DSS," for decision support systems, decision support usually involves accessing data on a data warehouse.

Direct marketing: Classic marketing practice of communicating directly to consumers, normally via the postal service. Has evolved to encompass a range of media, from e-mail to banner ads to wireless messaging services.

Electronic customer relationship management (eCRM or e-CRM): Activities to sell to, support, manage, and retain customers who do business through a company's Web channel. Online personalization is an example of eCRM.

e-marketplace: Online exchange that enables buyers and sellers in a supply chain to come together, providing better information (better than they would have with classic human-intensive supply chain processes) as well as automation of key business processes.

Enterprise application integration (EAI): Integration of often disparate corporate systems that routinely exchange or share data. Facilitating this data interchange between systems increases the likelihood of consistent data.

Enterprise CRM: Cross-functional CRM system used across various organizations and departments. A salesperson reviewing his customer's most recent open trouble tickets before making a sales call is an example of enterprise CRM.

Enterprise portal: User interface, usually Web-based, that provides a virtual window into different data sources and subject areas. Provides a common look and feel across the company for various business data, but can nevertheless be customized to provide user-specific information at various levels and from various sources.

Enterprise resource planning (ERP): Tying together and automating of diverse components of a company's operations, including ordering, fulfillment, staffing, and accounting. This integration is usually done using ERP software tools.

e-tailer: "Internet retailer." Usually refers to a company for whom the Internet is the exclusive sales channel.

Event-based marketing: Detecting a key event that triggers a tailored marketing communication or business action designed to increase customer loyalty or profitability. Example: Responding to a customer's inordinately large bank deposit with an offer for a high-interest certificate of deposit.

Exchange: Company partnership that leverages spending power and critical mass to negotiate more favorable deals with suppliers. Usually specific to a single industry and often involving companies that compete as well as cooperate with each other.

External data: Data acquired outside of a company's internal IT organization. Usually entails consumer data that has been cleansed, formatted, and updated with current information, but might also include market research, demographic statistics, and business and industry information.

Extranet: Secure Internet site available only to a company's internal staff and approved third-party partners. Flourishing in B2B environments where suppliers can have ready access to updated information from their business customers, and vice versa.

Field service management: Optimizing processes and information around support of a company's product or service on the customer's premises. Often involves a combination of CRM applications, wireless technology, and historical customer service data.

Frequently Asked Questions (FAQs): Usually a Web page wherein the company answers basic questions for its customers, such as "How do I change my name and address online?" or "How do I make a return?" Saves live service agents from repeating the same information over and over, allowing them to focus their support efforts on more specialized issues.

Front-office CRM: Customer-facing CRM capability. Usually pertains to sales force automation systems and other systems that involve direct customer interactions that can be recorded for back-office analysis.

Householding: Consolidating customer data to organize individuals into the households in which they live. Grouping customers within a household allows a company to be more prudent with its communications and at the same time to more accurately profile individuals in relation to one another.

Incremental development: Deploying periodic releases of software such that end-users receive functionality "in chunks" and not all at once.

Inferential personalization: Using analysis and extrapolation of customer behaviors and preferences, including performing collaborative filtering and other types of data mining, to tailor Web content and dictate the optimal marketing message.

Interactive voice response (IVR): Telephony software that recognizes human voice instructions or the pressing of numbers on a keypad to route customer calls to the appropriate call center or agent.

Iterative development: Desirable CRM approach of going through small, repeatable development steps to speed up software implementation and deliver small amounts of functionality more quickly. Reduces risk and allows for adjustments, enabling technical staff to refine the development plan as they go.

Knowledge management (KM): Centralized management of a company's corporate knowledge and information assets to provide this knowledge to as many company staff members as possible and thus encourage better and more consistent decision-making.

Knowledge management system: Centralizes a company's knowledge assets. Much of this documentation is widely dispersed both internally and externally, enabling KM users not only to access information in the system but also to supplement it with new or additional information as it's created.

Lead management: Sales force automation capability for tracking and monitoring sales prospects and a company's interactions with them, as well as enforcing

sales tactics and automating key tasks. Also enables telemarketing staff to pass leads along to the appropriate sales channel.

Life-stage marketing: Targeting consumers based on where they are on their life continuum. For instance, a bank might e-mail a promotion for a new credit card to a recent college graduate, but might market a home equity line of credit to a recent home buyer or financial planning to a recent retiree.

Lifetime value (LTV) modeling: Applying historical customer behaviors and financial information to calculate a given customer's value throughout her relationship with a company (as opposed to at a single point in time).

List generation: Automatically developing a list of customers for a marketing campaign, based on specific customer characteristics. Core feature of most CRM campaign management products.

Load balancing: See *Automatic call distribution*.

Market-basket analysis: Analysis of items purchased together during a shopping trip. Need not be retail specific but can also be applied to a bank's or telephone company's products. Classic example: Peanut butter being purchased with jelly.

Marketing service bureau: Third-party company to which marketing campaigns and mailings are outsourced for a fee. Many companies have historically relied on marketing service bureaus due to the company's lack of complete data or mailing infrastructures.

Mass marketing: Traditional practice of marketing a product to an undifferentiated group of consumers. Also known as "spray and pray" or "batch and blast."

mCRM: Mobile CRM. Communicating key information to customers or internal customer support staff via wireless technologies.

Metadata: "Data about data." Usually refers to agreed-on definitions and business rules stored in a centralized repository so business users—even those across departments and systems—use common terminology for key business terms. Can include information about data's currency, ownership, source system, derivation (e.g., profit = revenues minus costs), or usage rules. Prevents data misinterpretation and poor decision-making due to a sketchy understanding of the true meaning and use of corporate data.

Multichannel: Support of more than one sales or service channel; for instance a retailer's Web site and its catalog.

Multimodal: Numerous ways a customer can interact with a company, and vice versa. A call center that allows inbound customer interactions via fax, voice, telephone keypad, or handheld device is providing multimodal access.

Online analytical processing (OLAP): "Drilling down" on various data dimensions to gain a more detailed view of the data. For instance, a user might begin by looking at North American sales and then drill down on regional sales, then sales by state, and then sales by major metro area. Enables a user to view different perspectives of the same data to facilitate decision-making.

Operational CRM: Involves customer-facing business functions. Sales force automation and customer service are two examples. See also *Front-office CRM*.

Opportunity management: See *Lead management*.

Partner relationship management (PRM): Qualifying, tracking, and allocating leads to third-party sales partners (e.g., resellers) to understand how to price, market, and compensate channel partners. In effect, advocating to the partner relationship the customer differentiation inherent to CRM.

Permission marketing: A customer's implicit or explicit agreement to be communicated to or to communicate with a company. Usually implies customer perception of value in the relationship, suggesting a *quid pro quo* between the customer and the vendor.

Personalization: Company's ability to recognize a customer or prospect as an individual and differentiate its interactions with her. Although personalization usually means individualized content delivered on a Web site, it can also involve target marketing, tailored e-mail campaigns, or customized banner ads.

Pipeline Management: See *Lead Management.*

Private portal: See *Extranet.*

Proof of concept: Software trial that allows a prospect to try out the product before buying it. Delivers a realistic slice of functionality and is often used as the foundation for the first application.

Point solution: Piece of software used for a specific business purpose. Example: A product that performs only automated campaign management. Many companies decide to choose point solutions for discrete CRM functions to select the best-of-breed tool for each function (rather than relying on a CRM suite from a single vendor).

Pure play (n), pure-play (adj): Refers to a dot-com company without a brick-and-mortar presence.

Referential personalization: Using explicit customer data—such as survey responses, service requests, and satisfaction feedback—to determine the best selling strategies and marketing messages for a customer.

Relationship marketing: Marketing to customers based on your knowledge of their behaviors and their relationship with your company: what they do and don't purchase, how often they buy, and how they use your support services.

Retention: Company's ability to keep customers by offering products and services—and, by extension, the right messages—to keep the customers satisfied and avoid losing them to a competitor.

Return on investment (ROI): Measuring CRM's contribution to the bottom line versus its cost. Most accurately performed after CRM has been put in place and improvements can be measured. "Intangible" ROI such as increased customer satisfaction might be more difficult to measure but is nevertheless also a factor in CRM success.

Return on relationship (ROR): Applies to overall value of a relationship and how it has paid off. Can describe B2B relationships, as in measuring the uplift in sales triggered by certain partnerships, or B2C relationships, as in the increase of customer satisfaction rates. Can also imply a superset of a customer's financial value to a company, specifically in cases where a customer might refer other customers to the company.

Rules repository: File or database containing business rules to ensure they are tracked and understood. Example: Each time a customer opens an account online, e-mail him a welcome letter.

Rules-based personalization: Involves the coding of user-defined rules that are analyzed by the specific personalization software tool and used to create tailored customer messages.

Sales force automation (SFA): Electronic tracking and management of account activities by individual salespeople. SFA data is integrated at the corporate level to provide a company with a rich view of its customers and prospects.

Screen pop: Small window that appears on a user's workstation screen to provide contextual information. Could be a survey ("How do you like this Web site so far?") or a response to a marketing analyst's mouse click on a certain product, listing the product's specifications.

Scripting: Automatic "scripts" (prepared questions or comments) generated for customer service reps based on an individual customer's segment and/or customer profile contents. Scripts remove the guesswork from determining how to respond to a customer query or complaint, guiding reps through a dialog with the customer and thus optimizing discrete customer interactions.

Segmentation: Grouping customers (or products or other business metrics) to analyze characteristics or behaviors with an aim toward target-marketing specific products and services to the group.

Self-service: Customers can ask their own questions or resolve problems without the intervention of a live person. Usually performed over the Web.

Service-level agreement (SLA): Contract with a service provider—be it an internal IT organization, an ASP, or an outsourcer—specifying discrete reliability and availability requirements for a given system. Might also include such requirements as support of certain tech-

nology standards or data volumes. Outsourcer's failure to adhere to the terms laid out in an SLA could result in financial penalties.

Skunkworks CRM: Project being developed "under the radar," apart from the sanctioned CRM project that might be underway. Usually the result of unhappy political situations, skunkworks projects can jeopardize the reputation and funding of the authorized CRM project by raising questions about its value, timeliness, or planned deliverables.

Steering committee: Group of managers or executives charged with planning and prioritizing CRM functionality and allocating appropriate funds for CRM development, rollout, training, and usage. Can also influence CRM adoption rates and accompanying business process changes.

Sticky: Web site that grabs and keeps a visitor. Often juxtaposed with the term "eyeballs," implying that one's eyes (figuratively) stick to an effective Web site.

Supplier relationship management (SRM): Offshoot of CRM that focuses on improving relationships with vendors and resellers. SRM includes selecting the lowest-cost supplier and matching suppliers with their optimal sales channels and product sets.

Suite: Range of functional software modules that interact with each other. Often combines marketing, sales force automation, and analytical functions.

Advantage: CRM suites eliminate integration complexity.

Supplier relationship management (SRM): Ability of a company to optimize its choice of suppliers around the various attributes and historical performance of those suppliers. Often involves specific software that helps companies analyze various characteristics to use in approving suppliers and granting contracts.

Supply chain management (SCM): Integration and optimization of a company's supply chain, usually involving automation of business processes that bring a product or service to market. Can help to tighten integration and communication between a company and its suppliers and partners.

Target marketing: Dividing the sum of the customer base into discrete subsets that range from large (dividing customers based on whether or not they own a product) to small (even individual "segments of one").

Touchpoint: Point of interaction when the company communicates with a customer, or vice versa. One interaction—a customer order, for instance—can involve several touchpoints: comparing products on the Web (touchpoint 1), checking inventory levels (touchpoint 2), and placing the order with the sales representative (touchpoint 3).

Trouble ticket: Record of a customer's call into the call center. Usually contains identifying features such as the reason for the customer's call, the status of the problem, and the ultimate resolution of the call. Trouble tickets enable a company to track and monitor the superset of customer calls into the contact center to summarize the main reasons for inbound customer contacts, whether problems, questions, or service requests.

Up-selling: Motivating a customer to trade up to a more expensive or profitable product. The logic is, now that I know what this customer wants to buy, perhaps we can motivate him to buy a more profitable version or model. Example: A jeweler might convince the buyer of a diamond tennis bracelet to go for larger diamonds, at a higher price.

Vertical silo: An organization or system involving a specific and often narrow business function. Example: A financial analysis system specific to a certain car model and not the automaker's entire line. The opposite of a vertical silo is a *cross-functional* system.

Viral marketing: Word-of-mouth on steroids. Could be positive or negative, but is definitely effective.

Waterfall development: Methodical and linear approach to technical development. Although rigorous, usually implies going through an entire development life cycle before deploying functionality to end users. Possible only when exhaustive, detailed requirements are known up-front; has been known to take years. The opposite of the waterfall approach is iterative or incremental development, the ideal means of deploying regular CRM functionality.

Workforce management: Usually applied to staffing the customer support center.

Deals with optimizing staffing levels in terms of both numbers and skill sets. Workforce management tools can analyze historical call types and volumes and help suggest optimal call center staffing.

Index